PLANT-BASED EATING HAS AN OUTSIZE IMPACT ON OUR ENVIRONMENT AND WELL-BEING. Dominick Thompson's story and the eighty simple repertoire-building recipes and meal plans in this book will help you become your strongest self, inside and out, one meal at a time.

Dominick grew up on the West Side of Chicago, where he was lured into the drug trade, as much for comradeship as for power and money. One summer, he agreed to a last hustle; it was a sting, and Dom went to federal prison.

It was in this darkest hour that he had the revelation that brings us *Eat What Elephants Eat*: to heal his body and soul, he vowed never again to harm another sentient being. Like Earth's strongest herbivore, the mighty African elephant— an intelligent, gentle, and curious creature that fuels its body with plants—Dom, too, would eat only plants.

At the heart of *Eat What Elephants Eat*, Dom connects the dots among the social and environmental perils of the industrial food system, our health, and our global and local environments. And then, with humor and understanding, he guides us toward a plant-based diet, answering the most common questions vegan-curious people ask: How do I stay focused? What are the health benefits? Is it expensive? (No!) What about protein? (Yes! Lots!) And what are some great-tasting recipes?

DELICIOUS RECIPES INCLUDE:

BREAKFAST

- Saturday Morning Nostalgia Pancakes
- The "Duluth" Omelet
- Really Good Tofu Scramble

SOUPS AND BOWLS

- Watermelon Gazpacho
- Mushroom Ramen Noodle Bowl
- Buffalo Cauliflower "Chicken" Wings Bowl

SMALL PLATES, SANDWICHES, AND BURGERS

- Sweet Corn 'n' Jalapeño Fritters
- Mega Tofu BLT
- Lentil Sloppy Joes

MAINS

- Spaghetti 'n' Beet Balls
- Almond-Crusted Tofu "Salmon"
- Jackfruit Tacos with Mango-Corn Salsa and Avocado "Cream"

SWEET TREATS

- Brownies in a "Jiffy"
- Lemon Loaf with Lemon Icing
- Roasted Stone Fruit with Sweet Cashew Cream

Hopeful and beautiful, like the being that inspires the title, *Eat What Elephants Eat* clears a path for all of us to see ourselves as healthier people and instruments for change, simply by changing what we eat.

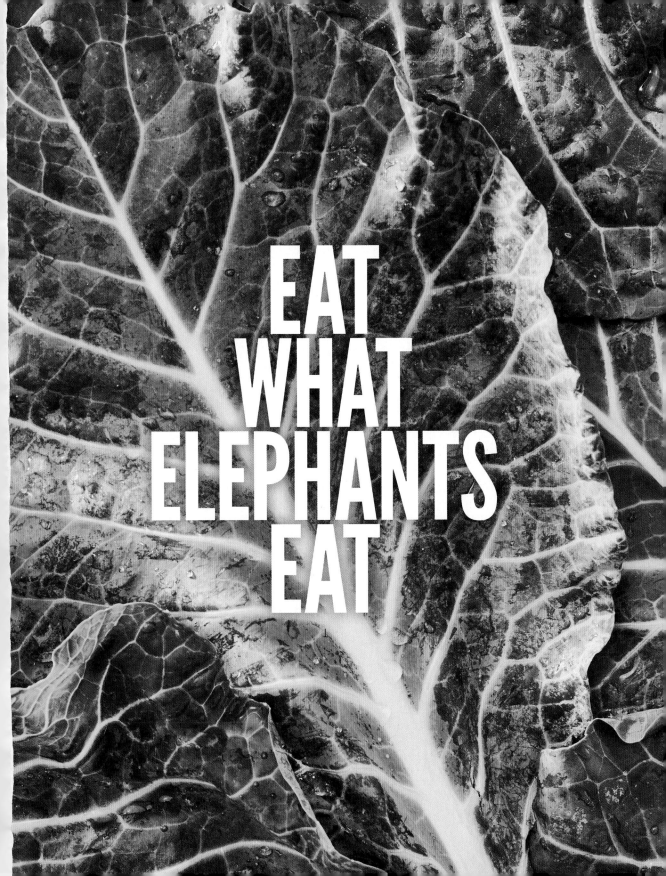

EAT
WHAT
ELEPHANTS
EAT

EAT WHAT ELEPHANTS EAT

VEGAN RECIPES FOR A STRONG BODY AND A GENTLE SPIRIT

DOMINICK THOMPSON
with Theresa Gambacorta

Photography by Caitlin Bensel

SIMON
ELEMENT

NEW YORK LONDON TORONTO SYDNEY NEW DELHI

The heroic journey is rarely a journey about love, it's about deeds that have to do with conquering and domination. Living as we do in a culture of domination, to truly choose to love is heroic.
—bell hooks

This book is dedicated to the three most important sources of energy and inspiration in my life: my mother, Maria; my fur-daughter, Soca; and my fur-son, Roc. I love you all to the moon and back.

CONTENTS

THIS KITCHEN IS FOR DANCING

I have a sign in my kitchen that says "THIS KITCHEN IS FOR DANCING." I hung it to honor my late fur-daughter, Soca, who was named for the upbeat Caribbean dance of the same name. Soca came into my life when my mother, Maria, brought her home after a trip to St. Thomas with her husband, Ken, a native islander. Ken's three chihuahuas (bitter and grumpy, each of 'em, probably 'cause Taco Bell wasn't hiring, and they were out of work!) couldn't stand the new addition to the family. And so, Soca came to live with me.

At the time, I was on house arrest—more on that in a bit—and from the moment I laid eyes on that little white and brown fur ball of energy with the most beautiful brown eyes I've ever seen, she opened my heart in ways I never dreamed imaginable. I'd often hold her in my arms, getting our groove on. Or sometimes, it would be just me, dancing for her while cooking.

While that sign reminds me of Soca, who has since transitioned on, and whose loving energy still fills my home, it has also taken on new meaning. "THIS KITCHEN IS FOR DANCING" is a reminder that here, in my kitchen, where I cook, eat, and share delicious vegan food, I am engaged in the most upbeat dance of all, the one called *life*.

Today, when you opened this book, you were transported to my kitchen. And I opened my heart to find you here. I named this book for Earth's largest herbivore, the mighty African elephant—an intelligent, gentle, curious, strong, and peaceful creature that fuels its massive body with plants. They are a reminder and inspiration that we, too, can move through the world as protectors, strengthening our bodies by "eating what elephants eat." Our hearts and minds will expand, too, with plants.

I am honored to share with you my story and how my do no harm mantra—"If It Requires Harm, Then Nahh"—set me on course for healing physically, mentally, and emotionally. By eating what elephants eat, I am on a path toward a healthier and more just world for all living things. I hope you will join me on my journey.

Are you feeling excited? Curious?

Me too.

I love that you showed up in my EWEE kitchen just as you are. It doesn't matter where you were born, how you were raised, or what obstacles you have faced; every day, you have the power to make food choices that reflect how *you* want to move through the world, too.

Eat What Elephants Eat is for everyone. And I do truly mean everyone. You *do not* have to be vegan to engage in the topics I discuss, nor to cook and enjoy my recipes. And for those of you who may be wondering what the difference between being vegan and being plant-based is, here is an explanation:

- The term "plant-based" has historically been associated with people who have adopted a 100 percent plant-based diet, free of all animal products. However, recently some people have opted to eat primarily plant-based while incorporating small servings of meat, poultry, seafood, eggs, and dairy instead of eliminating animal products entirely. These same plant-based eaters may also be consumers who directly and indirectly support industries that source materials from dead animals (think fabric used in clothing, car interiors, and more).

- Plant-based is not an absolute term, but overall, those who adopt a plant-based diet do so for its health benefits. Nutrient-dense, whole, unprocessed plant foods—including vegetables, fruits, seeds, nuts, and legumes—are central to plant-based and my EWEE recipes.

- *Veganism refers to both diet and lifestyle.* A vegan diet excludes animal flesh, animal by-products, including dairy and eggs, and any services or products from industries that harm, exploit, and kill sentient beings—animals and humans. There are many reasons that inform someone's decision to be vegan, such as animal protection, health, ethical, environmental, and social justice issues. A nutrient-rich vegan diet consists of whole, minimally processed plant foods but can include faux meat products, too. Processed plant foods can be an essential step toward embracing more plants among all types of eaters who wish to reduce or eliminate meat for any reason that resonates with them.

Whether you consider yourself plant-based or vegan or are just curious about either choice, this book is for you. It's divided into three parts to help guide you on your journey.

IN PART I, THE EAT WHAT ELEPHANTS EAT JOURNEY, I share my origin story, and my EWEE journey that led me to ethical veganism (and now, to you!). Along the way, we'll connect the dots among the factory farming system as well as other systems of oppression that are in opposition to the life-affirming values of veganism. We'll discuss ways in which you can begin to adopt the EWEE mindset, and I'll share how we can become protectors—of our health, all beings, and the planet. Finally, I will guide you toward your "why" for choosing an EWEE journey. (Because, if we know *why* we are doing something, we are much more likely to stay in the long game, reaping the maximum rewards of vegan living!)

This book is a judgment-free zone. Think of the information that I present in this section as heart-to-heart talks, like ones I had with my mom growing up. As you'll soon hear, these conversations gave me the foundation for the physical, emotional, and spiritual authenticity I discovered later in my life through veganism.

IN PART II, HOW TO EAT WHAT ELEPHANTS EAT, WE PUT our heart-to-hearts into a plan of action to meet you where you are on your journey. I offer you a choice of three "EWEE Pathways," each with a fourteen-day meal plan, along with cooking and shopping tips to set you up for success. The three pathways are:

1. **CROWD IT OUT (PAGE 77):** If you want to replace animal products gradually with plant-based foods, this gentle approach is for you. You'll add servings of grains, beans, legumes, and plenty of nutrient-rich fruits and vegetables to your meals every day, learning to eat what elephants eat by prioritizing whole foods. And, you'll have the option to cook EWEE meals and taste new plant flavors.

2. **FAKE IT TILL YOU MAKE IT (PAGE 86):** If you're vegan-curious or having trouble letting go of the cultural and social-emotional associations that accompany meat, this transitional approach is a great start. Think of it as an adventure, as you try new plant-based products, settling into the idea of relinquishing animal ones, and exploring easy plant-based eating with minimum kitchen prep.

3. **COLD TOFURKY (PAGE 90):** Looking to make a swift change and eliminate all meat, dairy, and animal products in one swoop? I will share what to expect and coach you through this shift. And I will provide a list of hidden animal products in some common foods.

Each of us moves through our food choices, kitchens, and wider communities differently. Our options depend on the moment, our traditions, circumstances, upbringing, and struggles. My story has elements of all of those. The information I share is easy to understand and designed to support you—whether you are eating for health, weight loss, or to manage diabetes or heart health. Perhaps you're an athlete who wants to reach peak performance, or a "junk food" vegan, wondering how to maximize your nutrition as you explore the many whole food recipes in part IV.

PART III IS THE EWEE KITCHEN. HERE, I INTRODUCE YOU to my EWEE Kitchen "dance partners"—the nutrient-dense ingredients, flavor enhancers, and whole foods I cook with most frequently—and the kitchen equipment and tools I use for easy prep. There are more than one hundred recipes in this section that are filling, delicious, and, best of all, within reach for any budget, making plant-based eating, in many instances, more affordable than an omnivorous diet. Whether you're new to eating plants or are already on board, the recipes are designed to be a part of your go-to repertoire.

Eating only plants has made me strong in body, mind, and spirit. And, as you read, I want you to know that I believe my setbacks in life were op-portunities to discover that the beauty of life, as in dancing, doesn't unfold in a straight line.

YOU READY TO DO THE SOCA IN MY EWEE KITCHEN?

Okay, now.

First, take a step back, allowing yourself some perspective.

Then raise your arms in joy and begin to make moves, marching forward with intention—it's okay, if you take a detour, side to side. That's called finding your groove!

That's right.

You're doing it!

You are now vibing!

"THIS KITCHEN IS FOR DANCING."

And I am so happy to move through *Eat What Elephants Eat* with you.

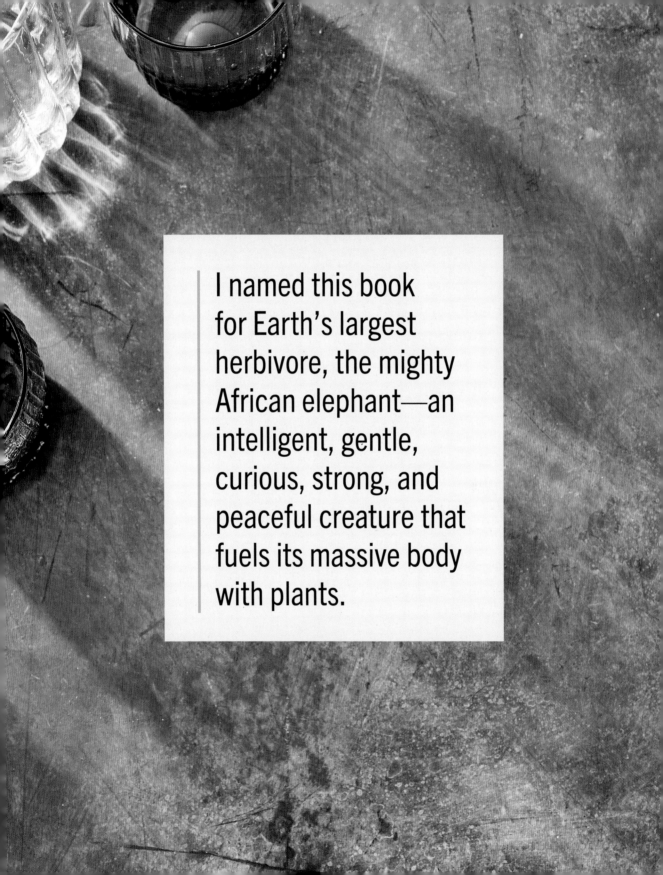

I named this book for Earth's largest herbivore, the mighty African elephant—an intelligent, gentle, curious, strong, and peaceful creature that fuels its massive body with plants.

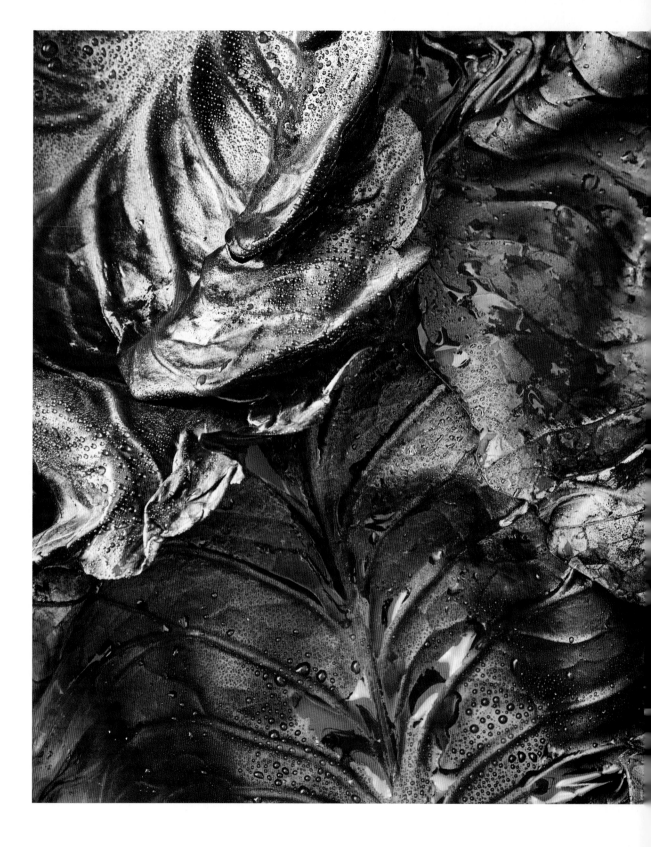

PART I

The Eat What Elephants Eat Journey

CHAPTER 1

MY ORIGIN STORY

Chi-raq

My journey to veganism began on the West Side of Chicago—notoriously known to many as Chi-raq because of the neighborhood's warlike violence.

I lived with my mother, Maria, and two older sisters, Tonia and Yalonda, until I was about six. Our home was a tiny, rundown one-bedroom apartment at the intersection of Lockwood Avenue and Crystal Street.

My father, whom many considered handsome and built like his nickname, Big Tank, was in love with my mom early in their union. She was the only woman he ever married, and I was his biological child; my sisters were born to two different men. Between my dad's odd jobs and chasing other women, he couldn't get it together to be financially supportive or present for our family. My mom, a no-nonsense woman with infectious energy and a self-starter's mindset, worked full-time and overtime as a pediatric nurse. Back in the 1980s, nurses, especially Black nurses, didn't get paid well at all. So, my mother put in as many hours as she could. She asked my father for help, including to buy a family car to make traveling to work and getting around town easier and safer for us. I remember countless times hanging on tightly to her dress at the hip, or with my arms around her neck, like a baby cub, while we waited at the bus stop making our way through the dangerous Chicago public transportation system just to get me to preschool and herself to work.

One day, my mother answered the pale-yellow house phone with the twenty-foot cord hanging on the kitchen wall.

"Hey Ree!" my father said on the other line, calling her by her nickname. "Come downstairs with the kids in about ten minutes!"

"Where are you?" Mama asked.

"I gotta surprise!" he said.

My mom, sisters, and I went down and stood on the corner in front of our building. Soon, he came around the corner driving a fancy, bright-white, T-top two-door Corvette with one of those heavy-ass 1980s car phones that set you back twenty bucks a call.

"This is our new car," he beamed.

My mother's face fell with heartbreak and disappointment as the realization set in that there was room neither in his car nor in his life for a wife and three children. That was the day she finally left him, kicking him out for good to go run the streets he never truly wanted to leave.

Big Tank, who had eight other kids by eight different women prior to meeting my mom (none of whom he supported), would pick me up a few times a year to spend time with me after the divorce. I was too young to understand his neglect. All I knew was that I loved running toward him, rushing into his big arms as he would lift me up,

and we'd make silly faces together. Eventually, though, he stopped putting in any effort to spend time with me, and we became unimportant to each other.

My mother, sisters, and the extended family who occupied other units in our building were my world. My mom's brother, Uncle Matt, a heavyset, easygoing, and charismatic guy, lived with his wife and my five older cousins across the hall. A jokester who was always doling out nicknames, Matt called me Pooh Bear—short for Winnie the Pooh because my skin was "high-yellow," which is how we in the Black culture in that era described other Blacks with fair skin. I was also chunky, husky, like Winnie the Pooh. He nicknamed my sister Tonia "Tiki," short for Tiki Bird, because he said she looked like a little yellow bird. And my sister Yalonda was Yogi, short for Yogi the Bear. She had a deep voice and was the darkest skinned of the three of us. My mom's sister, my aunt Sophie, and my quiet cousin Quentin lived below us. And directly across the hall from them lived my grandfather's ex-wife Mary and my cousin Derrick. My mother's other sister, Auntie Valerie, lived in the basement unit with her daughter, my cousin Tiffany.

My sisters and I slept in the living room in our little apartment, sharing the space with cockroaches we called "little vice lords," while our mom had the bedroom. We would sit on the couch at dinner, eating chicken wings and cheap cuts of pork—the only meals my mother could afford—off plates on our laps because we didn't have a kitchen table. To save money on the water bill, my mom and aunties would recycle the bath water, and we'd take baths with our siblings or cousins. I hated it. The little vice lords would sometimes float in the tub. Occasionally, we'd freak out when we'd spot an albino one that had shed its hard exterior during its molting phase.

My mother didn't believe in pity parties. After leaving my father, she bought a beat-up Chevy Caprice and took on a second nursing job. She put in more hours to make ends meet. She left our apartment by 7 a.m. and drove to her first job in the pediatric office at Humana Healthcare (now known as Advocate Health Care). Then, after her morning shift, several days a week, and most weekends, she'd drive two hours in traffic to Skokie, where she worked the graveyard shift at a nursing home. Sometimes she left my eldest sister, Yalonda, in charge of Tonia and me, making sure Yalonda cooked us something to eat. One of our aunties or older cousins was always around for adult supervision, or, in a pinch, my mother brought us to our grandmother Sophie's house. But much of the time, I had to fend for myself.

We Lived in a Danger Zone

One sticky, hot Chicago summer day, when I was five, we were on our way back home to Lockwood from my grandmother's house in the violent Holy City section of Chicago's West Side. I was in the back with Tiki while Yogi rode up front with my mom, who was catching up with us about our day.

We came to a stoplight, where a group of young teenage girls was crossing the street in front of our car, one of them lagging the others by a few feet. Suddenly, from the passenger side of our Chevy, a drunk driver sped by and veered into the crosswalk, hitting the slow-footed girl. We watched her fly up, up into the air, before falling and landing on her side. And then, charged with adrenaline, she sprung up and bolted to the other side of the street and collapsed in a heap again. The driver slowed for a split second, then accelerated and sped away. But in that moment before he peeled off, a group of Vice Lord gang members, who had seen the hit-and-run unfold in real-time from across the street, ran toward the drunk driver's car. They were armed with Uzis and sprayed him with bullets.

"Get down, now, now!" my mom screamed. "Now, Little Man! All y'all down! Duck! Duck!" she yelled frantically. But it was no use. I heard the rattle of the guns, and through the cracks between my fingers that covered my face, I had seen my first murder.

I may not have known it as a five-year-old in the back seat of my mom's car, but Uncle Matt and his sons ("Little Matt," Walter, and Aaron, whom everyone called "Boo-bee"), and just about every other man on my mother's side of the family, as well as some female cousins, were Vice Lords or affiliated with factions of the Vice Lords. Violence pierced my world that day. It was the first, but certainly not the last, time I would experience gun violence ending human life.

Back in our apartment building, across the hall from where we lived and one floor below, the family members I loved and the Vice Lords were one and the same.

My Vice Lord Roots

My family's involvement with the Vice Lords dated to the 1960s, when its mission was founded on community protection. From the early part of the twentieth century through the 1960s, Black families from the rural South migrated to the north, west, and Midwest, and to urban cities, such as Chicago, to escape segregation and oppression. The Vice Lord Nation, as they were known in the 1960s, was influenced by the Black Power movement. The members ran the group like a corporation, and they worked with community organizing groups to improve race relations among white, Latino, Italian, and Black residents. But by the 1980s, crack cocaine ruled inner-city Chicago, and the Vice Lords became involved in drug trafficking, which led to violence and turf wars. Boo-bee, and a few others in my family, held influential positions within the Vice Lords; they were known as "shot callers." Each was smart, confident, dominant in the streets, and out to make money. The men and women in these roles put food on the table and cared for their families.

They were important.

The Vice Lords were a part of my bloodline, and growing up, as natural as breathing, I knew that an influential role in the gang was ahead of me, too.

My mom was a fantastic listener.

When I was a boy, my cousin Boo-bee—the only other person besides my mother to call me Little Man—was my hero. He was so fly, looking like Michael Jackson from the early '80s before the surgeries. Boo-bee had a decade on me. He loved me like a little brother and scooped me under his wing. He'd pick me up in his Black Regal, wearing fresh sneakers and gold chain ropes, and we'd ride through the streets, bumping N.W.A through the loud customized speakers in his trunk:

Hanging tough, I'm the leader, ain't no need to pretend
Like an elevator up, I mean, I'm on the ascend

That same sweltering summer when I was five years old, I went swimming with a few of my other older cousins at La Follette Park public swimming pool. Boo-bee wasn't there, because what happened next wouldn't have happened if he'd been there to protect me. I couldn't swim, but I wanted to be in the water. So I held on to the rail, laughing, the youngest and smallest in that big pool, while my older cousins played, splashing and roughhousing. I was the most fair-skinned of all of us, and in their eyes, and the eyes of other Black Americans then, and still in some communities today, fair skin is associated with being soft, inferior, and weak. To some, I was not Black enough.

While my cousins would never dream of letting anyone in our neighborhood lay a finger on me, on that summer day, four of them got it into their minds that they had to toughen me up. So as a prank, they wrestled me and carried me to the pool's changing room and stuffed me inside a locker. They locked the door and left me there. It was dark, small, and hot. Alone and terrified, I yelled at the top of my lungs, beating on the locker door with all my might as much as possible with my limited range of motion, trying to bust it open and free myself. I couldn't breathe and began hyperventilating. I thought I was going to die. While everyone was off having fun in the pool, I could hear my screams echoing throughout the empty fieldhouse. After what seemed like an eternity, a worker finally heard me. He broke the lock and opened the door. I collapsed, sweaty and exhausted, into his arms.

I look back and see young Dominick, a kind, empathic boy. I was the kid who would break up pit bull fights or stop other kids from making homemade slingshots and pop cans to hurl at squirrels and cats. Nothing in me felt compelled to harm or bully others, especially those people and animals I knew to be more vulnerable than me. Perhaps this was because I knew what it felt like to be on the receiving end of what my cousins deemed "tough love," but was, in hindsight, cruel.

Mama's Heart-to-Heart Talks

My mom and Auntie Sophie, who also worked multiple jobs, eventually saved up enough money together to get us out of the 'hood and buy what we call in Chicago a "two-flat" or two story home, about a mile away from Crystal and Lockwood. It was still on the West Side but in the slightly better Austin neighborhood. We lived on the top floor and my Auntie Sophie took the bottom floor. Uncle Matt, who was handy, built another unit from scratch on the basement level for my grandma. For the first time, I had my own space—a sun porch extending off the bedroom my sisters shared. Uncle Matt tried to insulate it, but he couldn't fix the fact that my "room" was freezing in the winter, and hot as hell in the summer. It always felt like I was sleeping in a tree house. But at least we finally had a kitchen table.

My mom was a fantastic listener, and once my sisters moved out, I had more of those rare opportunities to be alone with her sitting at the kitchen table for heart-to-heart talks. We'd order Chicago deep-dish pizza, or she'd make hot water corn cakes and mac 'n' cheese or enchiladas. I loved her enchiladas, and when I was older, she knew I would come in from the streets if she made them. Sometimes, when pharmaceutical companies would visit the clinic where she worked, Mama would bring home leftovers from the big spreads of food they ordered to entertain the doctors. My mom always showed us her values in action through her hard work and love for us. But it was over the kitchen table that she planted the seeds in me to think about my future, telling me:

"Do what you can with what you are working with."

"Reach for the stars, Little Man, and don't ever give up on your dreams."

"Keep your word."

"Speak your mind without fear."

"Be loyal."

But events beyond my mother's kitchen table also shaped my Black boyhood. You can't control your kid's seeing a murder when he's five or protect him from getting a gun stuck into his stomach when somebody's trying to steal his football Starter jacket or gym shoes. Then his bike. A mom can't control shoot-outs in the barbershop or whether her child witnesses gang wars and drive-bys.

Feeling Powerless

When I was ten, Boo-bee was killed. And later, his brother Walter was murdered. I was in middle school, and I began acting out on my feelings of powerlessness and started punching holes in our apartment's walls.

My mother didn't know what to do. But she had health insurance, so she asked me to talk to a therapist. In Black culture at that time, the motto was "What goes on in the house stays in the house," and that was the way most people in the Black community dealt with their personal problems. But my compassionate mother was ahead of her time, and eventually I agreed to talk to someone. In the therapist's office, I spoke about

how my cousin Quentin and his drinking buddy Fred gave me my first taste of malt liquor at twelve. I got so drunk that I was practically flying through the street, my fast, strong, naturally athletic legs carrying me on an inebriated run that I felt could have gone on forever. Quentin, who had introduced me to football—how I looked up to him, coming through the building, like a warrior, with his helmet still on—was a powerful defensive tackle. He was fearful of my mother, known as "The Enforcer" among the aunties and uncles, and he tried to catch me and put me to bed to sober me up before she got home from work. As I sat in the therapist's office, I thought I might as well have been recounting my story to an alien: There was no way in hell that the white woman sitting across from me could ever begin to understand my life. *Do you know what I am? I'm a car rolling down the middle of a highway paved with my mother's hard work and values, but it's bumpy as all hell and full of potholes, and I just can't pull over.*

After school, I'd watch "dope boys"—slang for drug dealers—ride around in luxury cars, and the voice inside me said, "Money is tight; you have to earn money and help mama out!" That voice resounded in me like a chorus of other young Black men from humble beginnings, coming of age with me in the '80s and '90s. It didn't matter if one of us had our sights set on playing professional football or figuring out how to make the next wicked jump shot, like Michael Jordan, or we got into hustling dope. Our environment shaped us to "do something big" to lift ourselves out of poverty. My mother worked herself to the bone to keep the lights on and was driven by her love for us, and naturally, I thought: *I'm gonna go through them potholes. I'm gonna get my share of the fast money I see flying around and take care of my mother because there's nothing I won't do to help her and my fam. And eventually, I will roll toward better things.*

Hustling Drugs: A Short-Term Solution

Selling drugs came down to satisfying fundamental needs: food on the table and financial help for immediate and extended family. During my junior high football off-season, I began hustling nickel and dime bags of dope, and I was also a part of the notorious gang the Four Corner Hustlers. I never went back to the therapist.

I picked up drug hustling from watching my older cousins. By middle school, many of the men I depended on in my family were either dead or in jail. After Boo-bee was killed, my cousin Dre was shot in the back of his head over a dice game. Later, my cousin Walter was assassinated. Then my cousin Little Matt was sentenced to thirty years in prison when he was just fifteen for avenging his brother's murder. I had seen enough carnage to understand the cons of street life and had no intention of staying in the gang forever. I went to school and continued playing football. I was an excellent linebacker, and I excelled at art, architecture, and math. As soon as I turned fifteen, I found a job so that I could "clean" my drug money with a legit source of income.

My first job was bagging groceries at a store coincidentally named Dominick's. I applied to be a cashier since I was so good at math. Instead, my job at Dominick's was way mundane. Paper or plastic, stack the groceries, fetch the carts. Repeat. Repeat. Repeat. I lasted three months. I moved on to Kmart and other low-level jobs, as a utility clerk, cashing my paychecks and establishing credit so I could pay for a pager. I needed it for hustling. Minimum-wage jobs weren't taking me far, and although I wasn't proud of it, hustling channeled my ambition, and I rose through the ranks in the streets fast, wishing Boo-bee, Walter, and Dre, and others I had lost, were around to see me.

Eventually, along with the money came a lifestyle and the trappings of a masculine dude who was "doing it right": fast cars; $1,200 Coogi sweaters that emulated the rappers of the day—Biggie Smalls and 2Pac; the attention of women; and the feeling of power and respect.

The Tug-of-War: My Mother's Values versus Street Life

Still, I envisioned a life beyond hustling—making it past my twenty-first birthday, then twenty-fifth, a sustainable job, and a decent home. But my life was becoming a tug of war between my beautiful, kick-ass mother's strength, love, and positivity and the dark pull of fast cash and Chicago's Street culture. One summer, when I was still in high school, my mom told me about data entry summer jobs that her employer, Humana, offered. I recognized that it was a good opportunity and a chance for a "real job." I carpooled with my school friend Nick—his mom was a nurse, too—to affiliated clinics and hospitals, where we did office work and purged medical records. It was my first introduction to the administrative side of health care.

Despite the streets and because of my mother, I continued to work hard at sports, and I stayed in school, hoping one day to earn a football scholarship and attend college. I took advanced architecture courses and was good enough at drafting that the College of Creative Studies in Michigan aggressively recruited me for their automotive design program. But I did not apply.

Then, during my senior year, I broke my ankle. And with the injury went any hope of a football scholarship. Preferring to stay near Chicago than go to Detroit, I enrolled in Triton College to focus on design. I also took another legit job. My Auntie Valerie was a manager at a medical collection agency, and she suggested a temp job with MacNeal Hospital collecting claims for insurance companies. It later turned into a full-time corporate position as an account representative. We used to call the job "Dialing for Dollars," and I loved it! After all, I was a numbers guy. Hospital claims would be between $50 and $100,000, sometimes more, depending on the patient's procedure. Using the latest software tools to interpret contract rates and billing codes, I would problem solve, cleaning up the accounts receivable. My work made a significant impact on the revenue cycle, and I was promoted to managing the negotiations of all high-dollar claims.

I was carrying sixteen college credits, working forty hours a week, and still hustling drugs late nights on the street. Through my teenage years and into young adulthood, I was on a mission: *I gotta get mines, I gotta get this money, I gotta get this bread by any means necessary.*

By this time, I had made a name for myself and was known as a "shot caller," like my cousins before me, managing the distribution of cocaine.

An Exit Ramp or Death

I realize now that the larger my street status grew, the more Little Man got locked away. I felt myself becoming selfish, self-centered, and desensitized as I normalized the pursuit of money, power, and the material goods that came with hustling at the expense of others. I used human beings like lab rats: Every dealer had a drug addict or "hype" that we called when we needed to test our product before it went out into the streets. I wasn't happy to watch an addict's eyes roll back into their head or see their body shake while they snorted or smoked product, but in my mind it was a transactional relationship—there's no room for empathy when you are pressed for time and concerned about the money at the other end of the deal.

But I also had moments of clarity. I knew I had to find an exit ramp from a life of violence and dead ends, with more dead cousins and friends.

Life pivoted when I was nineteen. I was in my car smoking a blunt with my boy "P." We were on our way to do a cocaine drop-off across state lines, and the car panels were filled with concealed product. Having that much powdered cocaine in the car was as good as having cash. I had been running on two hours of sleep and had grown paranoid. *What if I get robbed, pulled over, or someone kills me on this trip?* I thought. Once we arrived at the "trap house"—abandoned houses where dealers store or transfer their products—a nightmare situation unfolded with the other crew. It's standard procedure during drug transactions for the product's recipient to check its quality upon delivery. But unknown to me and P, the cocaine we were carrying fell below the expected high-quality level. The other crew believed we were trying to pull one over on them. Angry crew members surrounded us. The mood turned tense. P and I now had our lives on the line. I stayed calm and talked the other guys down, de-escalating the situation and convincing them that the lesser quality goods we delivered were not intentional.

We returned home alive to Chicago, but after the life-or-death stakes of that drop-off, I decided to leave street life behind me for good.

One Final Pothole

When I was a sophomore, I transferred to Southern Illinois University Carbondale, about three hundred miles from inner-city Chicago, to make a clean break from the madness of my lifestyle. But even in Carbondale, Chicago gang culture was strong, and the design program I was enrolled in wasn't challenging. I returned home and began a design program at Columbia College. I resumed working full-time and focused on school, staying out of street-related activity.

Until one day, during the sticky hot "Chi-raq" summer of 2001, I received multiple phone calls from a childhood friend.

"I need your help," he said.

That summer, the streets of Chicago were "hot," meaning that the Feds had gotten wind of a large drug drop. When the streets are "hot," the idea is to stay "cold." Dealers pull their drug supply off the street, which causes a shortage, or drought. A drought means tough financial times in the 'hood. There are, however, a few people within the street's hierarchy who have the courage and audacity to release some of the drugs being held in reserve, giving the "green light" to "make it rain" and provide a source of cash flow.

"I can't do it," I told him.

"You're the only guy I know who can do it."

"I'm out the game. I can't help you."

"I really need your help. I'm getting pressured by these guys."

"That's not my problem."

I hung up the phone.

That didn't stop him from being persistent and calling me back-to-back for weeks.

"I can vouch for them on the lives of my family," he told me over the phone and on multiple voicemails. I sensed his life was on the line if I didn't help.

So I caved and arranged the deal.

You may be asking, how could you do that, Dom, when you decided to leave street life behind? Was it to help your friend? Or was it the thrill of "one last score" before retiring for good?

The answer is complex. Sometimes the human mind can't give a clear answer for why you do what you do in the moment. In retrospect, I think it was because, on my journey, I hadn't yet hit my bottom. This last pothole was the biggest of them all: its depth and width as grand as my misguided sense of strength and importance. I could not resist the power that came with being among the few street legends who would be brave enough to "make it rain."

The deal turned out to be a setup by the DEA working with the FBI and ATF. And the pressure my friend was receiving, unbeknownst to him, was from two informants.

The US attorney indicted me.

The United States of America versus Me

The first time I saw the indictment papers, I knew shit just got real. My older sister Yogi, who later went on to become a sheriff, helped arrange for me to have an experienced attorney with a high-level understanding of federal laws. She insisted on a Black man. We needed someone who understood the unfair biases young Black men face in the judicial system. Now, there were a lot of things I didn't like about my attorney. But up until that point in my life, he was the first Black man who sat down to speak with me, man to man, from an honest, hard place, with sound advice about my future.

"This is what is called karma," he said.

I had never heard the term before, referring to the Hindu and Buddhist belief that our actions decide our fate.

"The Universe is sitting you in a TIME OUT," he continued. "We can go to trial and fight this as an entrapment case, but listen carefully: *The federal government has a 90 percent conviction rate.* If you lose, they will make an example out of you. You're twenty-one years old—lose, and you're not coming home until you're in your thirties. Or you can go in there, chin up, and take full responsibility for your actions because you and I both know this could have been worse."

I took his advice. I was sentenced collectively to ten years: about five years of hard time in federal prison and another five years to be served on house arrest. Eventually, my lawyer was able to reduce my prison sentence by two and a half years on the condition that I enroll in a prison drug and alcohol program. The therapist I had seen once, at my mother's insistence, included a note in my medical record about drinking alcohol as an adolescent, and it was enough for the judge to grant me admission to the program.

Little Man Takes the Wheel

The Feds detained me for six weeks in Chicago's Metropolitan Correctional Center (MCC for short). It's an ugly, crowded twenty-eight-story high-rise with small block windows and a rooftop deck that provides the only access to sunlight. Think gladiator prison. Daytime at MCC was the only time I could find some privacy and peace of mind while my cellmates played cards on the deck.

When I found myself alone for the first time, my thoughts churned as I tried to figure out why the Universe had put me there. I understood I was in prison because of the consequences of my actions, but I was also searching for a deeper meaning. I don't want to say I was better than anyone else sitting in prison with me, but I knew my mother's love and the values she taught me shaped my heart and mind. And it caused me mental anguish to know that I had ambition and the potential to do more in this world than rot away in a jail cell. I felt vulnerable, alone, and afraid—not of others, since, trust me, I knew I could handle myself well physically. But for my mental health.

Now, I don't care if you are spiritual, religious, science-based, or atheist, all I know is a powerful Unknown Energy brought me to my knees in a prayerful search for a more significant meaning to my dire circumstances. And from my fear and emotional pain arose a vivid food memory: *I look at the chicken wings, and I look up at my mom, then I look back at the chicken wings, and then I look at my arms and back at my mom and I think to myself the chicken wings shouldn't be on my plate.*

"I'm not eating them."

"What do you mean you're not eating them?"

"I can't eat them. They look like ... little-bitty arms."

"Well, that's what's for dinner."

"Then I guess I'm not eatin' dinner."

It was as if the memory were a light bulb turned on in a dark room as Little Man. My empathic, innocent inner child broke through to me, showing me fragments of my life. And I began to piece them together for the first time. Through my childhood memory, I made the connection that for years I had lived in a way that differed from who I was meant to be: a protector. I decided then and there that if I was going to heal myself and heal from the violence of my life on the streets, then I had to denounce anything that had to do with causing harm to any living creature.

And as fast as the memory flashed across my mind, so did my new mantra: "If It Requires Harm, Then Nahh." And then, right there in prison, I immediately renounced eating meat.

So, what happened to eight-year-old Dominick after that chicken wings day? Well, for starters, I remember my mother wasn't too happy about my back talk. She busted her ass to put those chicken wings on the table. But it also showed her that I was willing to speak my mind, as she taught me. From then on, she went out of her way to buy fish sticks for me since their shapeless form masked their anatomy. (I think chicken nuggets and fish sticks are hugely popular for young children because they mask the connection between the life of a beautiful cow, pig, or chicken being sacrificed in the name of "food.") Life went on: junior football, video games, chasing girls in the streets, poppin' wheelies on my bike, another inner-city kid, lost among distractions.

But in my darkest hour, the compassionate energy of Little Man took the wheel and steered my life in a new direction.

Crazy! Weirdo!

At the time I renounced meat, I would have been labeled vegetarian, since I was still eating dairy and eggs. But calling myself vegetarian wasn't even a consideration. Back then, vegetarianism was still a fringe movement. And among Black people, eating vegetarian or vegan was asso-

ciated with white privilege, hippie dudes, and salads, and none of that was represented in my Black community. All I knew was that I didn't want to eat meat because if a living creature had to die, it inflicted harm and violence.

Mine was a fast and clean overnight transition.

When I began by trading my meat for veggies with my cellmates, they said:

"You're crazy."

"You're weird."

"You sure you don't want your meat!?"

I had never been more sure of anything in my life. Instead of meat, I intuitively reached for as much beans, rice, banana-filled oatmeal, apples, peanut butter, complex and simple carbs, and water, as I could. I wasn't getting enough vegetables in my diet, but I figured out that the inmates working kitchen duty for the prison staff were serving an abundance of fresh vegetables at lunch, and selling them on the side to inmates, like me, who wanted them; I would pay them in postage stamps for tomatoes, bell peppers, onions, lettuce, or any other produce I could get my hands on. I spent the little money I had purchasing more fruit and vegetables instead of chips and ice cream from the commissary. I didn't have access to supplements, the Internet, social media influencers, books, or documentaries, and so I didn't have a clue about how my body would respond without meat. Besides, it was the early 2000s, and most of those things didn't exist anyway.

My Outer and Inner Transformation

When I entered prison in my early twenties, I weighed more than 250 pounds. I'd spent plenty of late nights hustling and eating at Chicago sit-down staples like Portillo's, famous for its Italian beef sandwiches, and Pizzeria Due, with its deep-dish, or fast-food places we'd stop by in our cars. You'd catch me at JJ Fish (fried fish fillet sandwiches, fried chicken), Harold's Chicken (buckets of chicken there), and Mr. Submarine, aka "Mr. Sub's"—I loved a warm sub with a bag of fries and a Coca-Cola. I made my way to every mom-and-pop place, too: gyros, rib tips, French fries, soda, and sweets. It all contributed to weight gain and inflammation. No one I knew was really cooking; it wasn't something we did. My unhealthy diet of animal products, fried food, and processed carbs, and the negativity of street life, were taking their toll on my health. I had been a naturally gifted athlete as a boy, but by the time of my arrest, I was overweight, lethargic, and had gas pains in my chest and shortness of breath.

During my first three months without meat, my weight dropped from 250 pounds to a solid 190 pounds. I began weightlifting in the prison yard during recreation time to keep my mind occupied. Surprisingly, instead of discovering that I had become weaker, I started to emerge as the real person I was: As I became less inflamed, my former fast life fell away. I lost fat from my core (my love handles disappeared!). My arms and quads became muscular and defined, and my facial bone structure emerged. My chest was being rebuilt along with the rest of my body. Some guys leave prison with tattoos and unhealthy weight gain; I returned home with an ironclad chest and one incredible, strong body!

People often ask me what those days of transitioning from a diet of meat and terrible fats to plants felt like, and I tell them, "Honestly, it was the closest thing I have ever felt to feeling like I was a real-life superhero with a cape, superpowers, and incredible strength." I lifted weights two to three times a day to stay occupied, but also to burn off a surge of newfound energy. I became one of the strongest men among more than one thousand inmates in my prison compound. We would have what we called power "Lift-Offs," and I was always in the top five.

I was experiencing an organic, head-to-toe transformation.

My psyche also changed, a development I can only describe as a sense of inner peace. My mindset shifted when I adopted "If It Requires Harm, Then Nahh" as my mantra. For the first time in my life, I viewed the world with clarity, purposefulness, and reflection. I felt calmer and slept better. I started thinking critically about society's traditions and expectations, challenging the idea of the American Dream to make as much money as I could. By renouncing meat and removing myself from the cycle of inflicting pain on other beings, I felt like I was healing from the inside out. It was also my first experience being in touch with my "inner energy," or soul, for the first time.

My Understanding of Spirituality

Many ethical vegans don't discuss the spiritual aspect of their transition. But I came to my current vegan lifestyle through a crisis that forced me to confront my moral compass. My experience was nothing short of a rebirth from a life of violence and negativity. I understand this is not the case for everyone who chooses to eat a vegan diet. And it may not ring true for you. But before we move on, let's talk more about my understanding of the soul, which throughout this book I use interchangeably with the word "energy."

My mom raised us Christian and took us to church once in a blue moon. I had never explored other perspectives, beliefs, or theories about life in any meaningful way before prison. While incarcerated, I lived among men from different backgrounds and cultures, doing time for federal offenses. My "neighbors" were drug kingpins, white-collar criminals, executives, former military personnel, activists, politicians, Indigenous Native Americans, among others, and we all now had to get along. I studied and participated in religious rituals other than those rooted in Christianity. I attended open prayer groups, met Buddhists, and was exposed to different branches of Islam, including the Nation of Islam. When I was transferred to a prison in Colorado, I even participated in a teepee ceremony with Indigenous Native American inmates in the recreation yard, tapping out midway through since I couldn't handle the heat! (I'm sure my great-grandfather, who was an Indigenous Native American, wouldn't have been proud.)

As I sought to understand my place in the world during that time, I kept an open mind but never committed to a religious path. Instead, what I took from being exposed to different religious points of view was an awareness that we can *choose* what will inspire us on a moral and spiritual path.

"If It Requires Harm, Then Nahh" is my "why" for veganism. You will discover yours as we move through EWEE together.

Ultimately, I developed my spirituality and understanding of the soul, which I call energy. Most of my beliefs align more with science, which defines everything existing in the world as "energy stored in mass particle form." But also, energy, unlike flesh, can never be destroyed. As you continue reading, you will learn that plant energy is "live" energy, and "live" energy, like every energy composed of molecules, vibrates at different speeds. It is also fuel for your body, which I think of as a "temple," or the physical space your energy occupies in life. If you are dead, your molecules stop vibrating—everything comes to a complete stop. So do the molecules of dead animals; they do not vibrate. And your body, specifically your gut microbiome, sometimes called "our second brain," knows the difference between dead energy and live energy. By eating the "live" energy of plants, I am not just feeding my body; I am feeding my soul because I am fueling it with high vibrating whole-food plant energy.

A Dark and Challenging Test

Despite experiencing tremendous emotional, physical, and spiritual growth, one event caused me to hit a new rock bottom while incarcerated. I was playing chess with an inmate nicknamed "St. Louis" in the recreation room. It was close to our 4 p.m. mandatory head count, and the guards expected us to be in our cells without excuses or risk punishment. I rushed through my last moves on the board, eager to get to my cell, when St. Louis, who was about my size and build, called checkmate—game over. As retribution for losing, I owed him a set of pushups, but not wanting to be late for the head count, I told him I would pay him afterward. St. Louis became enraged. He insisted I drop and give him his due. We exchanged words, and as I turned to walk away, he picked up a heavy chair and swung it with all his might, striking me across the back of my head and knocking me out. I didn't see the blow coming. Everything went black as I fell face forward and hit the floor. I woke up with tubes through my nose, handcuffed to a cold hospital bed. Two correctional officers stood by my side.

I heard: "Inmate! Inmate! Do you know what happened to you?"

And then the doctor: "Please, he has head trauma; stop questioning him."

Numb, I closed my eyes. I had no hold on reality or who I was. I had no sense of what was happening or how to form words. I opened my eyes once more and fixated on the ceiling. And then, a warm sensation started from the top of my shoulders and moved up to my head. A cascade of my life's memories ran, in what felt like a billion directions, through my brain. It felt as if they were being downloaded, and I began to relive each one, in slow motion. Waves of horror and panic started to set in as the recollections flooded me, in chronological order, starting from childhood, right up to the recent memory of St. Louis's cowardly attack. I returned to the present with a tsunami of rage. I tried to bust out of my bed, but the officers restrained me. Against the doctor's recommendations, they transported me back to prison for interrogation, expecting me to implicate St. Louis.

Because we were inmates, St. Louis and I were federal property. And assaulting federal property is a crime. However, when interrogated, I denied knowing his identity. I wanted to ensure that the correctional officers didn't get to him first because I wanted REVENGE. Even though I had removed myself from the cycle of violence by not eating meat, it wasn't until years later that I realized how the incident with St. Louis was a test, challenging my process of dismantling the conditioning of My Life on the streets where violence is met with violence.

I chose not to name St. Louis as my attacker, and as punishment the officers sent me to the SHU— short for Segregation Housing Unit, also known as "The Hole," pending further investigation.

Hell Hole

The one detail Hollywood movies get right about prison life is portraying the living hell of The Hole. It is a maximum security six-by-eight-foot holding cell with three layers of steel doors and no ventilation, sunlight, or windows. My head injury, sleep deprivation—a fluorescent light remained on in the cell twenty-fours a day—and meals that lacked the sustaining nutrition left me weak and exhausted. The claustrophobia I developed from being stuffed in the public pool changing room locker worsened. I didn't think I would emerge from The Hole alive for fear of losing my sanity. It was the first time in prison that I feared for my life. I was kept in isolation for forty days and nights, returning on July 12—my mother's birthday—to the general prison population.

My experience in The Hole further tested my faith and fortitude. Of all the violence and scarcity that I had witnessed on the streets, I had never been on the receiving end of such deprivation.

Later in my journey, I could not help but draw connections between the inhumanity and unethical treatment I experienced and the lives of other sentient creatures, feeling their suffering as my own.

House Arrest

After nearly three years in federal prison, I was finally released to a halfway house to complete the house arrest portion of my sentencing and reenter society. I struggled with severe depression.

"If It Requires Harm, Then Nahh" is my "why" for veganism.

Despite my new mindset and physical transformation, I returned home angry at myself and bitter at the stigmas associated with my crime. I also developed increased sensory sensitivity—cars going by would make me feel nauseous and dizzy, and I despised hearing the music I had listened to growing up. I was distraught that I couldn't find a job—one of the conditions of being released was that I had to maintain employment; otherwise, I would be sent back to prison. My work hours were preapproved, but I didn't have permission to go to the gym before or after work. I was passionate about working out, and to lose that as an outlet increased my stress. So, I committed to basic home workouts—much like the ones people were doing during COVID lockdown. I held down odd jobs as a brand ambassador for a marketing company and another through a temp agency selling Verizon flip phones at Best Buy stores. I waited, with hope, to return to my former employer at MacNeal Hospital.

The hospital directors where I held my entry-level position during college were two women, a Black woman named Regina and a white woman named Kim. During my arrest and indictment, I remained honest with them, and because of their kindness, they allowed me to continue working during my pretrial. Once I was sentenced, they told me that if they were still employed with the hospital and able to help me, I had a home at MacNeal upon my release. They were nurturing, remarkable women in leadership positions who saw my potential and were willing to give me a second chance. When I returned home, I called them, and, true to their word, they fiercely petitioned the hospital, fighting like hell with the legal department, HR, and eventually the hospital president for my return to work. Because I was a convicted felon, it took several months to be approved.

My Fur Daughter, Soca

In the early days of my house arrest, I had plenty of time on my hands and no distractions. Smartphones didn't exist. I couldn't go on a date, take a walk, use the Internet, or see a movie. I was incredibly lonely.

Meanwhile, my mom told me that she was having a problem with her husband's Gremlin-lookin' chihuahuas ganging up on the little dog they had brought back from St. Thomas, and it was causing a rift in her marriage. I told my mom to bring me her puppy, thinking I could help raise her for six months—I had cared for stray dogs my entire life. One Saturday, my mom rang my bell, and I looked down to find a tiny fur ball she had named Soca hiding between her legs. I bent down, scooped her up with my right hand, and stood tall, holding her. I burst out laughing. And my mom started to cry: It was the first time since my return home that she had seen me

smile. Warmth flowed through me, where I had been so cold. I was in the presence of unconditional love.

During my house arrest, I spent hours with Soca—I would get on all fours to play, tickle, and slide around my wood floors with her. We'd watch Blockbuster movies surrounded by snacks on the couch, like two kids. And when I would return home from work, I would see her Disney Pixar–sized brown eyes bright, tail wagging, waiting for me at the windowsill. Throughout my life, I had never viewed animals as pets or property. I loved them as beings who shared my home, and I felt responsible for their lives. But I had never, before meeting Soca, connected to any other living being in the way I had attached to her. Soca was an intelligent, communicative life force, and she deepened my love for other species and helped develop my critical thinking about how we treat them. She was my best friend and my fur daughter.

She and my mother guided me through the challenge of claiming forgiveness, love, and patience toward myself.

A Second Chance

As we say in football, I took my fresh start at work, put it in a headlock, and ran with it, ascending the corporate ladder and parlaying my second chance into big career leaps. I took nothing for granted. The judge commuted my time, rewarding me for model citizenship, and I served only two years of house arrest. I moved from Chicago to Nashville and later to Atlanta for work, ultimately landing a job as a health care executive responsible for the business development and management of hospital systems across the eastern United States. In 2008, I went to New York City. My girlfriend at the time had taken a job in New York. Soca and I headed for the concrete jungle. I will never forget the first time I stood in my doorman building in Midtown. I looked at my girlfriend, a successful lawyer, and me, an executive, and I couldn't believe how my life had turned out.

I exhaled for what felt like the first time.

CHAPTER 2
OUR EAT WHAT ELEPHANTS EAT (EWEE) JOURNEY BEGINS

In New York, I could finally consider possibilities. Now in my thirties, I had moved beyond my childhood trauma and the legal issues of my early adulthood. I began to build a new life. I took up intense physical training: cycling, swimming, running, calisthenics, boxing, CrossFit, cross-training, and powerlifting. You name it, I did it. I competed in ten to twelve endurance races a year, including marathons, triathlons, and ultra-races.

My New Life

I became curious about the science of how I had come through such an intense physical transformation through eliminating meat from my diet. I went down online rabbit holes, educating myself on ways to fuel my workouts with whole fruits, grains, and vegetables. This was before the wealth of documentaries, such as *Forks Over Knives* and *The Game Changers*, offering robust, science-backed research and stories of elite athletes who improved their overall performance and recovery time through plant-based eating.

I read the *China Study* by T. Colin Campbell, PhD, and his son, Thomas M. Campbell II, MD. The elder Dr. Campbell was the first person to do a longitudinal study of how a modern Western diet comprising meat and animal products as primary sources of nutrition plays a significant role in promoting heart disease, cancer, and diseases associated with obesity. While many nutritional studies only focus on single nutrients and how they impact our health, the China Study was conducted over twenty years in rural China, where the participants lived for long stretches, sometimes their entire lives, on a diet of locally sourced plant-rich foods. Dr. Campbell and his team made significant, groundbreaking connections between lifestyle, diet, and disease prevention, showing that humans don't *need* meat and are, in fact, healthier without it.

But, Dom, Aren't Humans *Supposed* to Eat Meat?

Well, not actually. A ton of plants (and little meat!) is how humans have rolled for millions of years. Take a moment to stop and notice that your hands are soft and your fingers are long and suited for fine motor skills, which include picking rather than clawing or prying another animal open! And even though I've trained for and run in highly competitive endurance races, no human among us—even the most elite athlete—can reach the top speed of a big cat, who, when in pursuit of prey, can reach speeds up to eighty miles per hour!

Our flat molars are suited for grinding and are useless in tearing open the flesh and tendons of a captured animal. Humans' sharp incisors and canine teeth are for gripping and slicing; they're hardly sharp enough to tear raw flesh. Our teeth live in a tiny mouth compared to a carnivore's wide, hinged jaw that allows them to swallow huge chunks of meat. Ever looked at the intestines of a tiger? They're short and straightforward. Their highly acidic stomach chamber breaks down large amounts of protein, moving it rapidly through their digestive system without needing plant fiber. The human intestine is long by comparison—about three and a half times the length of our body. Plant matter passes slowly, assisted by fiber, to optimize the absorption of nutrients. And our alkaline saliva and salivary glands help us to predigest the fibers of fruits and grains and resemble those of herbivores—elephants, too!

True meat eaters—eagles, crocodiles, orcas, big cats, and bears (and other apex predators)—evolved to have complex sensory systems: enhanced vision, for example, that enables them to see deep into the night on land, air, or ocean, so they can track and corner another animal, and eat it raw. We humans need tools to corner, destroy, and slaughter defenseless animals in the wild.

Our physical engineering tells us that we are natural herbivores, designed to consume nutrient-dense live plant energy. We have existed and thrived for millions of years on a plant-based diet.

The Health Care Industry's Disconnect

Ironically, I worked in the health care industry and witnessed their failure to see the connection between chronic health problems and poor nutrition. My work required extensive domestic travel, and I discovered that you need only look at in-patient menus and hospital cafeteria food, with its animal-heavy SAD (Standard American Diet), to see what a hospital thinks of its community. Hospital kitchens are run with the same intention as the fast-food industry—feed as many people as possible while keeping costs down. And worse, there are often gaps in hospital communication among a patient's care team, the pharmacy, and the nutritionist. In the hospital culture I experienced, "patients" were dishearteningly referred to as "clients." I saw how hospital systems began billing yearly screenings, such as colonoscopies and mammograms, as diagnostic rather than preventive, which are covered by insurance, running up out-of-pocket costs to you, their consumer. Practices such as these aren't designed to promote good health or synthesize the data that links food and our well-being so that people can make healthy, plant-based choices. Instead, hospitals create environments that seem to look after their own bottom lines before they care for patients.

Black Americans are their sickest clients. They are 60 percent more likely to develop diabetes than a white American. In fact, the risks for Black Americans are significantly elevated in almost every potentially deadly disease, including cancer, diabetes, and high blood pressure. They have nearly double the first-time stroke risks. But there is some good news: Black Americans are starting to wake up, change their lives, and fight off obesity and other chronic health issues through veganism. A 2016 Pew Research Center survey shows that Black Americans are the fastest-growing vegan and vegetarian demographic in the country at 8 percent, compared to 3 percent of Americans overall.[1] An article published in the *Journal of Medical Ethics* questioned the ethical obligation of doctors to screen for their patients' ability to access whole food sources of nutrition,[2] similar to the way they screen patients for smoking or cancer, when we know the benefits of a whole food plant-based or vegan diet saves lives.

Our physical engineering tells us that we are natural herbivores.

Deepening My Awareness of Widespread Animal Abuse

One day, while living in New York, and doing some research, I stumbled across the documentary *Earthlings*, which exposed animal cruelty and unspeakable abuse in the factory farming, cosmetic, clothing, and entertainment industries using hidden camera footage. At the time, I had been committed to my "do no harm" mantra and hadn't eaten meat for more than a decade. And yet, I had not been aware of the rampant animal abuse in the dairy and agriculture industry. *Earthlings* left me shaken. It brought back memories of watching late-night television as a boy when commercials from PETA (People for the Ethical Treatment of Animals) would air portraying the violent slaughter of animals. I would cringe and close my eyes in fear, reaching for the remote, just as I did when a trailer for a scary movie came on.

The scenes of extreme violence and degradation of other living beings in *Earthlings* made me heartsick. This also made me aware of a new way to describe my true self—as an empath, or a person in tune with the feelings and emotions of others. I don't remember where I first heard the word "empath," but when I learned it, it impacted me much the same way as hearing "karma" for the first time. From that point on, defining myself as an empath made sense to me. I *am* in tune with the energy of other sentient beings and place as much value on their well-being as my own.

After watching *Earthlings*, I immediately eliminated eggs and dairy from my diet. I remember the look on my girlfriend's face when she came home from work to see our refrigerator no longer held her yogurt containers. She asked, "What happened to my yogurt?!" and I replied, "I threw it out. We will no longer have animal products in this home. You are lucky I didn't throw out your expensive designer purses and shoes because I threw out most of mine and will be donating the rest to charity."

Factory Farming: It's About Money, Not Food

The meat industry developed out of American capitalism—not as a necessity to feed people. Until the mid-nineteenth century, meat eating, for most Americans, was considered a privilege be-

cause it was so expensive. After the Civil War, however, technological advances, including chilled train cars that allowed for the transport of cattle and pigs from Midwestern pastures to the Chicago stockyards where the animals would be inhumanely confined before being sent to slaughterhouses, helped Chicago become the epicenter of the meat industry. Its railways connected to points west, where livestock were raised, and to points east, where there was a robust market for meat distribution.

In 1904, Upton Sinclair went undercover in Chicago meatpacking plants. In his book *The Jungle*, he exposed the filthy, inhumane conditions under which the animals were transported and slaughtered and where people, mostly immigrants, toiled in the excruciating conditions of the plants. Capitalism, which placed profit above the well-being of animals and humans, drove the widespread availability of cheap meat. There was no going back. As the price of meat dropped because of this new animal industrialization, Americans' demand for meat increased. No longer a privilege, meat moved to the center of our plates, bringing a range of health, social justice, and environmental problems, which worsened as killing animals fast became a necessity to meet the demand.

The 1930s saw the mechanized slaughtering of pigs, and then, by the 1950s, the rise of Concentrated Animal Feeding Operations (CAFOs), which have all the cold, hard feelings of their name, allowed for the housing of thousands of chickens in single indoor facilities to breed, mass-produce eggs, and make their meat widely available.

CAFOs, also called intensive farming, thrive in capitalism—maximum profits with minimum expenditure. Each year, CAFOs inflict atrocities on billions of pigs, chickens, cows, ducks, turkeys, sheep, and, in intensive aquacultures, fish. Of the seventy billion or more farmed animals around the world, fifty billion of them are factory-farmed. If you haven't yet watched a documentary such as *Earthlings*, with hidden-camera footage that shows the atrocities inflicted on factory-farmed animals, it may shock you. And you may want to make radical changes to your diet (see The Cold Tofurky Pathway, page 90).

Prepare yourself before watching one and have the comfort of a friend or loved one close by, if you need that. And if you don't plan to see one of the documentaries but would still like a sense of the cruelty inflicted on animals, read on for a list of the practices depicted. As you read, keep in mind that the workers employed to make this system operate are disproportionately people from surrounding marginalized communities. They also suffer. A person has to bury their empathy and compassion to stun, gas, electrocute, kick, slaughter, and slit throats to make ends meet.

- Farm animals are treated as property and housed in cramped, filthy indoor conditions without access to natural light or grazing.

- Cows must be pregnant to make milk for their calves. They are forcibly bred, and the factory workers tear calves from mothers at birth, causing distress for both.

- To keep cows, pigs, and turkeys "healthy" in cramped stalls, they are fed preventive antibiotics. The overuse of antibiotics contributes to the development of antimicrobial resistance (AMR), a condition in which humans develop a resistance to antibiotics. This is why people are increasingly getting sick and can't be treated through previously effective uses of antibiotics. Eating meat is literally making people sick, and costly hospitalizations from it are on the rise.

- Factory farms and slaughterhouses are death houses. The cries and moans of suffering are loud, and fear is palpable. Animals must walk into the slaughterhouse on their own, fully conscious. We kill twenty-five million unique creatures, each with distinct personalities, every day. Animals are stunned before they are slaughtered, but it often fails to make them unconscious. Cows and pigs are strung up alive and upside down to have their throats slashed.

- Over one thousand pigs are killed an hour in slaughterhouses. Pigs, whose intelligence is equivalent to that of a family dog, live without natural light on slatted floors, confined to sleeping and eating in their excrement.

- In aquaculture, fish are subjected to stressful, cramped living conditions, causing diseases and parasites. Their fins rot.

- Chickens are confined in small, wired cages and undergo a painful practice of beak trimming, to reduce pecking. They show signs of helplessness, pain, and an inability to eat. Some are beaten to death or thrown away and left to suffocate.

- Chickens, turkeys, and ducks are shackled to conveyor belts to be "processed"—the term for their mass slaughter by mechanized throat cutters.

Behind-the-scenes footage and what I just described exposes animal cruelty at the hands of large corporate-owned intensive farms, and so people often ask, "What about humanely raised animals, Dom?" I believe that there is nothing humane about imposing painful castration, branding, and death on innocent creatures in the name of "food"—even on small, family-owned farms.

"If It Requires Harm, Then Nahh."

My Animal Rights Activism

In New York, I became involved in animal rights activism, helping to raise awareness about the cruelties of factory farms. But until then, I had never met a cow, pig, or chicken up close and personal. One day, I was invited to meet the residents of a pig sanctuary in New Jersey. It was my first visit to a farm sanctuary—nonprofit forever homes for farmed animals rescued from the cruelties of abuse and slaughter of the factory farming system. For the first time there, I looked into the eyes of several of the resident hogs and experienced firsthand their strong personalities and life force—which I can only describe as their "energy" or soul—and I could feel my lifelong love of animals come full circle.

I understand that wrapping your mind around the idea that animals have souls may be new or feel challenging, especially if you're not yet used to the idea that all living things have a soul or source of energy that is infinite. But choosing veganism doesn't have to be about spirituality. Not all vegans are spiritual. In fact, many believe in secular humanism—humanity's ability to reason and be decent toward one another, and toward other species. Secular humanism is guided by the natural, physical world, and secular humanists believe that animals are sentient beings—that they have the ability to feel and perceive the world on their terms—and don't deserve to suffer. They experience pain, loss, anxiety, fear, dread, doom, love, and everything else that comes with a central nervous system.

Think of the beauty of a sunset, the joy of hearing your favorite song, or the exhilaration of fresh air. Animals may not express their responses to these stimuli in ways familiar to us—such as the excited wagging of my fur son Roc's tail—but we know more now than ever about the profound complexity of nonverbal communication among them. The more evidence we uncover, the more we understand that animals have unique personalities and feelings—yes, personalities! If you share your home with a dog or cat, you know what I am talkin' about.

This first visit to a farm sanctuary moved me to urgently communicate that just like the animals we care for and love in our homes, so, too, do sentient farm animals provoke adoration, feelings of wanting to care for and protect them, and move one to provide the best quality of life for them. I continued to visit other farm sanctuaries, befriending cows, chickens, turkeys, and pigs (and ducks, too!), so that I could have the privilege of doing good for their lives via my social media and activism. With each visit, I experience a remarkable range of personalities. Some residents, usually the turkeys, dogs, or pigs, will come right up and greet me. The body language of others is often more stand-offish, as if to say, "Who's on our turf!?" And who could blame them? I have also been wary of human interaction. I have experienced how people in positions of authority can treat others so cruelly.

Raising awareness about animal cruelty is about dismantling cognitive dissonance—a psychological term that means your beliefs and values don't align with your actions. For example, you might call yourself an "animal lover" and never dream of hurting one—the domesticated ones—yet you choose meat over plants. The agriculture industry works hard to keep factory farms and slaughterhouses out of sight, so we disassociate the meat on our plates from the harm that makes our meat-based meals possible. The less we see, the less we know, and the more we accept—and don't question—the cultural tradition of buying and eating dead animals. The cycle will carry on uninterrupted. Most of us have been raised in a culture that simply considers farm animals as food sources. Even if we know, in our innocence, that we do not want to eat them, just as I did as a child, it *is* hard to choose differently for ourselves.

It takes work to transform harmful traditions into "do no harm" practices. Our ability to reason, rationalize, make decisions, and create values that influence our behaviors and understand the harmful and beneficial actions toward animals is what sets us apart from them. Putting plants first asks us to celebrate human intelligence as compassionate caretakers of all animals rather than as their exploiters.

All species deserve our protection.

Emotional and Mental Strength

I knew for years how eating plants contributed to my powerful body. I also knew in my heart that my "do no harm" mantra and intentionally choosing a diet rich in fruit, whole grains, and vegetables played a role in my transformation into an emotionally and mentally strong person.

If you are wondering, *Dom, how can fruits and veggies make* me *happy or emotionally strong?* You need only to look to the dozens of recent studies, such as a longitudinal study of over fifty thousand participants in the United Kingdom called "Lettuce Be Happy." The data showed that the number of fruit and vegetable portions we consume daily is directly related to long-term physical health *and* the subjective experience of happiness.[3] A similar study in Australia that followed 12,385 people shows that while healthy changes to our diets can take years to show up in our physical well-being, feelings of "happiness," purpose, and self-worth happen much sooner. Participants' well-being in this study was reported as the equivalent of "moving from unemployment to employment."[4]

And while happiness is subjective, ongoing studies in the field of neuroscience paint a complex gut-brain connection that shows how our gut hormones and brain neurotransmitters participate in a two-way conversation via the gut-brain axis. The gut-brain axis is described by researchers as a kind of "superhighway"—each sending signals to the other and impacting our stress levels, emotional responses, hunger, and sleep patterns.

Throughout our gastrointestinal system, but mostly in our intestines, lives a population of trillions of bacterial microbes, or "little bugs," that make up our gut microbiome. Most of these microbes are vital to our heath and prevent us from getting infections and diseases. The bugs that live in *your* gut microbiome are more unique to you than your fingerprints, and they are impacted by the quality of your nutrition.

In the largest analysis so far to study the link between depression and the bugs in our guts—conducted in the Netherlands among 2,600 individuals and called "Gut Microbiome-Wide Association Study of Depressive Symptoms"—researchers revealed sixteen types of bacteria that were referred to as "important predictors" of varying degrees of depressive symptoms.[5] One of the best things we can do to keep the "good" gut microbes flourishing and the "bad" depression-causing gut microbes in check is to feed our bod-

My fur son, Roc.

ies nutrient-dense, fiber-rich vegetables and fruits.

Eating plant-based and feeding my gut whole foods filled in and paved the potholes of my life by creating a healthy, smooth superhighway within my body.

The Empathetic EWEE Mindset

Moving through the world with a mindset that fosters protection and love, rather than hurting and destroying, made me happier and more peaceful: It was clear to me that I had uncovered and deepened my natural-born empathy through my food choices.

The gratitude, calm, and ability to regulate my

emotions that I experience living my mantra "If It Requires Harm, Then Nahh" is borne out in global studies. The one that has most affirmed my identity as an empath and vegan is an Italian study conducted in 2010 among twenty omnivores, nineteen vegetarians, and twenty-one vegans. Using functional MRI (a type of MRI used to measure subtle changes in blood flow to different brain areas), researchers tracked participants' empathic responses as they observed images depicting human and animal suffering. The empathy quotient average of vegetarians and vegans was more than ten points higher than that of the omnivorous participants.[6]

Human connection to all living creatures builds empathy. And to instigate meaningful change—on society's quest for human and animal rights, for social justice, environmentally, and our own health—we must first understand and cultivate empathy. It is at the heart of our ability to value one another.

In 2012, I set out to disrupt the vegan narrative—one that's often associated with being meek and eating lots of "rabbit food"—to help build a more inclusive vegan community. I began sharing my "do no harm" mantra, animal rights activism, and my strong body on social media. I wanted to show what a vegan triathlete who cares for all living beings can look like. And all kinds of folks, from the plant skeptical to the plant- and vegan-curious to the plant-fueled athlete, began direct messaging me. They wanted to know how I was able to reap the physical, mental, and emotional benefits of my compassionate vegan life. I led by example, sharing my athletic content—my body on plants spoke for itself! In 2017, I shared my origin story on ultra athlete and bestselling author Rich Roll's podcast. I reminded people from all walks of life that it's okay to accept your past and be vulnerable. It's okay to talk about mental health and show your feelings. And I wanted people to know that making changes in their lives and evolving, and thinking of themselves as compassionate protectors of all beings, has a direct impact on us as individuals, on our communities, and on our planet.

My Way of the Elephant

For years I believed strength meant being a physically, financially, and emotionally dominant *man*. Back in the day, you wouldn't want me to whoop your ass with my big arms and "boxer's reach" if I had to. It rained money when I was a "shot caller." And I wouldn't let anyone get through my protective shell for fear of being seen as vulnerable, or what some men culturally in those days would describe as "weak."

The gut-brain axis is described by researchers as a kind of "superhighway."

But as I matured and followed my "do no harm" path, my new definition of strength became a nongendered one, based on compassion, empathy, and vulnerability. My vision of strength is inspired by two sources: my mother's kindness, integrity, ability to overcome challenges, and her willingness to communicate; and from the strength of our world's largest herbivore and my ancestral guide: the mighty African elephant.

The deeper into my vegan journey I traveled—reaching for whole, unprocessed foods—the more I reconnected to my native African roots, specifically precolonial Africa when people there subsisted mainly on plants, fruits, seeds, and nuts. I traced my bloodline and family history to Nigeria and the Congo, where elephants are esteemed and protected. And I began to feel a natural, effortless pull toward them—as if my love for them was part of my DNA. They became my guides for the next phase of my life.

The words scientists use to describe elephants—intelligent, community-oriented, and compassionate—are the same words that I use to describe my choice to be vegan. Veganism embodies the ethical, environmental, and social justice values that lead to taking care of one another. Elephants, more than any other animal (although I love them all), take care of one another, too, replenish the planet, and are, above all, strong.

Additionally, strong herbivorous mammals, such as elephants, can recognize other living beings and exhibit conscious, purposeful, goal-directed behavior. They can also understand the physical competence and emotional state and intentions of others.

Glorious elephants in African forests make their way over land, using their trunks and large feet, paving the way for other animals to travel. In times of drought, they use their strength and trunks to dig for water—a source of life—for themselves and other species. A complex ecosystem depends on elephants for existence and survival. Through their grazing and stomping, forest elephants of Central Africa contribute to the growth of rainforest trees, which trap carbon.

The more I saw humans' health and environmental issues intersect with justice and animal protection, the more I understood how the fabric responds as soon as you pull at one thread. The issues are interwoven.

CHAPTER 3

CONNECTING THE DOTS

The vicious cycle of cruelty and injustice that begins in the factory-farming industry is inextricably linked to the well-being of people and the planet. An EWEE journey shows us how to shift our mindset so we can change course and choose a life affirming path to healing people, the environment, and animals.

The Oppression of People

Factory farming is an oppressive system built on dominating, controlling, disempowering, and inflicting harm on animals. That much is obvious. But it's also detrimental to people. In the 1970s, the English philosopher Richard Ryder coined the word "speciesism." Speciesism drives the idea that animals are on Earth just for our needs. But speciesism is also closely related to racism, xenophobia, and other discriminatory practices.

At the center of these destructive mindsets is a flawed definition of strength: that disregarding the inherent rights and desires of another human or a nonhuman species makes one powerful. A misguided sense of strength supports the belief system that one species or race or nationality or gender or religion is more intelligent or deserving than another. Such justification and righteous resolve in pursuit of resources and power elevates one group by oppressing another. It lies at the center of all oppressive systems. Think about these atrocities against humanity:

- The Atlantic slave trade

- Manifest destiny and the practice of driving indigenous people off their land

- The Holocaust

The oppressors justified the exploitation of races and cultures with the belief in the supremacy of one race over another. These horrors, and all the "isms" that accompany them, rely on an "Us" versus "Them" mentality. An intersectional mindset, rather than a single-issue approach, such as just focusing on animal advocacy (although that may be a "why" that led you here), allows us to practice *all-encompassing compassion.*

An Intersectional Mindset

For vegans, an intersectional mindset means we look to our allies in the human rights movement and move animals *and* humans forward into a space of love and well-being. Intersectionality asks us to look at our privileges—whether that means making better food choices, or the way we move through life with social and material privileges— and recognize the injustices and cruelties that impact the marginalized people who make animal products available.

For years, veganism was associated with petite white women, picky eaters, and the wealthy. An intersectional mindset is inclusive: It shows veganism through a broader lens and with diverse voices and stories, and acknowledges the common ground between the exploitation of animals and the oppression and exploitation of humans. Take the production of cocoa powder, for example, a naturally vegan food. It may "do no harm" to animals, but it harms humans: Slave labor and the exploitation of children occur in horrendous conditions among leading exporters of cocoa beans in Brazil and West African countries. Intersectionality asks us to raise our awareness to make ethical choices that benefit all species involved. Intersectionality recognizes that our society is complex and built on an oppressive and unjust patriarchal system—men hold power, at the exclusion of women (a flawed idea of strength!). It recognizes that capitalism, which prioritizes profit over the good of all species, and the well-being of our planet, is at the center of exploitation and is fundamentally unethical.

Race and Class in Our Food System

When the first Black-owned McDonald's franchise opened in Chicago in 1968, it was a symbol of desegregation and Black small business ownership. McDonald's saw a huge market in Black patronage and franchising opportunities and tapped it greedily. But what happens when you add nutritionally poor, cheap "foods" to a meat-based Southern food tradition in Black communities? Higher risk for chronic illness and disease.

The poorer quality and convenience foods that people in these communities buy, the more companies spend on advertising—disproportionally targeting Black and Brown communities, placing them at risk for obesity and diet-related disease. The cycle is vicious. Some of these neighborhoods of color are classified as food deserts—neighborhoods where access to fresh food, or transportation to get some, is limited. The genetic predispositions to chronic disease and nutritionally deficient, inexpensive food in these communities intersects with systemic racism and oppression rooted in domination.

Environmental Racism

Rural Black communities also experience "environmental racism." Environmental racism is when policies and regulations violate and disregard the rights of communities living near farm factories to ensure the privilege of the lives and well-being of "other" communities. It is a human rights issue. No law regulates where CAFOs can be built, so corporate agricultural companies choose poor zip codes where land and labor are cheap and where residents lack the resources to advocate for themselves.

Poverty is not just about lacking money in your hand to buy things. The lack of money affects your physical, mental, and emotional well-being. It is destabilizing to live day to day without job security, access to healthy food, or access to health care. Poverty makes you feel small and unimportant, vulnerable, and alone. It makes you feel like you have no control, even when you know what is happening outside your window is wrong. Poverty forces people into compromising

situations that threaten their health and cause suffering. It removes your ability to *see possibilities* in your future, for a better life—like changing homes or improving your health. Getting from one day to the next is exhausting. And so it stands that marginalized, poor, rural communities are ideal places for large corporations to build CAFOs. A small group of people fighting alone will not change corporate greed. But if we advocate in large numbers for marginalized people, and refuse to buy animal products, then they will have to listen. Because they will lose the one thing they care most about—money.

Environmental Health and Social Justice Issues

Let's look at one food—pork—to connect the dots and illustrate how factory farming impacts surrounding communities of color, and those who live in poverty.

Eighty percent of the pork at grocery stores comes from North Carolina. It is home to more than seven thousand massive factory farms, where millions of animals live in windowless enclosures. Black, Latinx, and Indigenous Native Americans make up almost half of the people living near CAFOs in North Carolina. They breathe the nauseating stench of methane produced by the animals, and that induces respiratory illness, such as asthma, and headaches. Landfills in these communities are filled with sludge and carcasses that leak into flood zones during storms and cause animal waste to flow into waterways, polluting rivers and air. What's more, foul-smelling pig-waste lagoons—open ponds of dark-brown wastewater—get converted into sprayable airborne fertilizer. More is sprayed than the ground can absorb, and it contaminates the ground water and drinking water and spills into the nearby rivers and streams. When residents complain, pork producers harass and intimidate them.

Can you imagine this happening to you or where you live?

Environmental health and social justice are inextricable in marginalized communities: Factory farms employ undocumented workers and people of color. They work in dangerous and abusive conditions: Exposure to deadly toxins from manure and airborne pathogens sickens them. They are exposed to stressful noise from thousands of screaming animals in a confined space. The risk of injury from sharp equipment is ever present. All for a low wage, often below the legally mandated minimum wage.

Children are harmed, too. While schools with white children are located far from factory farms, schools with larger populations of children of color are closer to those farms because they are situated in poor communities. These kids have disproportionate rates of asthma and symptoms of other health issues.

Protecting marginalized communities begins with a light-bulb moment: Aha! The food I buy impacts other people—not only animals.

How to Be an Ally

Shifting purchases from animal products to plant-based foods is one way to advocate for protecting people (and it's a benefit to your health, too!). So, too, is deepening your commitment to becoming part of a sustained social resistance movement through veganism. Disruption is already making an impact. Food producers see the demand for plant-based products rise; they are investing, if not fully pivoting, to include them on their menus and in stores—you can get a nonmeat burger just about anywhere these days. And advocates on the federal level are listening, too. In 2019, vegan New Jersey Congressman Cory Booker drafted the Farm System Reform Act (FSRA), which recognized that exploitative CAFOs are a food issue and a racial justice issue. The bill proposes the end of CAFOs by 2040.

For now, if your "why" is to become part of the resistance and protect people, you can begin by moving more plant foods to the center of your plate, one meal at a time, one day at a time, crowding out harm, and practicing compassion for all.

Our Planet Is Suffering

Factory farming does more harm to our planet than any other human activity. And according to a 2022 report from the United States Intergovernmental Panel on Climate Change,[1] the most important move we can make to save our planet is to adopt a plant-based diet.

Let's start with greenhouse gases. These gases in the Earth's atmosphere—some naturally occurring, others human-produced—trap heat from the sun. The major ones are carbon dioxide (CO_2), methane (CH_4), nitrous oxide (N_2O), and fluorinated gases. They are called "greenhouse" because, just as a greenhouse's glass roof traps heat from the sun, so the gases trap heat in the atmosphere. At the start of the European and American Industrial Revolution in the eighteenth century, human activity triggered the release of these gases. Think the invention of cars, burning fossil fuels, more machinery and factories. This ignited "the greenhouse effect," which increases global temperature and changes climate patterns—it's one reason why extreme storms and floods increase each season. It also causes polar ice caps to melt, which is disastrous since they protect our atmosphere by reflecting the sun's heat away from the Earth back into space. And when polar ice caps melt, they add water to the ocean, raising the sea level. A rising sea level causes serious floods and endangers and disrupts the lives of people living in coastal cities, the surrounding infrastructure, and wildlife. Factory farming is the biggest contributor to the rise of these worst offending greenhouse gases:

- **CARBON DIOXIDE:** Factory farms rely on fossil fuels for energy to produce animal feed, to transport truckloads of live animals to slaughterhouses, and to heat CAFOs. This produces unsustainable amounts of carbon dioxide. Clearing land for animal factories and to plant animal feed crops removes trees as natural environmental protectors, since they absorb carbon dioxide.

- **METHANE:** Cows, pigs, and chickens produce excess methane through manure and digestion. When billions of cows expel gas and burp out the methane that naturally occurs in their guts, they release about 19 percent of the overall 42 percent percent of methane that animal agriculture contributes to the climate crisis.

- **NITROUS OXIDE:** The large-scale use of synthetic fertilizers releases nitrous oxide. It depletes the ozone layer, which protects us from the sun's ultraviolet B (UVB) rays—these medium-wave rays cause sunburn and damage skin cells, which leads to skin cancer. The only way to reduce nitrous oxide is to decrease the global demand for meat, which, in turn, will reduce the use of fertilizers.

The Misuse of Resources, Toxic Waste, and Other Environmental Harms

The harms that follow are just a brushstroke of a larger picture of the environmental damage caused by the agricultural industry. Everyday resources, such as land, fresh water, and oxygen are at risk.

- Most farmland is used to grow food to feed animals, and yet more than 10 percent of Americans experience food insecurity. This land could be reallocated to grow good-quality, nutrient-dense food. I mean, really, WTF?!

- Specialty farming—growing the same crops year after year to sustain farmed animals—creates a reliance on pesticides and fertilizers. They deplete the soil, run off into waterways, and contribute to the release of nitrous oxide into our atmosphere.

- Fresh water is diverted away from people to grow crops for animal feed. Wait a minute: We breed animals purposely and irresponsibly, and now, we take water from people to give to animals? YES. And this: It takes twenty times more water to produce cow meat than to grow vegetables.

- Excess nitrogen from fertilizers and animal-waste runoff pollutes the Mississippi River and contributes to the Gulf of Mexico Dead Zone, where algae overgrow and fish can't survive.

Let's talk about the other parts of the globe: To meet the demand for beef in South and Central America, rain forests are cleared to create farmland for cattle. As a result, biodiversity suffers with the extinction of organisms and the habitats of other animal species—tigers, orangutans, chimpanzees, elephants, monarch butterflies. This deforestation destroys trees (which provide oxygen for breathing), plants and flowers (many of them with healing properties), and insects that pollinate and aerate the soil and control pests that harm vegetation.

Our planet's biodiversity is critical to humanity's survival.

For millions of years, humans lived among stable and expanding resources of rich biodiverse organisms that adjusted and adapted with us, supporting and ensuring our survival as a species.

We never have, in the history of humanity, experienced "low biodiversity."

Until now.

We are living in the era of the sixth mass extinction, and the only one caused by human action.

It is only reversible if we change our behavior and greatly reduce, if not eliminate, our meat consumption.

CHAPTER 4

NINE STEPS TO THE EWEE MINDSET

In some ways, EWEE living "happened" to me. I had been so low, that apart from death, the only way I could go was up. Nobody sat me down and showed me how to do it. I didn't have a compassionate guide or manual. I just made my way, one day at a time, one meal at time, reaching for life-affirming energy to nourish me, and living my "do no harm" mantra.

I know what it means to feel challenged to take on new habits, and also let old ones fall away.

I want you to know that all change, no matter which areas of our life you want to shake up, is fueled by your ability to learn, grow, reflect, and adjust.

Growth Mindset

Learning, growing, reflecting, and adjusting are the hallmarks of what world-renowned psychologist Dr. Carol Dweck calls the "growth mindset theory." Her theory says "fixed-minded" people—those who believe they came into this world "as they are" with little room for improvement—find making lasting changes in their lives difficult. "Growth-minded" people—those willing to learn, grow, and reflect—have an easier time developing new skills and habits, such as learning to shop, cook, and eat plant-based or vegan. In Dweck's theory, I recognize my mom's positive can-do attitude, motivation, imagination, and value-based living, even as she faced the financial and emotional stress of keeping it together as a Black single mother with three kids. That's why Dweck's work speaks to me. Her research, along with that of other scientists, in neuroscience (the study of the human brain) has shown the neurons in our brains—the cells responsible for transmitting messages—can strengthen in their connections, meaning that if we put our minds to it, we can change our behaviors at any time in our lives. As my mama always said: "It's never too late to learn."

Whether on the streets or working as an executive, I was always looking to move up in rank. I didn't call it a "growth mindset," it was just a part of my attitude and perspective on life that I gleaned from my mom. You can call it your "hustle," your "know what to do when the shit hits the fan," or that "walk the walk" when you "talk the talk" mentality. Your mindset is the lens through which you see the world—also called your perspective, aka "what makes you tick."

Check Your Mindset

Adopting a new diet can feel uncomfortable at first. These seven questions will put you in touch with how you feel about making changes or adjustments in your current diet to Eating What Elephants Eat.

1. First, start by asking yourself: Am I someone who avoids challenges and gives up quickly?

2. Next, think back to a time when you were aware that poor eating habits would not pay off for good health in the long term. Perhaps you felt overwhelmed or stuck, not knowing where to

start to change them, or as an omnivore you were afraid to deal with discomfort or conflict that might unfold if you tried something new. ("You're crazy.") ("Weirdo.")

3. Now, ask yourself if you believe in your capacity for change. Do you have thoughts such as "I wasn't born with a knack for self-care, cooking, or athletics"?

4. Do you have a hard time seeing yourself breaking away from cultural or familial meat-based food traditions because they are deeply ingrained in your identity?

5. What associations or feelings do you have with the plant-based eaters or vegans you may know? Positive, negative, neutral? A plant-based or vegan identity may be important to you. Or you may choose to eat more nutrient-rich plant foods without "labeling" your choices—that is great, too. Which one works for you?

6. What feelings/comments do you think people would have toward you if you chose to bring faux meat to the family BBQ instead of eating your cousin's pork ribs? Or your grandmother's gumbo?

7. And finally, consider this question, if applicable to you: Do you believe that to enact any change for your health, and the well-being of others, going plant-based or vegan requires perfection?

Nine Steps to the EWEE Mindset

If you can identify with any of those "fixed mind" questions above, you'll benefit from the nine steps below. They are foundational to the EWEE "growth mindset" and to this book, and I hope they help you embrace change and give you information that may perhaps be new to you.

1. **ACCEPT YOUR PAST:** Your past is not who you are today. You may not have had access to the information you needed or were ready to make a change to plant-based eating. Accept the limitations you experienced as integral parts of shaping the strong person you want to be today and tomorrow.

2. **LEARN FROM YOUR MISTAKES:** Mistakes are not failures; they are opportunities to deepen your learning. Practice in the kitchen, get better at reading food labels for hidden animal products (see Look Out for Animal-Derived Ingredients, page 94), or dive deeper into plant-based eating, veganism, and the intersecting issues through further reading and documentaries (see Resources, page 284).

3. **RECOGNIZE POSSIBILITIES OVER LIMITATIONS:** When you focus on what you can do rather than what you can't, the Universe, God, Allah, Zeus, Ziggy Stardust, whoever or whatever is out there, will conspire in ways—from the simple to sublime—that support your growth. View the Universe as your partner, waiting for you to show up and say YES rather than NO, and suddenly, you'll notice some funky coincidences: That high-powered blender you've wanted to buy? It's on sale! Or a friend tells you they want to go plant-based, too, and now you have an ally, when before you felt alone.

4. **PRIORITIZE GROWTH OVER MASTERY:** I have not "mastered" veganism, but I have gotten better at making sure, in all areas of my life, that my choices reflect my "do no harm" mantra (aka my "why"). And I have grown in my nutritional know-how, preparation of delicious vegan food, and teaching others, like you, all about it: In the early years of my animal activism. I used to think that if I wasn't convincing people to adopt a vegan lifestyle, I wasn't doing all I could do as an activist. However, today I know that when inspiring people to change the world, it's important to bring some nuance. Veganism is not a journey to perfection but a journey to feeling and doing better for animals, others, our health, and our planet. Growth also means having the humility to step out of a comfort zone and acknowledge privileges that you may have that others don't share.

5. **ACTIVATE YOUR COMPASSION:** Empathy is the ability to feel others' suffering, and compassion is the part of you that wants to do something to help. Compassion cannot exist without empathy. Start with having

compassion for yourself and eventually reaching outward toward others, including nonhuman species. It is at the heart of my animal and human rights activism. Both are necessary to begin to see yourself as a protector.

6. **BE A PROTECTOR:** A protector is strong and caring, and actively participates in safeguarding the wellness of all living beings. For me, strength and protection and masculinity were wrapped up together. Now I see that being a protector is rooted in empathy and compassion.

7. **BE VULNERABLE:** This is one of the most challenging things to do in life, especially if your culture considers vulnerability a "weakness." But being vulnerable is paradoxically one of the most powerful ways to show your strength. Being vulnerable—communicating our emotions, wants, and needs to others—exposes us to judgment and criticism. When going vegan, allow for deeper connection with people who care about you, so that you can feel their support.

8. **MAKE SPACE FOR SELF-REFLECTION:** The first thing I do when I rise each morning is head to my patio, face the sun, kneel quietly, and connect to its energy before I meet my day. For me, sunlight is an expression of an indefinable, powerful energy source, which some refer to as their Higher Power. Whatever you call your practice—meditation, prayer, or a "pause"—set aside time to unplug and look at the mirror inside yourself.

9. **BE LIKE AN ELEPHANT:** Take a cue from these gentle giants and LIVE LARGE! Here are some ideas to get you started:

Our planet's biodiversity is critical to humanity's survival.

- Expand your plant-based repertoire with new recipes starting on page 117.

- Widen and deepen your knowledge of animal cruelty and the health and environmental issues that plant-based eating and veganism can solve.

- Excitedly share your experiences with plant-based food: Post on social media or cook and share new foods with friends. Don't push an agenda; just allow delicious food to be delicious, and they (and you!) will come back for more.

- Engage with like-minded people who share similar values and contribute to the wellness of their community and our planet—"join a herd!"— see Resources (page 284).

CHAPTER 5

FIGURING OUT YOUR "WHY"

Like the mantra—"If It Requires Harm, Then Nahh"—that bubbled up from deep inside me, your "why" is the reason you are compelled to make changes. The more I grew in empathy and educated myself, the more I grew in my compassion for human rights and the health of our planet.

There is nothing wrong with taking as much time as you need to figure out your "why," especially if some of the topics we've unpacked are new to you. Maybe you want to do some parallel reading (see Resources, page 284). Each EWEE Pathway in chapter 7 has a recommended timeframe, but there are no hard and fast rules when it comes to being a protector and making better choices.

The Difference Between a Mantra and a "Why"

The word *mantra* or *mantram* is specific to Buddhism. It is a sacred or holy word or phrase that steadies your mind when faced with stressors, and some believe it gets rid of negative energy. "If It Requires Harm, Then Nahh" is my mantra because it anchors me by reminding me of the spiritual crisis—and revelation—I experienced while incarcerated.

You do not have to have a mantra, which holds spiritual resonance. But you will want to find your "why," which is secular and rooted in psychology. A "why" statement contains your reason for moving toward a new goal, providing focus, clarity, and a conscious understanding of "what makes you move."

It's *Your* "Why"

Perhaps this is you: As you learn about the health benefits of plant foods, you become curious about how to cook and eat more of them. Therefore, your "why" at the start of your journey may be: "Because I am curious." To add more whole foods to your life, see the Crowd It Out Pathway (page 77), which shows you what to include at each meal rather than what to eliminate! The Fake It Till You Make It Pathway (page 86) might also be a beautiful place to take some steps. You'll learn to swap dairy for plant-based milk, yogurt, and cheese and animal products for faux meat and fish products, and see possibilities in fruits and vegetables that you may have never considered trying before.

Or, perhaps, you are not only compelled by health but also moved to disrupt the systems of oppression that intersect with our food system. That may be your "why." Is anyone out there planning on taking a hard turn toward a Cold Tofurky Pathway (page 90)? Well, sweet potato, that could be the point at which you discover your "why" may require more self-reflection. As you move your ethically fueled vegan self into more socially and emotionally complex situations, you will likely see that they require you to be vulnerable with friends, family, and a wider social circle.

The deeper you dig (self-reflection) for a "why" that aligns with your core values in life, the easier your journey will be on your way to becoming the strongest and most authentic expression of glorious *you*. Why? Because identifying your "why" as an extension of what you value sets you on course for a value-based life. A value-based life is one in which you have developed a set of beliefs that drive your choices. And when you internalize those beliefs, your reasons for going plant-based or vegan will become as unshakable as a two-ton elephant.

And being the kind of protector that YOU want will be effortless.

Values and a Value-Based Life

My nephew Travon and I are a lot alike; he is tenacious, passionate, and doesn't get discouraged when a door closes. We both see possibilities where someone else might see limitations. He, like me and his grandmother, my mom, has a natural "hustler" gene—he's gonna accomplish whatever he sets his mind to, with or without help. Sometimes, when I try to give him life advice, we bump heads. (That happens with people who are so similar.) But I have come to understand that what he really needs is to be left alone to figure out life on *his* terms, not mine. I have learned to take a nonjudgmental step back, while he, and others (like you?), sort out their value system.

My values are intimately connected not only to what I feel is best for me but also to my belief in the sanctity of life for all species. This belief has been shaped by my life circumstances, challenges, and the oppressive systems I have faced. My journey to veganism was driven by a total emotional, physical, and spiritual or "energetic" transformation rooted in my mantra and core value: "do no harm." Your "why" may reflect some of your core values.

If you haven't yet questioned your core values or given them much thought, I get it. Much the same way my mom's heart-to-heart conversations weren't written out for me on a fancy chalkboard, you, too, probably internalized familial or cultural values by watching what people *did* rather than listening to what they *said*. Remember: Even the most incredibly beautiful choreographed dances are created one step at a time. Making a commitment to deepen your awareness is enough.

I cannot impose my values on you. But I can tell you this: The moment I rose from my knees from my praying position on the cellblock floor of MCC and decided to stand tall with my chin up high and take steps toward living my life as a reflection of the values I internalized, the trajectory of my life—my mental, physical, and spiritual well-being—changed dramatically. And as my values deepened, my well-being continued to climb.

I keep my core values simple. Each one holds powerful resonance within me.

- Do no harm: Show power, bravery, and strength through living as a walking example of my higher self in all my vulnerable authenticity.

- Protect innocent living things, especially the vulnerable, whenever ethically possible.

- Put my family first.

- Be assertive. Not aggressive. Be decisive.

- Speak my mind with clarity, transparency, and with compassion.

- Keep my word. This is the core foundation of my integrity.

- Show loyalty to my community and genuine friends, both online and in real life.

- Tell the truth.

Give yourself the space to learn from your mistakes. Each morning, you have a chance to reassess, strengthen, and shape your values to reflect the strong person you wish to become.

Be a Protector

If you begin to think of yourself as a protector, choosing a vegan lifestyle is about more than changing your diet. It has the potential to change your relationship with the world. The more in touch we are with our values, the more the issues will touch us.

Here are some "why" phrases for being a protector and eating what elephants eat:

- "I want to protect my health."

- "I want to protect the health of people I love."

- "I want to be a protector of billions of animals."

- "I want to protect other humans."

- "I want to protect the planet from the devastating effects of factory farming."

- "I want to protect the money in my pocket." (I do!)

Even if you take a "reducetarian" approach—a mostly plant-based diet that focuses on eating more plants and less meat—you will feel like a protector, and you will be made stronger.

My EWEE Kitchen Is a Sanctuary

Once I was back on my feet after being released from prison, I deemed my kitchen a sanctuary. In there, I could grow freely; it was a sacred space that I filled with plant-based ingredients for cooking delicious, filling food.

In the before times, I associated food with hardship: my poverty-stricken childhood; poor health from the cheap, fast, mass-produced "food" I ate during my toxic drug-hustling days and that led to weight gain; scarcity and humiliation that descended on me in solitary confinement where my drinking water was recycled from the toilet in my cell.

In my kitchen now, I am finally in the driver's seat. I find immense joy creating whole-food vegan dishes with abundant flavor and texture. I am grateful and at peace knowing that I am doing better for my body, my world, and anyone who breaks bread with me.

You have already done 99 percent of the work by showing up here.

I am going to be your partner the rest of the way.

PART II

How to Eat What Elephants Eat

Photography by Caitlin Bensel

CHAPTER 6

PROTECT YOUR HEALTH: EWEE NUTRITION

I think of my body's metabolism as a car's combustion engine and plant or animal food sources as my fuel. Plant energy, or "live" energy, is a positive, life-affirming fuel that powers my physical and emotional health today and for the long haul. Animal food products, or "dead" energy, are harmful fuel sources that weigh me down, putting up roadblocks to health and well-being. By eating what elephants eat, you, too, can thrive on plant fuel. Make food choices that lift your energy levels. Having more energy can mean something different for each of us, physically and emotionally. It may mean having enough energy to haul the kids to school, put in a full day of work, and keep the household together. Or it can mean heading to the gym for a strenuous workout and reducing your recovery time. It can mean dancing the Soca, playing football, training for your first marathon, or lifting weights—or your grandkids—in the air, feeling like a superhero!

It can be all of these.

It's now time to unpack the nutrition information you need to drive yourself toward health, strength, and a better world.

Macronutrients and Micronutrients

I began my vegan journey making "dirty rice" in a plastic bag of scalding water and scrounging for vegetables from a prison kitchen. I was unsure whether I was getting enough to eat to survive! But you will survive. And you'll thrive. A plant-based diet will transform your physical and emotional health, as it has done for me. Following is a list of the necessary macronutrients—protein, carbohydrates, and fats to fuel our bodies—followed on page 70 by the micronutrients—smaller doses of food-sourced minerals and vitamins that everyone needs, regardless of what kind of eater they are.

Protein

But Dom, "Where do you get your protein?" (Oh, man, if I had a dollar—nah, make it five dollars—for every time someone asked me that!) *Protein is not a food group*, although you may be used to thinking about it as animal meat, fish, eggs, and dairy. Here is what protein is: large molecules made from a chain of smaller linked molecules called amino acids. Our bodies contain a pool of twenty amino acids. We produce eleven of these amino acids, but it's up to us to get the other nine (called "essential amino acids") through food. Protein is called the "building blocks of life" because of its crucial role in forming every structure of our bodies—muscles, organs, every strand of hair, nails, blood, skin, and so on. And protein supports the everyday *function* and regulation of our cells, tissues, and organs. We are made of protein. We cannot live without protein. When we say we need to "eat protein," we really mean that we need to "get enough amino acids" to grow, build, and repair strong bodies.

And the most important proteins come from the essential amino acids, and those are found in plants.

Carbohydrates—"Carbs"

Like protein, carbohydrates are made up of smaller units. They are called saccharides, which are also known as sugars. And that's the root of carb confusion or "fear" of carbohydrates. While protein helps grow, repair, and rebuild muscle, it is not a source of fuel for your body. Instead, carbohydrates are our bodies' source of energy. Once we eat them, our digestive process converts carbohydrates into glucose, or sugar, to fuel us. Carbohydrate-rich foods also contain protein, nutrients, and minerals that contribute to your overall health and well-being.

But not all carbs are created equal. There are two types of carbohydrates: simple (not good for you) and complex (good for you). And they have different impacts on our health.

- **SIMPLE CARBOHYDRATES** are foods that our bodies easily convert to energy (glucose) and are digested quickly. These include refined white sugar, milk, and fruit. A "sugar high" comes from glucose entering your bloodstream rapidly. The rate at which carbohydrates are converted to glucose and enter your bloodstream is called the glycemic index. Eat foods low on the glycemic index for sustained energy.

- **COMPLEX CARBOHYDRATES** are whole foods with a lot of fiber. Our bodies need more time to break down fiber, making the conversion to blood sugars slower. Sources of complex carbohydrates include whole grains, legumes, and starchy vegetables, all of which have provided energy to humans for millennia.

PLANTS PROMOTE HEALTH

Minimally processed fruits, vegetables, whole grains, legumes, nuts, seeds, herbs, and spices are the sources of "live" plant energy. Plants are the cornerstones of health because they contain the following essential nutrients:

- **All three macronutrients—protein, carbohydrates, and fat.** The fat is in the form of essential fatty acids (EFAs), such as linoleic (omega-6s) and alpha-linolenic (omega-3s). These EFAs support major bodily functions in our nervous, immune, cardiovascular, and reproductive systems

- **Micronutrients in the form of vitamins and minerals,** which play an essential role in protecting and bolstering our immune system, as well as growing, healing, and producing energy

- **Essential macro minerals,** such as calcium, magnesium, potassium, phosphorous, and sodium, vital to cell growth and repair

- **Essential trace minerals,** such as iron, zinc, copper, and selenium, that support the function of our body's tissues

- **Sulfuric compounds** with anti-inflammatory, antibacterial, and antiviral properties, and that also promote immune function

- **Important enzymes**—protease, amylase, lipase, and cellulose—that play a role in our digestive health

- **Antioxidants**—powerhouse compounds that protect our cells from unstable molecules that cause damage to cells, as well as disease and aging

- **Phytochemicals** that reduce inflammation, protect our cells from cancer, regulate our hormones, and can reverse disease

- **Dietary fiber,** which is essential for gut health and digestion and keeps poops on the regular! It improves glucose tolerance and reduces heart disease risk factors, such as high cholesterol and hypertension (high blood pressure).

- **Peptides,** which are building blocks of protein and protect your skin

ANIMAL FOODS CAUSE DISEASE AND HARM

"Dead" energy is the dead flesh (meat) of once living beings, such as cows, chickens, pigs, sheep, and goats, as well as their milk, and eggs. Here's why animals and animal products cause harm:

- Meat has saturated fat, which elevates blood cholesterol, which in turn contributes to heart disease by clogging your arteries, which can lead to a stroke or heart attack.

- When we eat dead animals, we also ingest the antibiotics, pathogens, hormones, and industrial toxins that are stored in animal tissue and muscle, and that are the by-products of breeding, feeding, and slaughtering animals in our factory-farming system.

- Meat does not contain fiber and sits in our longer digestive tract for two to four days before it passes through us. Excess meat in our digestive tract resists digestion and rots, making us feel sluggish and creating conditions for chronic disease.

- Meat and dairy weaken our bones. When we consume meat and dairy as primary sources of protein, the amino acids (the building blocks of protein) create an acidic environment in the bloodstream and our bones release calcium minerals to counterbalance, which over time weakens them.

- The World Health Organization classifies meat, including beef, lamb, and pork, and processed and cured meat products, as carcinogens—substances that cause cancer.

- To meet the global demand for animal food energy, we must rely on mass-scale cruelty, torture, and killing of other innocent living beings that can sense fear, danger, and death. This, along with the exploitation of people and the planet in the cycle that supports mass meat production, carries heavy, harmful, and negative feelings.

Fiber and Our Gut Microbiome

Dietary fiber is classified as a carbohydrate and is found only in plant foods. There are two types of fiber: soluble fiber (fiber we can digest) and insoluble fiber ("roughage," or the bulky fibers of nuts, seeds, grains, and veggies such as cabbage). Fiber helps slow down digestion, making you feel full for longer, and softens your poop. Adequate intake of both types of fiber (25 to 30 grams per day) has been linked to a lower risk of heart disease and bowel cancer, plus it lowers cholesterol and stabilizes your blood sugar.

Good gut bugs thrive on a type of soluble fiber called prebiotic fiber. And when good gut bugs flourish, they produce short-chain fatty acid compounds (SCFAs), which strengthen your gut cells, in turn aiding in digestion and absorption of nutrients and preventing diseases, including diabetes, some cancers, and inflammatory bowel issues. Our gut is called "our second brain" because these compounds communicate with our immune systems, metabolism, and endocrine system via the vagus nerve—a nerve that runs through our bodies from our brains to our guts—that superhighway I told you about in our Emotional and Mental Strength discussion on page 40. SCFAs stimulate the production of our body's natural "feel good" chemical, serotonin, which helps us stabilize our emotions and stress levels and promote a feeling of calm.

Vegetables, fruit, and fiber impact and strengthen your emotional health.

Or, as I like to say: EWEE for EWEE (Eat What Elephants Eat, for Emotional Wellness Every day, for Everyone).

Fat

We need fat. It's a source of energy, protects vital tissues and organs, and keeps us warm. Fat is necessary for many important processes, including hormone production, cell membrane development, and vital bodily functions. And we crave fat—creamy avocado, rich cashews, smooth olives. Fat is satisfying and makes us feel full.

HOW MUCH PROTEIN DO YOU *REALLY* NEED?

Many Americans following a Standard American Diet (SAD) don't realize that they are consuming more protein than they need. Our bodies cannot store excess protein, so once your daily requirement has been reached, excess amino acids are excreted in your urine. High protein meat-based diets burden your body's liver, bones, and kidneys. Follow this guide from the Dietary Reference Intake Report[1] to see where *your* dietary protein needs may land.

- An average person eating for optimal nutrition: 0.8 grams of protein per kilogram of body weight

- A person eating for muscle gain: 1.2 grams of protein per kilogram of body weight

- A person eating to fuel workouts: 1.5 grams of protein per kilogram of body weight

To figure out your protein needs, first covert your body weight from pounds to kilograms. Since 1 kilogram is 2.2 pounds, divide your body weight by 2.2 to get the kilograms.

- Example: A 150-pound person weighs 68 kilograms

- Next, multiply your weight in kilograms by the number of grams per kilo for your dietary needs.

- 68 kg × 0.8 = 54 grams of protein per day

When it comes to healthy, plant-based eating, what matters more than the overall amount of fat we consume, is the *type* of fat we eat. Saturated fat is the main kind of fat we get from animals—it's "dead" energy. Saturated fat in our diets leads to clogged arteries, which leads to heart disease and stroke, eventually threatening your life. Unsaturated fat is derived from "live" plant energy, and each one protects our heart health and strengthens our bodies and minds.

Focus on these types of unsaturated fat:

- Monounsaturated (MUFAs)

- Polyunsaturated (PUFAs)

- Essential fatty acids (omega-6 and omega-3s)

PLANT PROTEIN FUEL

Plants and the amino acids in them are the reason massive herbivores like elephants can fuel their muscles! Here are my go-to protein-rich plant foods. Add any of the below to an EWEE Bowl (page 190) or build yourself an EWEE Plate (see page 72) for a dish that is just as rich in beauty, texture, color, and flavor as it is in protein.

Plant Protein Fuel

FOOD	SERVING SIZE	PROTEIN (GRAMS)
Almonds	1 ounce	6
Beans, black, cooked	1 cup	10
Beans, kidney, cooked	1 cup	17
Beans, pinto, cooked	1 cup	16
Cashews	1 ounce	5
Chia seeds	1 ounce	4.7
Chickpeas, cooked	1 cup	18
Edamame, cooked	1 cup	16
Flaxseeds	1 ounce	5
Hemp hearts	1 ounce	8.8
Lentils, cooked	1 cup	18

FOOD	SERVING SIZE	PROTEIN (GRAMS)
Peanut butter	2 tablespoons	8
Pine nuts	1 ounce	7
Pistachios	1 ounce	6
Pumpkin seeds	1 ounce	9
Quinoa, cooked	1 cup	8
Rice, brown, cooked	1 cup	5
Sunflower seeds	1 ounce	5
Tahini	2 tablespoons	5.2
Tempeh	4 ounces	21
Tofu	4 ounces	9
Whole wheat pasta, cooked	1 cup	7.5

CARBOHYDRATE FUEL

The carbohydrate-rich foods listed here are sources of soluble, insoluble, and prebiotic fiber. Though some of our healthiest fruits, such as fresh strawberries and melons, are considered "simple carbohydrates," I have included them here, too, because they are also rich in micronutrients and contain fiber.

- Almonds
- Apples
- Asparagus*
- Bananas*
- Beans* (such as black, kidney, and pinto)
- Beets
- Berries (blueberries*)
- Broccoli
- Chia seeds
- Citrus fruits
- Flaxseed
- Garlic*
- Leafy greens (such as kale* and spinach)
- Leeks*
- Lentils
- Mangoes
- Melon
- Oats
- Onions*
- Pasta, whole wheat
- Pears
- Pistachios
- Popcorn
- Potatoes, cooked and cooled
- Rice, cooked and cooled
- Strawberries
- Sunflower seeds
- Sweet potatoes
- Watermelon
- Whole grains

*This food is a good source of prebiotic soluble fiber.

HEALTHY FATS

Here are healthy unsaturated fats, and the ways they
protect your health.

TYPE OF FAT	WHAT IT DOES	WHERE TO FIND IT
Monounsaturated fats (MUFAs)	Protects our hearts by lowering our bad cholesterol (LDL), reducing our risk of heart attack or stroke	Olives and olive oil, avocados and avocado oil, cashews, almonds, macadamias, pistachios, nut oils, soybean oil, flaxseed, and tahini
Polyunsaturated fats (PUFAs)	Protects our hearts, reduces inflammation that triggers disease. Supports healthy bones and joints.	Sesame seed oil, canola oil, sunflower oil, and safflower oil
Omega-6s	Powers our brains, maintains bone and reproductive system health, and stimulates skin and hair growth	Avocado oil, peanut butter, walnuts, hemp hearts, sunflower seeds
Omega-3s (ALA)	Increases blood flow to our brains, supporting memory and cognition; reduces inflammation, preventing chronic illness	Tofu, walnuts, pumpkin seeds, flaxseeds, chia seeds, soybeans, soybean oil, canola oil
Omega-3s (EPA and DHA)	Protects our hearts and reduces triglycerides (dietary fat) in our bloodstream. Increases dopamine—a neurotransmitter in the brain that helps us feel happy and motivated.	Kelp powder, nori (dried seaweed), spirulina, chlorella (a type of algae), hemp hearts

Micronutrients: Vitamins, and Minerals

In addition to the macronutrients—protein, carbohydrates, and fat—your body needs micronutrients for optimal health: Here are the essential vitamins and minerals, and where I source them.

VITAMIN/ MINERAL	WHAT IT DOES	WHERE TO FIND IT
Vitamin A (beta-carotene)	Necessary for liver, heart, and lung health, and supports our vision and reproductive health	Sweet potatoes, carrots, winter squash, mangoes
Vitamin B$_{12}$	Converts the foods we eat into energy	Nutritional yeast, tempeh, fortified cereals, some plant-based milks, mushrooms, chlorella, nori (dried seaweed)
Vitamin C	Alleviates cold symptoms, protects our immunity, and is a crucial antioxidant for collagen production, healthy joints and skin, healthy cholesterol levels, and blood vessels	Bell peppers (yellow peppers have the highest amount!), grapefruit, oranges, strawberries, broccoli, kale, cherry tomatoes
Calcium	Essential for healthy bones and teeth, a healthy nervous system function and regulating our heart rhythm	Collard greens, kale, turnip greens, mustard greens, broccoli, okra
Vitamin D	Calcium's partner, helping our body absorb it to maintain strong bones	Sunshine, fortified plant-based milk, yogurt, mushrooms (when exposed to sunlight or UV light)
Vitamin E	Helps prevent plaque from sticking to the inner lining of our blood vessels	Almonds, mangoes, avocados, sunflower oil, sunflower seeds

VITAMIN/ MINERAL	WHAT IT DOES	WHERE TO FIND IT
Iron	Transports oxygen to our cells. Iron from plants (nonheme iron) is better absorbed by your body when you pair the food with vitamin C.	Cashews, kidney beans, spinach, spirulina, lentils, organic blackstrap molasses, tofu, tempeh, and skin-on potatoes—in combination with vitamin C–rich citrus fruits, bell peppers, and dark leafy greens
Selenium	Fights free radicals, which are unstable atoms in our cells linked to aging and disease, and is necessary for our thyroid gland's hormones	Ground cornmeal, fortified cereal, bread, and Brazil nuts (just 1 nut a day will provide all you need!)
Iodine	Controls the production of thyroid hormones, which regulate our metabolism	Sea salt enriched with iodine, seaweed, seaweed powders, (such as chlorella or nori), cabbage, broccoli, brussels sprouts, potatoes, cranberries, strawberries
Magnesium	Plays a role in more than three hundred life-sustaining chemical reactions in our body, such as muscle and nerve function and blood pressure regulation	Brown rice, beans, almonds, spinach, cashews
Zinc	Helps our bodies heal and powers our metabolism	Tofu, lentils, sunflower seeds, pumpkin seeds, cashews, oats

THE EWEE PLATE

Here is an EWEE plate. When preparing meals, aim to fill in each section of the plate with foods recommended in this chapter to cover your macronutrient and micronutrient needs. Use this template to help you visualize an EWEE Bowl (page 190), too!

Fill about one-quarter of the plate with complex carbohydrates (page 68).

Fill half of the plate with a mixture of vegetables (fresh or frozen), such as leafy greens and cruciferous vegetables, and fruit (fresh or frozen). This ensures you are getting a wide range of micronutrients and phytonutrients (pages 70–71).

Fill about one-quarter of the plate with protein-rich plants (pages 66–67).

Include a small portion of healthy fat, such as a scoop of guacamole, a handful of nuts, or nut butter (page 69).

CHAPTER 7

THREE PATHWAYS TO EATING WHAT ELEPHANTS EAT AND MEAL PLANS

Strong hearts.

Strong bodies.

Strong minds.

All through plants.

So, how *are* you feeling?

Closer than ever before to eating what elephants eat?

Wanting to make a swift change?

Or do you need to "fake it" for a while—your curiosity piqued?

Maybe you want to fill your tank with some "live" energy foods, take yourself for a spin, and see how it feels while you push some animal foods out the door.

Now is an excellent time to remind you that an EWEE journey is not a journey to perfection—rather, it's a journey to feeling better, and doing better, through the choices we make for ourselves, other humans, nonhuman species, and our planet.

As you move through this chapter, I want you to know that failure is not possible. We only fail if we stop moving forward. The well-being of our species depends on our evolving, and moving forward from a place of awareness, empathy, and compassion, dismantling and disrupting oppressive systems as we do. We each have the power to define strength on our terms. We can express it through our food choices.

Now, some of you reading this may be at your lowest energetically—physically, emotionally, spiritually (whatever that means for you). I have been there. But by reaching for "live" energy, plant-based foods, you will move forward, even if you feel stuck. You will rise, even when you feel like you are falling.

I tell people repeatedly, and they are in awe each time I say it: My life's trajectory kept ascending from choosing "If It Requires Harm, Then Nahh" as my mantra.

And the Universe had my back.

Now I have yours.

What lies ahead are three pathways to eating what elephants eat, plus meal plans. Each one covers you for fourteen days. Follow as much as you can each day. And if it helps to break it down into smaller steps at first—by committing to one meal, then increasing to two meals and so on, until you're following the entire plan—and it takes you longer than fourteen days, that's okay, too. I suggest that you read all three—Crowd It Out (page 77), Fake It Till You Make It (page 86), and Cold Tofurky (page 90)—to see where you'd like to begin. With Crowd It Out, you'll do just that— "crowd out" animals gradually as you focus on adding whole foods. When you're ready, move on

to Fake It Till You Make It using faux meat products to transition away from animal foods entirely. Stay on this pathway until you feel ready to reap the benefits of a "do no harm" whole-food vegan diet, which is Cold Tofurky. You can mix and match the meal plans and recipes from the plans. You know yourself better than anyone, but let Mother Nature take the wheel whenever possible.

The view out your window can change.

You are evolving, with compassion, for yourself, and other species, too. And I am by your side.

Tips for Every Pathway

Each pathway has tips to help you along, such as Tips for Cooking with Faux Meats (page 90) and My Guide to Plant-Based Milks (page 83). But every EWEE pathway has the following moves to set you up for a smooth and joyful ride.

- **DANCE IN YOUR KITCHEN EVERY DAY (DO THE SOCA!):** Because you are beautiful, because you are trying your best, and because we are connected.

- **CLEAN AND ORGANIZE:** Make space in the refrigerator and freezer for whole plant foods.

- **CHECK YOUR MINDSET:** Turn to page 52 for a refresher on the Nine Steps to the EWEE Mindset. Connect to your "why."

- **BE VULNERABLE:** Ask a trusted friend or family member for their support and compassion. Do not be afraid to share your intention to reduce or eliminate animal products from your diet.

- **CHECK OUT MY MOST FREQUENTLY USED KITCHEN "DANCE PARTNERS":** Read EWEE Kitchen Ingredients (page 98) before heading out to browse or shop. Be open to new food choices.

- **SET YOURSELF UP FOR EARLY SUCCESS:** Smoothies (pages 168–75) and Overnight Oats (page 149) are easy EWEE breakfasts for transitioning—check out my EWEE Smoothie Formula (page 174) and pick up some ingredients you may want to add to your smoothies, such as plant-based milk (see My Guide to Plant-Based Milks, page 83).

- **SHOP FOR INGREDIENTS TO MAKE WHOLE-FOOD SNACKS:** Check out recipes like Date and Fig Energy Balls (page 277). Store-bought vegan snacks are fun on occasion, but they are highly processed, and expensive.

- **PICK ONE DAY OF THE WEEK TO DO SOME BATCH COOKING:** Check out Good Morning, Sweet Potato! (page 160), Batch Cooking Whole Grains 101 (page 138), Batch Cooking Beans 101 (page 140), and EZ EWEE Veggies (page 142) to have "live" energy plant foods at your fingertips.

- **CHECK OUT VEGAN RESTAURANTS IN YOUR AREA:** Take a night off from cooking and go out or order in—whatever fits your budget. Make a commitment to try a new dish, something from outside your culture and comfort zone—Thai, Ethiopian, and Burmese cuisines, for example, all have vegan-friendly foods. If you enjoyed it, post a picture of it on social media. Describe how yummy it was—focus on the food instead of an agenda. It doesn't matter that you didn't make it yourself—you are publicly acknowledging your choices.

- **IF YOU LOVE THESE RECIPES AND ARE NOT NEW TO VEGAN LIVING,** consider throwing a "Soul" Food Redefined feast (page 225) or potluck in your home, inviting like-minded friends or any food-loving friend who wants to feed their "soul."

1. The Crowd It Out Pathway

"Crowding it out"—or pushing animals off your plate—is a transitional pathway. It guides you toward adding more "live" energy whole foods into your diet at each meal: budget-friendly fruits, fresh and frozen vegetables, frozen or bulk whole grains, canned or bulk beans and legumes, nuts, seeds, and healthy fats. You can continue eating animal foods if you're not ready to let go—no judgment here. Crowd It Out is a gentle and flexible pathway that gives you room to grow. It's a great place to practice your "why" and learn more about making whole-food vegan meals without the pressure to transition immediately.

For each meal on the Crowd It Out plan, you can either try my suggested EWEE recipe or add a serving of whole food to your choice of meal. But if you choose the latter, try eating the entire serving of whole food first before any other food. Why? Because when you eat that whole food first, you will feel full more quickly, naturally reducing how much of the animal food you eat and eventually crowding it off your plate.

For example, for the first week, you might want to start by making the easy EWEE smoothie breakfast recipes. Then for lunch and dinner you can "crowd out" your traditional choices by adding my suggested portion of whole food.

Get into the habit of crowding out animal foods—and harm—for as long as you need, eventually moving all animals right off your plate and out the door. Follow the meal plan to take the guesswork out of what to make.

WHAT TO EXPECT FROM ALL THREE PATHWAYS

- You may feel lighter energetically, knowing you are doing good for all beings.

- As you introduce beans and vegetables, the increase in fiber will impact your bathroom time—gotta go!

- Your taste buds may become sensitive—leafy greens taste more bitter, you can pick up on flavors in tap water, and fruit seems sweeter. You are adjusting to new eating patterns.

- You'll may lose weight, since nutrient-dense plant foods have fewer calories. (Put a belt on those saggy pants!)

- If you have any skin issues, they may clear up, since you have eliminated dairy. Your cholesterol may drop! Hallelujah and pass the corn bread (page 234).

Crowd It Out Meal Plan

Week 1

MEAL	BREAKFAST	LUNCH	DINNER
Day 1	Strawberry Cashew Smoothie (page 173) or add 1 cup fresh berries, 1 piece whole fresh fruit (such as an apple, banana, pear, citrus), or a handful of grapes	EWEE Bowl (page 190) or add 2 cups leafy greens with plant-based dressing or 1 serving A Mess of Greens (page 233)	Mushroom Ramen Noodle Bowl (page 184) or add 1 cup cooked mushrooms (see Caring for and Cooking Mushrooms, page 104)
Day 2	Good Morning, Sweet Potato! (page 160) or add ¼ cup unsalted nuts, such as cashews, almonds, or pistachios	Really Good Tofu Scramble (page 154) or add 1 cup EZ EWEE Veggies (page 142)	Loaded Chipotle Chili (page 185) or add 1 cup cooked lentils or beans, such as Great Northern or kidney. Save leftovers for lunch the next day.
Day 3	Berry Beet Smoothie (page 169) or add 1 cup fresh berries, 1 piece whole fresh fruit (such as an apple, banana, pear, or citrus), or a handful of grapes	Leftover Loaded Chipotle Chili or add 1 cup cooked beans, such as black, pinto, or chickpeas (garbanzos)	Spaghetti 'n' Beet Balls (page 240) or add 1 cup EZ EWEE Veggies (page 142). Save leftovers for lunch the next day.
Day 4	Overnight Oats (page 149) or add 1 plain Good Morning, Sweet Potato! (page 160)	Leftover Spaghetti 'n' Beet Balls or add 1 cup EZ EWEE Veggies (page 142)	Lentil Sloppy Joes (page 219) or add 2 cups leafy greens with plant-based dressing or 1 serving A Mess of Greens (page 233)
Day 6	Bold 'n' Beautiful Beet Waffles (page 148) or add 1 plain Good Morning, Sweet Potato! (page 160)	Good Morning, Sweet Potato! (page 160) or add ¼ cup nuts, such as cashews, almonds, or pistachios	Mom's Plant Loaf with Skillet Cabbage (page 258) or add 1 cup whole grain, such as bulgur, farro, or freekeh. Save leftovers for lunch the next day.
Day 7	The "Duluth" Omelet (page 152) or add 1 cup EZ EWEE Veggies (page 142)	Leftover Mom's Plant Loaf with Skillet Cabbage or add 2 cups leafy greens with plant-based dressing or 1 serving A Mess of Greens (page 233)	Mac 'n' "Cheese" (page 242) or add 1 cup EZ EWEE Veggies (page 142). Save leftovers for lunch the next day.

SHOPPING SMARTS

The Food Empowerment Project—a nonprofit group that seeks to create a more just and sustainable world by recognizing the power of our choices through food—is one of several nonprofits I have worked with to offer shopping tips for plant-based and vegan people living in communities of color, where sometimes transportation, low incomes, and lack of availability of fresh foods is a deterrent to going plant-based. Below is some "do what you can with what you are working with" advice for everyone. Because no matter your background or your budget, we all want to get the most for our dollar. An EWEE journey, even on a tight budget, is entirely possible.

- Focus on shopping the perimeter of the grocery store where fruits and vegetables are stocked. These can be the center of budget-friendly meals, such as bowls (see EWEE Bowl Guide, page 186), smoothies (see EWEE Smoothie Formula, page 174) and pasta dishes (pages 240–43).

- Try new things—plantains, spaghetti squash, brussels sprouts. They may not have been part of your repertoire before, but buy them if they are on sale!

- Eat seasonally. Buy in-season fruit and freeze it for later.

- Join a CSA (Community Supported Agriculture). Ask a friend to share the cost with you.

- You can save a buck by choosing conventional produce over the more expensive organic option. (See Should I Buy Organic?, page 82.)

- Buying whole grains, beans, pulses (lentils and peas), nuts, and seeds is the most affordable way to get plenty of plant protein and fiber. Expand your palate beyond brown rice to include amaranth, teff, and spelt, which have been part of indigenous cultures for centuries. See Batch Cooking Whole Grains 101 (page 138) for batch cooking times.

- Nuts and seeds are expensive but cost less in bulk. To prevent spoilage and waste, store them in an airtight container in the refrigerator for up to 6 months or in the freezer for up to 1 year.

- Choose the store brand for most pantry items, such as oils or grains. Be sure to read labels for hidden animal-derived ingredients (see Look Out for Animal-Derived Ingredients, page 94).

- Make homemade condiments and dressings from EWEE pantry items. (See Pantry, Fridge, and Freezer recipes, pages 119–43.)

- Instead of plant-based milk as a smoothie base, mix it up and use water. It will still taste great.

- Rely on faux meats for a transitional period only, rather than making them the center of your meals for the long term; they are often just as expensive as animal products. (See Fake It Till You Make It, page 86.)

Week 2

MEAL	BREAKFAST	LUNCH	DINNER
Day 8	Choco Power Smoothie (page 172) or add 1 cup fresh berries, 1 piece whole fresh fruit (such as an apple, banana, pear, or citrus), or a handful of grapes	Leftover Mac n "Cheese" or add 1 cup EZ EWEE Veggies (page 142)	"Clean" Dirty Rice (page 252) or add 2 cups leafy greens with plant-based dressing or 1 serving A Mess of Greens (page 233). Save leftovers for lunch the next day.
Day 9	Good Morning, Sweet Potato! (page 160) or add ¼ cup unsalted nuts, such as cashews, almonds, or pistachios	Leftover "Clean" Dirty Rice or add 1 cup beans, such as mung, navy or pinto.	The "Duluth" Omelet (page 152) or add 1 cup EZ EWEE Veggies (page 142)
Day 10	Green Mango Smoothie (page 168) or add 1 cup fresh berries, 1 piece whole fresh fruit (such as an apple, banana, pear, or citrus), or a handful of grapes	Mega Tofu BLT (page 212) or add 2 cups leafy greens with plant-based dressing or 1 serving A Mess of Greens (page 233)	Fantastic Fritters (page 203) or add 1 cup chickpeas or Crispy Chickpeas (page 134)
Day 11	Blueberry Oatmeal Smoothie (page 172) or add 1 cup fresh berries, 1 piece whole fresh fruit (such as an apple, banana, pear, or citrus), or a handful of grapes	"Egg" Salad Collard Wrap (page 210) or add 1 cup fresh cauliflower or broccoli paired with EZ Hummus (page 130)	"Beef" 'n' Bean Enchiladas (page 264) or add 1 cup beans, such as black, cannellini, or chickpeas (garbanzos)

MEAL	BREAKFAST	LUNCH	DINNER
Day 12	Really Good Tofu Scramble (page 154) or add 1 cup EZ EWEE Veggies (page 142)	Tomato Soup with Grilled "Cheese" (page 182) or add 1 cup fresh cherry tomatoes	Auntie Valerie's Stuffed Peppers (page 256) or add 1 cup lentils, brown rice, or other whole grains. Save leftovers for lunch the next day.
Day 13	Build a smoothie using the EWEE Smoothie Formula (page 174) or add 1 cup fresh berries, 1 piece whole fresh fruit (such as an apple, banana, pear, or citrus), or a handful of grapes	Leftover Auntie Valerie's Stuffed Peppers or add 1 cup lentils or brown rice, or 1 cup fresh cauliflower or broccoli paired with EZ Hummus (page 130)	"Iron Man" Spinach and Broccoli Soup (page 180) or add 1 serving A Mess of Greens (page 233) or 1 cup fresh or frozen broccoli or cauliflower. Save leftovers for lunch the next day.
Day 14	Overnight Oats (page 149) or add 1 plain Good Morning, Sweet Potato! (page 160)	Leftover "Iron Man" Spinach and Broccoli Soup or add 2 cups leafy greens with plant-based dressing or 1 serving A Mess of Greens (page 233)	Buffalo Cauliflower "Chicken" Wings Bowl (page 194) or add 1 cup fresh cauliflower or broccoli paired with EZ Hummus (page 130)

Should I Buy Organic?

Synthetic pesticides used to grow conventional produce pollute our environment and are toxic to humans—even natural pesticides used for growing organic produce can be harmful to fish and other animals! But I would rather eat plants than consider the other option. I mix up my grocery cart by buying organic produce for potatoes, tomatoes, and leafy greens, such as kale, as they are more vulnerable to the absorption of pesticides. I buy conventional produce for foods that have a protective skin or outer shell, such as melons, bananas, oranges, lemons, and limes. Check the list of the Clean Fifteen and the Dirty Dozen posted annually by the Environmental Working Group (EWG) to see which foods carry the highest pesticide residue, so you can make an informed choice to buy conventionally grown or organic produce.

MY GUIDE TO PLANT-BASED MILKS

Each brand I recommend is GMO-free and does not contain added sugar. Avoid brands with carrageenan, a thickening agent that is tested on animals and can cause digestion issues; and whenever possible, make your own plant-based milk from scratch at home.

MILK	FLAVOR	RECOMMENDED BRAND
Almond	Lighter in body than soy, but has a creamy texture, with a light nutty taste	Elmhurst Milked Almonds
Coconut	Refrigerated carton coconut milk for drinking has coconut flavor and creamy body. (Canned coconut milk is best for cooking.)	So Delicious, Unsweetened; Silk, Unsweetened
Oat	Creamy, with a light toasted oat flavor. It's a great alternative for those with soy and nut allergies.	Elmhurst Milked Oats
Rice	Light in body, a touch sweet, and the least allergenic of all the plant-based milks	Rice Dream, Unsweetened
Soy	Rich body and taste that most mimics that of dairy milk	Pacific Foods, Original Unsweetened; EdenSoy Organic, Unsweetened

MY RECOMMENDED BRANDS FOR ANIMAL REPLACEMENTS

Before the availability of faux meats—such as Impossible Burgers, smoked tempeh meant to stand in for bacon, and "beef" crumbles—ethical vegans, like me, made whole food replacements from scratch. We cooked up mushroom "bacon" or blended rich, finely ground walnuts, herbs, spices, lentils, beans, and beets to make vegan versions of dishes we love. You can do that, too! But if that's not convenient for you, meat replacements, or faux meats, are available in every supermarket.

FOOD	BRAND	WHAT TO LOOK FOR
Bacon	Lightlife	Smart bacon strips or tempeh smoky bacon
Chicken	Gardein	Chick'n Filets, Chick'n Tenders, and Chick'n Wings
Cream cheese	Kite Hill	All flavors, especially chive, garden veggie, and strawberry
Deli meat	Tofurky	All flavors, especially oven roasted
Enchiladas	Amy's	Plant-Based Enchiladas with Spanish Rice & Beans, or Black Bean Vegetable
Fish fillets, fish sticks, burgers	Good Catch	Breaded Fish Fillets, Crab Cakes, and Salmon Burgers
Eggs	JUST Egg	Liquid egg replacer in a bottle
Meat	Beyond Meat	Frozen burger patties or bulk ground "meat," breakfast sausage links, "beef" crumbles, and meatballs
Parmesan cheese	Violife	Cheese block for grating
Pizza	American Flatbread	All flavors, especially pepperoni
Pulled pork	jack & annie's	Jackfruit-based pulled "pork"
Ribs	Herbivorous Butcher	Smoky House Ribs (online ordering: theherbivorousbutcher.com)
Sandwich cheese or cheese spread	Miyoko's	All flavors, especially Garlic Herb
Soup	Amy's	All flavors, especially chunky Tomato Bisque
Tuna	Good Catch	Water-packed "canned tuna"
Waffles (frozen)	Van's	Organic Whole Grain Waffles: Blueberry, Flax, and Totally Original

2. The Fake It Till You Make It Pathway

"Faking it"—or swapping faux meats and plant-based replacers for animal products—can be beneficial if you want to eliminate animal foods but still crave their taste and texture. Look at them as products for transitioning or transition tools.

If "crowding out" was your first stop on your EWEE journey, now it's time to get comfortable cooking more plant-based meals and eliminating meat entirely by replacing it with faux meat products, while still emphasizing the whole-food "live" energy goodness of plants. Stay on this pathway for as long as you need to, but know that I do not believe faux meat products are a long-term solution to eliminating animals from your diet. Even though my recommended brands (see page 84) are "better for you" than the alternative meat-based products on the market, they are still ultraprocessed. The products I recommend are lower in fat and calories and offer some fiber, but more brands in the ever-widening field of plant-based products, such as snacks, pizza, and faux meat and fish, contain more sodium and saturated fat than their traditional counterparts. And they can be expensive.

For each day on the Fake It Till You Make It meal plan, you'll choose an EWEE recipe or a store-bought vegan option for each meal. After two weeks, try scaling back your dependence on faux meats, chicken, or eggs, to one meal per day, and make the whole food recipes I provide.

A little faking.

A little making.

Fake It Till You Make It Meal Plan

Week 1

MEAL	BREAKFAST	LUNCH	DINNER
Day 1	Overnight Oats (page 149) or vegan cereal with plant-based milk	Mega Tofu BLT (page 212) or vegan BLT made with organic smoky tempeh bacon	Buffalo Cauliflower "Chicken" Wings Bowl (page 194) or vegan chick'n wings and 2 cups leafy greens
Day 2	Strawberry Cashew Smoothie (page 173) or store-bought plant-based smoothie	BBQ Pulled Mushroom Sandwich (page 222) or plant-based pulled BBQ jackfruit sandwich on any bread	Crispy, Crunchy, Creamy Chickpea Caesar Bowl (page 192) or chick'n tenders with a plant-based Caesar salad
Day 3	Really Good Tofu Scramble (page 154) or plant-based breakfast burrito	Tomato "Tuna" Poke Bowl with "Yum Yum" Sauce (page 198) or plant-based tuna sandwich, with lettuce and tomato, on any bread	"Beef" 'n' Bean Enchiladas (page 264) or plant-based frozen enchiladas and 2 cups leafy greens
Day 4	Saturday Morning Nostalgia Pancakes (page 146) or vegan pancake mix with vegan butter and maple syrup	"Egg" Salad Collard Wrap (page 210) or vegan tofu egg salad or wrap	Lentil Sloppy Joes (page 219) or plant-based sloppy joe sandwiches
Day 5	Overnight Oats (page 149) or vegan cereal with plant-based milk	Tomato Soup with Grilled "Cheese" (page 182) or plant-based tomato soup and your choice of vegan sandwich	EWEE Beet Burger (page 216) or plant-based burger on any bun, with 2 cups leafy greens
Day 6	Bold 'n' Beautiful Beet Waffles (page 148) or vegan waffles with maple syrup	Fantastic Fritters (page 203) or chick'n tenders with 2 cups leafy greens	Chicago Taco Bowl (page 196) or vegan burrito
Day 7	The "Duluth" Omelet (page 152) or liquid egg substitute omelet with faux sausage links	Create an EWEE Bowl (page 190) and add your choice of plant-based faux protein	Orange "Chicken" (page 251) or order in a vegan dinner. Save leftovers for lunch the next day.

Week 2

MEAL	BREAKFAST	LUNCH	DINNER
Day 8	Choco Power Smoothie (page 172) or store-bought plant-based smoothie	Leftover Orange "Chicken" with Brown Rice or order vegan takeout	"Crab" Cakes with Rémoulade Sauce (page 206) or plant-based fish sticks or crab cakes and 2 cups leafy greens
Day 9	Overnight Oats (page 149) or vegan cereal with plant-based milk	Mega Tofu BLT (page 212) or plant-based deli meat and cheese double-decker sandwich, with tomato and lettuce	BBQ Tofu "Ribs" (page 230) with Creamy Coleslaw (page 232) or plant-based ribs. Save leftovers for lunch the next day.
Day 10	Green Mango Smoothie (page 168) or store-bought plant-based smoothie	Leftover BBQ "Ribs" with Creamy Coleslaw or plant-based "ribs"	Spaghetti 'n' Beet Balls (page 240) or spaghetti with plant-based meatballs. Save leftovers for lunch the next day.
Day 11	Saturday Morning Nostalgia Pancakes (page 146) or vegan pancake mix with vegan butter and maple syrup	Leftover Spaghetti 'n' Beet Balls or spaghetti with plant-based meatballs	Yalonda's Jerk Tempeh with Coconut Rice and Plantains (page 229) or plant-based Jamaican jerk jackfruit. Save leftovers for lunch the next day.
Day 12	Really Good Tofu Scramble (page 154) or plant-based breakfast burrito	Leftover Yalonda's Jerk Tempeh with Coconut Rice and Plantains or plant-based Jamaican jerk jackfruit	Create an EWEE Bowl (see page 190) and add your choice of plant-based faux protein (page 84)
Day 13	Blueberry Oatmeal Smoothie (page 172) or store-bought plant-based smoothie	Create an EWEE Bowl (see page 190) and add your choice of plant-based faux protein (page 84)	Kale-L Pesto Pasta (page 241) or use vegan pesto sauce. Save leftovers for lunch the next day.
Day 14	The "Duluth" Omelet (page 152) with Mushroom "Bacon" (page 155) or liquid egg substitute omelet with faux bacon	Leftover Kale-L Pesto Pasta	EWEE Chickpea Tahini Burger (page 217) with Maple-Roasted Brussels Sprouts (page 220) or plant-based burger on any bun with 2 cups leafy greens

3. The Cold Tofurky Pathway

I respect the efforts, pace, and comfort level everyone needs to undertake an EWEE journey. Maybe you have arrived at this destination after completing the transitional pathways Crowd It Out (page 77) and Fake It Till You Make It (page 86). Or perhaps you are, as I was more than two decades ago, experiencing a crisis—moral, emotional, health-related, or spiritual—and you need to make swift changes. Perhaps you have always been plant-centric behind closed doors but are called to LIVE LARGE in your identity. Maybe your "why" is informed by the topics we discussed in part I and now, you're thinking: "I can no longer eat animal-based food."

Sudden changes can be jarring, but also immensely rewarding—and physically, socially, and emotionally right for some. Each day on the Cold Tofurky meal plan provides a range of macro and micronutrients in easy-to-prepare dishes and comforting whole-food versions of standbys. After fourteen days, repeat, changing up a dish here and there with the variations I suggest throughout the EWEE recipes. For example, if you like Kale-L Pesto (page 241), try it with a different leafy green. Change up your Good Morning, Sweet Potato! (page 160). Create a new Fantastic Fritter (page 203). Make your own signature EWEE Bowl (page 190) and share it with friends! You got this, Sweet Potato.

Tips for Cooking with Faux Meats

Each brand of faux meat cooks up differently. Here are tips that will work for all brands.

- Use nonstick cookware because plant-based meat sticks to hands and stainless steel and cast-iron skillets.

- Use less salt when cooking! Faux meats contain quite a bit of sodium.

- The texture of plant-based meat is softer and doesn't hold together as well as traditional meat when you're making meatballs, meatloaf, or burger patties. Refrigerating the meat to make it cold before you start cooking will help it hold together.

- If you have a little extra time and want to save money, buy plant-based meat loose, rather than preformed and seasoned, which is more expensive. You can season the meat with your own Taco Seasoning (page 128).

- Save plant-based crumbles for taco meat and faux meat ragu since they do not hold their shape for any other damn dish.

Before You Begin Cold Tofurky

- **REMOVE ALL ANIMAL PRODUCTS FROM YOUR HOME.** Donate them to your local food pantry or bring them to an omnivore friend. Or if you are making a switch based on ethics and have decided "Hell no, I don't want to give these products to anyone," well then, just throw them out. I did the latter when I transitioned from vegetarian to vegan.

- **DEEPEN YOUR "WHY."** Write out your values or consider creating a mantra—or use mine! Post it to your wall or refrigerator or carry it in your pocket. Say it to yourself, as often as you need. Throughout this book, you will find support and advice on every page to reinforce your "why."

- **IF YOU SHARE YOUR HOME WITH A ROOMMATE OR LOVED ONE, TALK OPENLY WITH THEM.** They may want to join you on this pathway. If not, you may have to step up and take over the cooking for the household or cook separately for yourself. If you do, offer your food generously! Good food is good food! You can make plant-based dishes the central part of household meals and invite your loved ones to round out their meal with their food choices.

- **YOU DON'T HAVE TO EXPLAIN YOURSELF IF SOMEONE THINKS YOU ARE A "CRAZY" OR A "WEIRDO."** If you feel like sharing your "why," then do that. If not, you can direct them to this book or any of the resources on pages 284–85.

- **REPLACE YOUR USUAL SOURCE OF EGGS, MEAT, FISH, AND DAIRY WITH AS MANY WHOLE, NUTRIENT-DENSE FOODS AS POSSIBLE**, and limit processed meat replacement foods. Choose fresh whole or frozen fruits and vegetables—food without labels. The reason I don't have you reaching for faux meats from the get-go with this approach is to ensure that you include a wide variety of foods to support your daily nutritional needs.

- **RELY ON THE EASY-TO-MAKE RECIPES INCLUDED IN THIS BOOK.** Smoothies (pages 168–75) and juices (pages 165–68) will give you a nutritious, flavor-packed flush of good feelings. And EWEE Bowls (page 190) will provide crunch and texture. Overnight Oats (page 149) and batch-cooked Good Morning, Sweet Potato! (page 160) will have you eating breakfast in no time and with little prep.

- **DEPENDING ON YOUR DIET AND HOW MUCH ANIMAL PRODUCT YOUR BODY IS USED TO, YOU MAY EXPERIENCE YOUR BODY ADJUSTING.** For example, you may feel bloated, need more trips to the bathroom, or feel hungry. Everyone is different. Pay attention to how you feel. Refer to the Crowd It Out meal plan (page 78) to add more whole foods and snacks to your meals.

- **MAKE FRIENDS WITH MUSHROOMS** (see A Guide to Mushrooms, page 244) and other "dense" and "meaty" tofu and tempeh dishes (see Tofu Prep, page 103).

The Cold Tofurky Meal Plan

Week 1

MEAL	BREAKFAST	LUNCH	DINNER
Day 1	Blueberry Oatmeal Smoothie (page 172)	Mega Tofu BLT (page 212)	Buffalo Cauliflower "Chicken" Wings Bowl (page 194)
Day 2	Strawberry Cashew Smoothie (page 173)	Create an EWEE Bowl (page 190)	Mushroom "Cream" Penne (page 243). Save leftovers for lunch the next day.
Day 3	Really Good Tofu Scramble (page 154)	Leftover Mushroom "Cream" Penne	Almond-Crusted Tofu "Salmon" (page 248) and Spicy Sweet Green Beans (page 250)
Day 4	Saturday Morning Nostalgia Pancakes (page 146)	"Egg" Salad Collard Wrap (page 210)	Jackfruit Tacos with Mango-Corn Salsa and Avocado "Cream" (page 253)
Day 5	Overnight Oats (page 149)	Tomato Soup and Grilled "Cheese" (page 182)	"Crab" Cakes with Rémoulade Sauce (page 206)
Day 6	Good Morning, Sweet Potato! (page 160)	Fantastic Fritters (page 203)	Mushroom Ramen Noodle Bowl (page 184)
Day 7	The "Duluth" Omelet (page 152)	Create an EWEE Bowl (page 190)	Vegan takeout. Save leftovers for lunch the next day.

Week 2

MEAL	BREAKFAST	LUNCH	DINNER
Day 8	Choco Power Smoothie (page 172)	Leftover vegan takeout.	BBQ Tofu "Ribs" (page 230) with Sophie's "Famous" Potato Salad (page 232). Save leftovers for lunch the next day.
Day 9	Green Mango Smoothie (page 168)	Leftover BBQ Tofu "Ribs" with Sophie's "Famous" Potato Salad	Auntie Valerie's Stuffed Peppers (page 256). Save leftovers for lunch the next day.
Day 10	Overnight Oats (page 149)	Leftover Auntie Valerie's Stuffed Peppers	Make an EWEE Plate (page 72)
Day 11	Saturday Morning Nostalgia Pancakes (page 146)	Mega Tofu BLT (page 212)	EWEE Beet Burger (page 216) or EWEE Chickpea Tahini Burger (page 217) with Maple-Roasted Brussels Sprouts (page 220). Save leftovers for lunch the next day.
Day 12	Bold 'n' Beautiful Beet Waffles (page 148)	Leftover EWEE Burger with Maple-Roasted Brussels Sprouts	Spaghetti Squash with Cauliflower Alfredo (page 246). Save leftovers for lunch the next day.
Day 13	Really Good Tofu Scramble (page 154)	Leftover Spaghetti Squash with Cauliflower Alfredo	Mom's Plant Loaf with Skillet Cabbage (page 258). Save leftovers for lunch the next day.
Day 14	The "Duluth" Omelet (page 152) with Mushroom "Bacon" (page 155)	Leftover Mom's Plant Loaf with Skillet Cabbage	Tomato "Tuna" Poke Bowl with "Yum Yum" Sauce (page 198)

LOOK OUT FOR ANIMAL-DERIVED INGREDIENTS

Reading labels is key when deciding to eliminate animal products. But it takes some practice! Below is a list of common animal-derived ingredients that appear in foods you might think are fully plant-based. Some manufacturers now label their goods as "certified vegan," making shopping for vegan and plant-based foods easier. When in doubt, remember this: The healthiest foods you can ever put in your ever-loving body *do not* have labels!

INGREDIENT	DERIVED FROM	COMMONLY FOUND IN
Albumen	Chicken eggs	Baked goods, pastries
Carmine, red dye #40, cochineal	Beetles	Fruit juices, candy, yogurt
Fish oil	Fish	Fruit juices fortified with omega-3s
Gelatin	Cows or pigs	Candies, marshmallows, gelatin desserts, gummy bears
Glycerin	Animal fats	Baked goods, premade pasta and rice, dried or canned vegetables and fruits
Isinglass	Fish bladders	Some beers
Lanolin	Sheep	Cereals fortified with vitamin D_3
Lard	Pork fat	Tortillas, refried beans, cupcakes, pie crust
Shellac	Lac insect	Chocolate-covered candies and nuts
Tallow	Beef or lamb	Ice cream, pastries, gum, potato chips

PART III

The EWEE Kitchen

Building an EWEE kitchen pantry may be a new chapter for you—not just in this book, but in your life—as it was in mine. So, to start, I will take you through every item needed for the recipes, focusing on my most often-used ingredients for plant-based dairy, meat, and egg swaps. Each ingredient is widely available at grocery stores and farmers' markets. Even bodegas and 99-cent stores carry beans and other canned goods, dried herbs, plant-based milk, and flavor enhancers. For somewhat harder-to-find ingredients, such as kelp powder and liquid amino acids, I provide alternatives. I want you to see possibilities and celebrate curiosity while you adapt and grow on your EWEE journey at your own pace.

My kitchen is for dancing! And what follows are my most frequently used EWEE kitchen "dance partners."

EWEE KITCHEN INGREDIENTS

Water

Clean, fresh drinking water is the most important ingredient for your health and cooking. Although most people wouldn't consider it an "ingredient," water is the primary component in of Veggie Broth (page 120), soups (pages 178–84), and even smoothies (pages 168–75). As you grow on your EWEE journey and remove processed foods from your diet, your taste buds will change, and you may experience increased sensitivity to the chemicals in most public water systems. I recommend using a water filter. I use the all-natural Berkey microfiltration system since it removes more than 99.9 percent of harmful contaminants in water. It will pay for itself over time. If you do not have a water filtration system for your tap water, I recommend glass bottles of spring water (bottled at the source) for drinking and cooking.

Salt

Fine Sea Salt

Salt is essential for balancing sweet and bitter flavors. I use sea salt over table salt because sea salt retains trace amounts of the minerals calcium, potassium, and magnesium, all key nutrients. There's no need to buy fancy pink salt (unless pink is your favorite color) or an expensive brand, because they all contain similar nutrients. Sea salt comes in coarse and fine salt crystals, but I use fine because it dissolves well. If iodine intake is a concern, use sea salt enriched with iodine.

Himalayan Black Salt (Kala Namak)

I also use Himalayan black salt (kala namak) in my "Egg" Salad Collard Wrap (page 210). It is a mined rock salt that has naturally occurring sulfurous compounds that mimic the taste of traditional eggs!

Oils

I use cold-pressed oil whenever possible for cooking and baking because it provides flavor, unsaturated fats, and satisfaction. Avocado, grapeseed, and olive oil come in for sautéing and roasting since they can withstand high temperatures.

Flours

White Whole Wheat Flour

White whole wheat flour is naturally vegan and has the same nutrition as whole wheat flour. It's made from a winter wheat that is pale in color, mildly sweet, and, while not as soft as all-purpose flour, it's also not as hearty as regular whole wheat flour, so it behaves more like white flour and bakes up less rustic. King Arthur is my go-to brand, but you can try others. I don't bake vegan treats or eat sugar often, but when I do, I want them to taste like the brownies (page 268), cookies (page 278), muffins (page 282), and cobbler (page 280) I remember from childhood.

Gluten-Free Flour

For those who need or prefer gluten-free recipes, I've noted where you can easily swap white whole wheat flour for gluten-free 1:1 flour. I recommend Bob's Red Mill brand. It is formulated from a blend of rice flours and potato starch. I also use naturally gluten-free almond flour in the batter for my Buffalo Cauliflower "Chicken" Wings (page 194) and oat flour to make my gluten-free Saturday Morning Nostalgia Pancakes (page 146).

Grains

Old-Fashioned Rolled Oats

In one ½-cup serving of old-fashioned rolled oats, you get 4 grams of soluble fiber (which nourishes your gut microbiome), 5 grams of protein, and plenty of B vitamins; and they are also an excellent source of iron. This is why they are a staple in my diet. Add a scoop to a smoothie, make Overnight Oats (page 149), or cook a bowl of oatmeal as directed on the package. I also use them as a binder in my EWEE Burgers Two Ways (page 214).

Whole Grains

Whole grains have their bran and germ intact and are a great source of complex carbohydrates (fiber and starch), vitamins, and minerals. They are filling and give you elongated energy. You can buy frozen whole grains, or batch cook them (see page 137) and use them as a base for a bowl (see EWEE Bowl Guide, page 186), or include them on an EWEE Plate (page 72). See a list of whole grains in Batch Cooking Whole Grains 101 (page 138).

Plant-Based Swaps for Eggs

Chickpea Flour

Chickpea flour is naturally gluten-free and protein-rich. When mixed with water it makes a great egg swap in an old-school "Duluth" Omelet (page 152) and adds deep flavor to the batter for Fantastic Fritters (page 203) and Buffalo Cauliflower "Chicken" Wings Bowls (page 194). In some parts of the country, it is sold as garbanzo bean flour.

Applesauce and Bananas

Unsweetened applesauce and mashed bananas add moisture and smooth texture to a crumb, plus a hint of sweetness, which is why they are great egg swaps in baking. I use applesauce in my Sweet Corn Bread (page 234) and mashed banana in my Bold 'n' Beautiful Beet Waffles (page 148).

Flaxmeal (Ground Flaxseeds) and Egg Replacer

Flaxmeal is made by grinding flaxseeds, which are rich in omega-3 fats and fiber. When you combine flaxmeal with water, you get a thick, gel-like mixture that makes a nutritious egg substitute called a "flax egg." I use flax eggs and store-bought egg replacer, which comes in a powdered form, interchangeably. You can buy whole flaxseeds and grind them in a spice grinder to make a flaxmeal if you like. Store both flaxmeal and flaxseeds in the refrigerator.

I recommend that you prepare the amount of "flax egg" or egg replacer called for before beginning each recipe so that it is ready to mix in, as you would a traditional egg.

How to Prepare a "Flax Egg" or Egg Replacer

TO MAKE A "FLAX EGG": In a small bowl, stir together 1 tablespoon flaxmeal with 3 tablespoons warm water until well combined. Let stand for 10 minutes before using in a recipe.

TO PREPARE A STORE-BOUGHT EGG REPLACER: Follow the directions on the package before using in a recipe.

Plant-Based Swaps for Meat and Fish

Tofu and Tempeh

Tofu is made from mature soybeans (edamame are young soybeans) and has been a vital part of Asian cuisines dating to second-century BC China. To make tofu, mature soybeans are boiled to make soy milk. Once liquefied, a natural coagulant called nigari (a compound extracted from sea water) is added, which helps the soy milk form curds and whey. The curds are pressed and formed into blocks—think of tofu as an O.G. cheese.

Tempeh is fermented tofu that is pressed into a cake, and it is full of fiber and protein and is a good source of vitamin B_{12}, a vital micronutrient that keeps our nerve and blood cells healthy (among other important functions).

Beans (Dried and Canned) and Lentils

I rely on beans and lentils as whole-food meat substitutes in many recipes. You can choose to make them "from scratch" (see Batch Cooking Beans 101, page 140) or use canned. Buying dried beans in bulk to cook later saves you money, and I think they are more flavorful. For canned beans, use beans labeled "no salt added," and drain and rinse them thoroughly to remove their starchy liquid before adding to a recipe.

Mushrooms (Fresh and Dried)

My life is more beautiful with mushrooms in it! They are a super-filling, whole-food substitute for animal or processed faux meat products with an umami flavor. *Umami* means "delicious taste" in Japanese and it is one of the five basic tastes, along with sweet, sour, salty, and bitter. Make Mushroom "Bacon" (page 155), add cooked mushrooms to pasta, or make a savory broth from dried mushrooms for a Mushroom Ramen Noodle Bowl (page 184). Cook up Mushroom Brown Gravy (page 263) to experience love on the back of a wooden spoon.

Jackfruit

This tropical tree fruit is rich in vitamin C and potassium and when unripe (or "young") has a fibrous texture and a neutral flavor that is great for absorbing sauce. It shreds easily, making it a good swap for pulled pork or chicken! I use it to make Jackfruit Tacos with Mango-Corn Salsa and Avocado "Cream" (page 253). Look for cans labeled "young" or "unripe" green jackfruit in brine.

Hearts of Palm

Hearts of palm come from the inner core of a palm tree and are slightly sweet. They are cut into cylinders and sold canned. Like jackfruit, they shred easily and make an excellent substitute for crab when blended with chickpeas (garbanzos) in my "Crab" Cakes with Rémoulade Sauce (page 206).

Plant-Based Swaps for Dairy

Cashews

Cashews are a little miracle; they are rich in protein, fiber, minerals, and monounsaturated and polyunsaturated fats (MUFAs and PUFAs) to protect your heart. Blend them into a delicious, rich plant-based dairy substitute to use in savory and sweet dishes (see Cashews Four Ways, page 122). Protect your investment and store cashews and other high-fat nuts, such as walnuts, in a glass con-

tainer in the refrigerator; their fat content makes them perishable. Pre-soak cashews for easier blending.

TO SOAK CASHEWS: Place the cashews in a bowl and add hot water to cover by about 1 inch. Soak for 20 minutes, then drain and proceed with the recipe.

Plant-Based Milk

Plant-based milks are naturally rich in vitamins and minerals and lower in calories and saturated fat than animal-based dairy. See page 83 for My Guide to Plant-Based Milks. I recommend specific plant-based milk in some of my recipes because they work better in baked goods.

Vegan Butter

Vegan, or plant-based, butter is made by combining water with a plant-derived oil, such as olive, avocado, coconut, palm kernel oil, or a combination of oils. Miyoko's brand is widely available, tastes like dairy butter, and comes in sticks for baking and tubs for spreading, which is nice.

Plant-Based Cheese

Food manufacturers have cracked the code (they rely on cashews) to make dairy-free versions of Parmesan, blocks of cheddar, feta, Gouda, and more that melt, stretch, and taste like their dairy counterparts. Experiment with brands that appeal to your budget and flavors that appeal to your taste.

THE WONDERS OF SOY AND TOFU

Tofu, tempeh, edamame, soy milk, soy "cheese," and soy protein powder are cholesterol-free protein sources with all nine essential amino acids, plus omega-6 and omega-3 fatty acids. Tofu also contains isoflavones—compounds that occur naturally in legumes, such as soybeans. Tofu and other soy products are also known to prevent certain cancers, type 2 diabetes, and osteoporosis.

TOFU PREP

You need to press and drain tofu of excess liquid before using it in a recipe. This step improves the texture, helps tofu hold its shape, and allows it to absorb a marinade or crisp in the oven or pan. Here are two easy methods:

TOWEL METHOD: Wrap the tofu block in a clean kitchen towel or a double layer of paper towels, then place it on a plate with a cast-iron skillet or heavy cutting board on top for about 20 minutes to squeeze out the water.

TOFU PRESS METHOD: A tofu press is a kitchen gadget that comes in handy if you plan on cooking tofu frequently! Most cost less than $25 and use a spring mechanism to press excess liquid out of a block of tofu. Press the tofu for a minimum of 15 minutes before using it.

TYPES OF TOFU

SILKEN, SOFT, OR JAPANESE-STYLE: The high water content makes this tofu very soft. You do not need to press soft tofu since its texture gets creamy once it breaks apart. For this reason, you may see it as a dairy replacement in plant-based and vegan desserts. Add soft tofu to smoothies (see EWEE Smoothie Formula, page 174) for creaminess.

FIRM: This is the Goldilocks of tofus. Its texture makes it firm enough to crisp up in a hot pan, yet it's still porous enough to absorb a marinade. Use firm tofu for a Really Good Tofu Scramble (page 154), "Egg" Salad Collard Wraps (page 210), and Almond-Crusted Tofu "Salmon" (page 248).

EXTRA-FIRM: Its name says it all! This tofu has the least amount of water and is the most compact and cooks up super crispy. You do not need to press it—a pat dry with a paper towel will remove excess water after draining. Use extra-firm tofu for Mega Tofu BLT (page 212), BBQ Tofu "Ribs" (page 230), Mushroom Ramen Noodle Bowls (page 184), and Orange "Chicken" (page 251), where I use previously frozen extra-firm tofu to achieve an incredible texture.

CARING FOR AND COOKING MUSHROOMS

TO STORE: Fresh mushrooms are highly perishable and susceptible to moisture and mold. Store them in a brown paper bag, refrigerated, and use within 1 week. Dried mushrooms are a cost-effective pantry staple. Store them in a cool, dry place. Add them to a bowl with enough warm water to cover and soak for 1 hour to rehydrate them. Drain, chop, and save the liquid for broth.

TO CLEAN: Mushrooms are like sponges. Rather than getting them wet, wipe mushrooms thoroughly with a damp paper towel; otherwise, they get soggy.

TO PROTECT YOUR WALLET: Save money and buy mushrooms in bulk. You can freeze fresh and precooked mushrooms: Spread them on a sheet pan and freeze first (so they don't clump) before transferring to a freezer storage bag. Cool precooked mushrooms thoroughly before freezing.

TO COOK: I prefer to use a large cast-iron skillet without added oil, or a nonstick skillet. Cast iron gets hot and stays hot, which will help mushrooms brown evenly, and the more browned they are, the more flavor they have. Arrange them in a single layer, since mushrooms, like people, need their space. If you put them too close or pile them up, they will steam instead of brown. And, when possible, cook mushrooms separately from other ingredients. When alone in a skillet, they will release their moisture faster, which concentrates their natural sugars and gives a ton of mushroom flavor to the whole dish. They will also then retain their texture and not become soggy.

TO SALT: Salting mushrooms not only helps them release moisture but also preserves their texture. But adding salt too early toughens them, so follow the directions in each recipe as to when to salt mushrooms.

Sweeteners

Pure Maple Syrup

Maple syrup is my go-to sweetener for everyday use in savory and some sweet treats. I love its caramel and vanilla flavors, plus it has antioxidant and anti-inflammatory properties. Not all maple syrup is vegan, since some small-batch maple syrup producers use an old-fashioned method of adding animal fat to "defoam" the syrup when reducing the sap. Vegan maple syrup labels should read one ingredient: pure maple syrup. If you have doubts, contact the producer directly and ask!

Medjool Dates

Medjool dates are large, thin-skinned dates full of antioxidants. They lend a deep caramel taste to Sweet Cashew Cream (page 122) and make the base for my Date and Fig Energy Balls (page 277). Medjool dates are a fresh fruit, so look for them in the produce section of your grocery store. Buy ones that are soft and pliable. To keep them moist, store them in an airtight container in the refrigerator for up to 6 months.

Organic Blackstrap Molasses

Blackstrap molasses is a by-product of sugarcane production, but unlike refined sugar, it's naturally rich in antioxidants, iron, and vitamin B_6. Use it as you would use brown sugar to bring balance to the Scotch bonnet pepper heat in my sister, Yalonda's, jerk marinade (see Yalonda's Jerk Tempeh, page 229) and for deep flavor in Pumpkin Chocolate Chip Cookies (page 278).

Organic Cane Sugar (and Other Sugars)

I use ORGANIC CANE SUGAR in my recipes rather than conventional white sugar, which is highly processed, often with animal bone char. Organic cane sugar has a full-bodied taste and because it is unrefined, it retains amino acids and other nutrients. I use COCONUT SUGAR in my Brownies in a "Jiffy" (page 268), because it lends a caramel sweetness. I also use ORGANIC POWDERED SUGAR in the lemon icing for my Lemon Loaf with Lemon Icing (page 272). Powdered sugar is made from pulverizing granulated white sugar, so look for certified USDA organic, or a vegan label on powdered sugar brands, or make your own!

TO MAKE YOUR OWN ORGANIC POWDERED SUGAR: Place ¾ cup organic cane sugar in a blender and blend until powdered. It will yield about 1 cup of fine, fluffy sugar.

Flavor/Texture Enhancers

Nutritional Yeast

Nutritional yeast, aka "nooch," is deactivated yeast loaded with minerals, essential amino acids, and B vitamins. Its taste resembles traditional Parmesan cheese and brings that "cheesy" taste to Mac 'n' "Cheese" (page 242) and Smoky "Queso" (page 202). Nooch shines as a flavor enhancer for many dishes. Sprinkle it over Crispy, Crunchy, Creamy Chickpea Caesar Bowls (page 192).

Liquid Amino Acids

Liquid amino acids, naturally vegan and gluten-free, are a concentrated form of sixteen amino acids derived from soy. It tastes like soy sauce but has less sodium, more nutritional value, and a more intense savory flavor, which is why I prefer it. Of course, you may use reduced-sodium soy sauce or the denser Japanese version of soy sauce, tamari (also gluten-free), interchangeably if you like. Liquid coconut amino acids, which are derived from coconut sap, give your dish a hint of sweetness.

Hemp Hearts (and Hemp Seeds and Powder)

HEMP HEARTS are the shelled centers of hemp seeds. They have a nutty taste, tender texture, and contain all nine essential amino acids, making them a nutritional powerhouse! I use hemp hearts and HEMP POWDER (made from pressed and dried hemp seeds) for a protein boost in my smoothies (pages 168–75). HEMP SEEDS are great for adding crunch to Overnight Oats (page 149), Good Morning, Sweet Potato! (page 160), over bowls (see EWEE Bowl Guide, page 186), and Blender Berry Muffins (page 282). The labeling can be a little confusing: Hemp seed packages are labeled as hemp seeds, but hemp hearts can be labeled either "hemp hearts" or "shelled hemp seeds." Once opened, store hemp hearts, seeds, and powder in the refrigerator.

Kelp Powder or Organic Nori Sheets

Kelp is a large brown seaweed that is often dried and sold in powdered form. You can find it at health food stores and, increasingly, at the grocery store. I use it as a good source of omega-3 fatty acids and to give seafood-like flavor to "Crab" Cakes (page 206), Tomato "Tuna" Poke Bowls (page 198), and Almond-Crusted Tofu "Salmon" (page 248), as well as deeper flavor to Mushroom Ramen Noodle Bowls (page 184). If you can't find kelp powder, look for organic nori sheets (or seaweed snack packs) and grind them to a fine powder in the food processor. Store in an airtight container in a cool, dry place for up to 2 months.

Dietary Supplements (Optional)

Spirulina Powder and Chlorella

SPIRULINA is a blue-green algae that grows in fresh and salt water. I buy it in powdered form at the health food store or in the supplements section of the grocery store. It's rich in essential amino acids and immune-supporting vitamins. Add a scoop to smoothies (see EWEE Smoothie Formula, page 174); its bitter taste blends away!

CHLORELLA is a type of algae that grows in salt water and has a similar nutritional flavor profile to spirulina but has more omega-3 fatty acids per serving, plus a good dose of iodine. Consult with your physician before using any dietary supplements.

STOCK UP!

These pantry and refrigerator/freezer items appear frequently in my recipes—but you don't need to buy them all at once. I mention specific brands of some of these items throughout, but feel free to shop on sale or try a different brand.

Produce: Fresh, Frozen, and Canned

- Chiles: jalapeño, Scotch bonnet, canned chipotle peppers in adobo sauce
- Citrus: lemons, limes, and oranges
- Corn
- Dates
- Edamame, precooked and frozen
- Garlic
- Ginger
- Green beans
- Leafy greens
- Leeks
- Mushrooms
- Olives, jarred and canned
- Onions: yellow and red
- Pickles: jarred jalapeño peppers, pickle chips
- Pumpkin puree, canned
- Russet potatoes
- Scallions (green onions)
- Seasonal fruit, such as mango and pineapple
- Seasonal vegetables, such as asparagus, broccoli, cauliflower, and brussels sprouts
- Shallots
- Snap peas
- Spaghetti squash
- Sweet potatoes: Japanese and orange sweet potatoes (yams)
- Tomato paste
- Tomatoes, fresh and canned whole peeled

Nuts, Seeds, and Butters

- Almonds
- Chia seeds
- Coconut, shredded
- Nut butters
- Peanut butter
- Pine nuts
- Pistachios
- Pumpkin seeds
- Sunflower seeds
- Tahini
- Walnuts

Dried Fruit

- Cherries
- Figs
- Raisins

Herbs (Fresh and Dried), Spices, and Seasonings

- Basil
- Black pepper
- Cumin, ground
- Celery seed
- Chile flakes
- Chili powder
- Cilantro
- Cinnamon
- Dill
- Garlic powder
- Italian seasoning (or make your own; page 128)
- Mustard powder
- Onion powder
- Oregano
- Paprika: regular and smoked
- Parsley

- Pumpkin pie spice
- Rosemary
- Sage
- Taco seasoning (or make your own; page 128)
- Thyme
- Turmeric

Whole Grains and Legumes: Dried, Canned, and Frozen

- Amaranth
- Beans: black, pinto, kidney, chickpea (garbanzo), and cannellini
- Barley
- Buckwheat
- Bulgur
- Farro
- Freekeh
- Lentils: brown and green
- Pasta: whole wheat and gluten-free
- Quinoa
- Rice: brown rice, Japanese sushi rice, jasmine
- Spelt
- Teff
- Wild rice

Condiments, Sweeteners, and Flavorings

- Chocolate sauce (or make your own; page 276)
- Cocoa powder
- Coconut sugar
- Dijon mustard
- Dressings, plant-based (or make your own; pages 125–26)
- Hot sauce
- Ketchup
- Liquid aminos
- Maple syrup
- Mayonnaise, vegan (or make your own; page 123)
- Mirin (sweet Japanese rice wine)
- Molasses
- Sriracha
- Soy sauce, reduced-sodium, or tamari
- Tamarind paste
- Vanilla extract
- Vinegar: apple cider and red wine

Bread and Bread Crumbs

- Buns, vegan sesame-seed
- Corn tortillas
- Panko bread crumbs: whole wheat and gluten-free
- Sandwich rolls, vegan

MY RECOMMENDED BRANDS FOR EWEE RECIPES

I am not a brand stickler, but I figured you might want to know what brands I rely on most for my recipes to help get you started. Feel free to experiment with different brands, shop on sale, or buy store brands for some vegan foods—do you.

FOOD	BRAND
BBQ Sauce	Primal Kitchen Classic BBQ Sauce Organic Unsweetened
Beet juice, cold-pressed, no sugar added	Pomona
Butter, vegan: sticks and tubs for baking and cooking	Miyoko's
Chickpea flour (garbanzo bean flour)	Bob's Red Mill
Chocolate chips	Enjoy Life
Corn grits, white or yellow	Bob's Red Mill
Flour, white whole wheat	King Arthur
Gluten-free 1:1 baking flour. Use this flour as you would an all-purpose flour.	Bob's Red Mill
Gluten-free pasta	Jovial, Banza
Hot sauce	Truff

FOOD	BRAND
Ketchup, organic	365 Whole Foods
Marinara, jarred	Organicville
Mayonnaise, vegan	Hellmann's
Mirin (sweet Japanese rice wine)	Eden Foods
Orange juice, cold-pressed	Trader Joe's
Sour cream, vegan	Kite Hill
Sweet relish	365 Whole Foods
Tofu, all types	House Foods
Vegetable broth, low-sodium	Imagine
Yogurt, plain	Kite Hill

ESSENTIAL TOOLS AND EQUIPMENT

You need only the basics to make the recipes in this book. Eventually, as you make more plant-based food and expand your cooking skills, you might want to consider adding items to your kitchen if you think it will make your life easier and if you'll use them regularly. An EWEE journey is about seeing possibilities while also keeping things simple and streamlined. I love my tofu press, but it is not essential—clean kitchen towels and a heavy skillet or book do the trick (see Tofu Prep, page 103). And if you can't splurge right now for a juicer, you can still make many fresh juices with a high-powered blender and a fine-mesh sieve. In the meantime, here's all you'll need to get set up for success in your EWEE kitchen.

Stovetop

Stainless Steel Soup Pot

An 8-quart soup pot with a lid is a sturdy, roomy, all-purpose pot for making Veggie Broth (page 120), "Clean" Dirty Rice (page 252), cooking pasta, making soup (pages 178–84), and cooking whole grains (see Batch Cooking Whole Grains 101, page 138) and beans (see Batch Cooking Beans 101, page 140). I prefer stainless steel since it's lightweight and easy to clean.

12-Inch Cast-Iron Skillet

No other cookware can compare to cast iron's heat-retaining power. If you are only buying one piece of cookware, this is it! A 12-inch heavy cast-iron skillet will give you crispy-on-the-outside Fantastic Fritters (page 203), perfect Homie Hash Browns (page 158), fried plantains for draping over Coconut Rice and Plantains (page 227), and excellent EWEE Burgers (page 214). My mom owned one cast-iron skillet, and she used it to cook everything from pancakes to pork chops and fried chicken! (I think it was one hundred years old.)

Nonstick Skillets and Sauté Pans

I use a 9-inch nonstick skillet for my Really Good Tofu Scramble (page 154) and browning mushrooms, since it releases food quickly and is easy to clean. Look for nonstick cookware free of toxic chemicals, such as lead, cadmium, PFAS, and PFOA (two types of manufactured chemicals that don't break down). Stainless steel sauté pans have high sides and come with lids.

Appliances

High-Powered Blender

A powerful blender is a must-have. Working with fibrous plants, frozen fruit, or hard nuts requires a heftier motor than a traditional countertop blender has. I use mine for making smoothies (pages 168–75), Cashews Four Ways (page 122), and other creamy, dairy-free sauces, EWEE dressings (pages 125–26), Soft-Serve Banana Nice Cream (page 274), and Blender Berry Muffins (page 282).

Food Processor

I use my 6-cup food processor more than any other kitchen tool besides my juicer and high-powered blender. It's essential for EZ Hummus (page 130), Kale-L Pesto Pasta (page 241), finely chopping nuts for my Date and Fig Energy Balls (page 277), and mincing mushrooms. If you are on a budget, a mini chopper is a versatile, affordable alternative.

Immersion Blender (aka Stick Blender)

Creamy soups are comforting, but transferring hot soup to a stand blender to get them smooth is a pain! An immersion blender lets you puree soups in the pot and gives you more control over texture. It's inexpensive, easy to clean, and fits in a drawer.

Baking

Sheet Pans

These are my go-to baking sheets for oven-roasting vegetables. Their side rims keep oils and juices from sliding off. I recommend half-sheet (13 × 18 inches) sizes for your oven and quarter-sheet (9½ × 13 inches) size for freezing produce for smoothies, since two smaller sheets can easily fit in your freezer. Look for sheet pans that come with a wire cooling rack insert, which allows air to circulate beneath and around baked goods so they don't wind up being overcooked.

Silicone Mats

Silicone baking mats protect your baking sheets from stuck-on foods and make for easier cleanup. Plus, they are reusable. If you don't have a silicone mat, line baking sheets with parchment paper for use in the freezer and oven temperatures for up to 425°F.

Parchment Paper

I use parchment paper for lining any baking pans of unusual shape or size, since a silicone mat doesn't work for them. For example, for Brownies in a "Jiffy" (page 268) and Lemon Loaf with Lemon Icing (page 272), I cut parchment paper to fit the size of the pans. When using parchment paper, measure a piece twice the length of your pan. Fold it in half lengthwise, then use scissors to cut it into two smaller rectangles. Brush the bottom of the pan with a bit of oil, then place the pieces flush along the bottom in a crisscross pattern, allowing for an overhang on both sides.

Storage

Bowl Covers

I don't use plastic wrap for covering dishes since it's harmful to the environment. Instead, I do what my mom and grandmother did—use an upside-down plate to cover dishes or store leftovers in airtight glass containers with lids.

One-Pint (16-Ounce) Mason Jars

One-pint Mason jars are the perfect size for prepping Overnight Oats (page 149)—the bigger size makes it easier to stir them up before eating. They are also great for storing juices and smoothies and making Quick Pickled Red Onions (page 132).

Tools

Knives

You only need one 10-inch chef's knife for slicing, dicing, and chopping fruits and hearty leafy greens, such as kale, or thick-skinned veggies, such as spaghetti squash. A serrated knife (bread knife) is excellent for slicing tomatoes and cutting bread.

Fine-Mesh Sieve

A 40-mesh screen sieve is my go-to tool for straining out solids such as for Veggie Broth (page 120) and for draining cooked whole grains or soaked cashews. It's my secret weapon for extra Creamy

Mashed Potatoes (page 262), too. And you'll need one to strain the pulp from fresh juices if you make them in your blender.

Silicone Spatula

I love my silicone spatula since it's the best tool for scraping the sides of a bowl, blender, or food processor to get every bit of sauce/pesto/batter/you name it out and into my bowl/dish/mouth!

Balloon Whisk

A balloon whisk is a big whisk essential for making smooth Mushroom Brown Gravy (page 263), "Cheesy" Grits (page 147), and Beet BBQ Sauce (page 132). Use it instead of a sifter for combining and aerating dry ingredients in Bold 'n' Beautiful Beet Waffles (page 148) and baked goods.

Microplane Grater/Zester

The cutting edges of a Microplane grater/zest are very fine and extra sharp, making it the best tool for zesting citrus or grating ginger or garlic.

Other Tools

- Box grater
- Kitchen towels
- Food scale
- Measuring cups and spoons
- Mixing bowls
- Tongs
- Vegetable peeler
- Wooden spoons

PART IV

Recipes

Here we are, Sweet Potato. We've arrived at the heart of this book: the better-for-you, better-for-the-world, whole-food vegan recipes that I love to cook and share with the people I love. Many are vegan versions of the foods I enjoyed growing up: Saturday morning breakfasts, hearty sandwiches, and mains like my mom's enchiladas. Others capture the smoky, earthy-sweet, and umami-rich flavors and textures I discovered on my EWEE journey.

Now it's *your* time to shine in the kitchen. I give you many ways to "do you" with these recipes. Whether you're searching for filling, easy-to-pull-off smoothies and full-flavored bowls or wondering how to create easy swaps and variations for every meal, you've come to the right place. And if you've been traveling a vegan road for a while and want to freshen your repertoire, you'll discover abundant, crowd-pleasing recipes, too—"soul food" get-together, anyone? (See page 225.)

Before you pick up a spoon/knife/pan, read the recipe from beginning to end. You'll save yourself time and avoid errors. Some recipes include notes about the preparation or an ingredient; in others, you may see a "Think EWEE" tip at the end. I want to help you get ideas flowing about incorporating many of these dishes into a sustainable EWEE journey!

PANTRY, FRIDGE, AND FREEZER

VEGGIE BROTH

4 medium carrots, scrubbed and roughly chopped

6 celery stalks, scrubbed and roughly chopped

2 large skin-on onions, roughly chopped

4 medium skin-on garlic cloves, smashed

2 or more sprigs fresh parsley

2 or more sprigs fresh thyme

2 bay leaves

1 cup vegetable trimmings (optional), such as mushroom stems (well cleaned), fennel fronds, scallion greens, and tomato cores

2 tablespoons tomato paste (optional)

It's great to have homemade vegetable broth on hand as a base for soups or a nutritious, warming snack on a cold day. It's easy to make, and more flavorful than store-bought since you can choose the ingredients that go into it. Preparing broth will also use up the mix of vegetable odds and ends— whatever you have on hand or need to prepare before it goes bad. I store veggie trimmings and peels, such as mushroom stems and scallion greens, in a reusable, resealable freezer bag and save them for my next batch. A spoonful of tomato paste adds deep color and umami flavor. Avoid adding sulfur-rich leafy greens and cruciferous veggies such as broccoli, cauliflower, or cabbage to a broth. They protect your body from inflammation but make a broth taste bitter.

In a large soup pot, combine the carrots, celery, onions, garlic, parsley, thyme, bay leaves, vegetable trimmings (if using), and 6 quarts water, or more if needed to cover the vegetables by 2 inches. Bring to a boil over high heat, add the tomato paste (if using), then reduce the heat to a gentle simmer and cook for 1 hour.

Let the broth cool slightly, then strain it through a fine-mesh sieve into a large bowl. Discard the solids. Use immediately or cool completely before storing in an airtight container in the refrigerator for up to 1 week. Or divide among freezer-safe containers and freeze for up to 6 months.

CASHEWS FOUR WAYS

Add cashews to a high-powered blender or food processor with water and—bam!—like Optimus Prime transforming from trailer form to selfless and wise Autobot, they become a versatile nondairy substitute for heavy cream, whipped cream, sour cream, and mayonnaise. If using a food processor, stop now and then to scrape down the sides, as necessary. Here are four ways to take cashews for a spin.

BASIC CASHEW CREAM

Makes about 1½ cups

Blended cashews make a rich, creamy, and versatile base that can take on a range of flavors, such as fresh herbs, "cheesy" nutritional yeast, or smoky chipotle peppers. You can control the thickness by adding more water if you like. Store refrigerated in an airtight container for up to 5 days.

1¼ cups raw cashews

½ teaspoon fine sea salt

Place the cashews in a bowl and add hot water to cover by about 1 inch. Soak for 20 minutes, then drain well.

In a blender (preferably high-powered) or food processor, combine the soaked cashews, salt, and 1 cup cold water. Blend on high for 2 to 3 minutes, until smooth and creamy. For a looser cashew cream, add more water, 1 tablespoon at a time, and continue blending, until the desired consistency is reached.

NOTE: To soak cashews, place them in a bowl and add hot water to cover by about 1 inch. Soak for 20 minutes, then drain and proceed with the recipe.

SWEET CASHEW CREAM

Makes about 1½ cups

Dates give basic cashew cream a beautiful vanilla and caramel sweetness. You'll want to lick the spoon each time you make it. Add a dollop to Roasted Stone Fruit (page 269), layer it in "Banana Cream Pie" Oats (page 150), spoon onto a Good Morning, Sweet Potato! (page 160), or enjoy it with Bold 'n' Beautiful Beet Waffles (page 148) or Saturday Morning Nostalgia Pancakes (page 146).

1¼ cups raw cashews

6 soft pitted dates, such as Medjool or Deglet Noor

½ teaspoon fine sea salt

1 teaspoon pure vanilla extract

Place the cashews in a bowl and add hot water to cover by about 1 inch. Soak for 20 minutes, then drain well.

In a blender (preferably high-powered) or food processor, combine the soaked cashews, dates, salt, vanilla, and 1 cup water. Blend on high for 2 to 3 minutes, until smooth and creamy. Transfer to an airtight container and refrigerate for 1 hour before using. Store refrigerated in an airtight container for up to 1 week.

THINK EWEE: Use the basic cashew cream in Smoky "Queso" (page 202), Mushroom "Cream" Penne (page 243), Ranch Dressing (page 126), and Southwest Dressing (page 126).

SOUR CASHEW CREAM

Makes about 1¼ cups

Apple cider vinegar and lemon turn basic cashew cream into nondairy sour cream! I like to drizzle it over soups (pages 178–84), "Beef" 'n' Bean Enchiladas (page 264), and Loaded Chipotle Chili (page 185).

1¼ cups raw cashews

1 tablespoon fresh lemon juice

1 teaspoon apple cider vinegar

½ teaspoon fine sea salt

Place the cashews in a bowl and add hot water to cover by about 1 inch. Soak for 20 minutes, then drain well.

In a blender (preferably high-powered) or food processor, combine the soaked cashews, lemon juice, vinegar, salt, and 1 cup water. Blend on high for 2 to 3 minutes, until smooth and creamy. Transfer to an airtight container and refrigerate for 1 hour before using. Store refrigerated in an airtight container for up to 1 week.

CASHEW MAYO

Makes about 1¼ cups

Dijon mustard and lemon juice give my egg-free, cholesterol-free mayo the tang of the very best mayos. I especially love this mayo because it thickens up once it's refrigerated.

1¼ cup raw cashews

½ teaspoon fine sea salt

1 tablespoon Dijon mustard or 1 teaspoon mustard powder

2 tablespoons fresh lemon juice

2 teaspoons apple cider vinegar

Place the cashews in a bowl and add hot water to cover by about 1 inch. Soak for 20 minutes, then drain well.

In a blender (preferably high-powered) or food processor, combine the soaked cashews, salt, mustard, lemon juice, vinegar, and ¼ cup water. Blend on high for 2 to 4 minutes, until smooth and creamy. Store refrigerated in an airtight container for up to 1 week.

THINK EWEE: Use the cashew mayo as a base for rémoulade sauce (to go with "Crab" Cakes, page 206), "Yum Yum" Sauce (page 127), and Jackfruit Tacos with Mango-Corn Salsa and Avocado "Cream" (page 253). Or use it as a condiment for Creamy Coleslaw (page 232), Sophie's "Famous" Potato Salad (page 231), and Mega Tofu BLT (page 212).

RANCH DRESSING

SOUTHWEST DRESSING

"YUM YUM"
SAUCE

CHICKPEA CAESAR DRESSING

Makes ¾ cup

Woosh-ter—lemme try again. WOOST-ER-SHEER sauce—a key ingredient in traditional Caesar dressing and an easy-to-mangle name—often contains anchovies or fish sauce. Liquid aminos are animal-free, and my savory replacement for Worcestershire. You can also use reduced-sodium soy sauce or tamari, too. I love the flavors of a classic Caesar, and my version delivers on that funky umami flavor without harming fish. Protein- and fiber-rich chickpeas make this nut-free dressing very creamy. Use the dressing on the Crispy, Crunchy, Creamy Chickpea Caesar Bowl (page 192).

¾ cup cooked chickpeas (garbanzo beans) or ¾ cup canned chickpeas, drained and rinsed

2 garlic cloves, roughly chopped

3 tablespoons fresh lemon juice (from 1 large lemon)

2 teaspoons Dijon mustard or 1 teaspoon mustard powder

2 teaspoons ground cumin

2 tablespoons liquid amino acids, reduced-sodium soy sauce, or tamari

¼ teaspoon fine sea salt

¼ teaspoon freshly cracked black pepper

In a blender or food processor, combine the chickpeas, garlic, lemon juice, mustard, cumin, liquid aminos, salt, pepper, and ¼ cup water. Blend for about 2 minutes, or until smooth and creamy. Store refrigerated in an airtight container for up to 1 week.

RANCH DRESSING

Makes ¾ cup

My cashew cream–based ranch dressing includes lots of fresh dill. I love its bright, grassy flavor. I use this dressing for my Buffalo Cauliflower "Chicken" Wings Bowls (page 194), and, by using just a little less water, it's great a as a thick ranch dip for Fantastic Fritters (page 203) or to complement freshly cut vegetables. For a nut-free dressing, substitute unsweetened, unflavored plant-based yogurt for the cashew cream.

½ cup Basic Cashew Cream (page 122) or plain plant-based yogurt

2 tablespoons apple cider vinegar

2 tablespoons chopped fresh dill or 1½ teaspoons dried dill weed

1 tablespoon chopped fresh parsley or 1½ teaspoons dried parsley

3 garlic cloves, minced

1 small shallot, minced

½ teaspoon paprika

1 teaspoon maple syrup

½ teaspoon fine sea salt

¼ teaspoon freshly cracked black pepper

In a small bowl, stir together the cashew cream, vinegar, dill, parsley, garlic, shallot, paprika, maple syrup, salt, pepper, and ½ to ¾ cup water, depending on desired consistency—less water for a thick dip, more water for a pourable dressing. Continue stirring until smooth and creamy. Store refrigerated in an airtight container for up to 1 week.

SOUTHWEST DRESSING

Makes ¾ cup

EWEE Spice Mix gives my cashew cream–based Southwest dressing a smoky lift, making it perfect for a drizzle over Chicago Taco Bowls (page 196). For a nut-free dressing, substitute ½ cup plain plant-based yogurt for the cashew cream.

½ cup Basic Cashew Cream (page 122) or plain plant-based yogurt

2 tablespoons fresh lime juice (from 2 limes)

2 teaspoons EWEE Spice Mix (page 127)

1 teaspoon maple syrup

¼ teaspoon fine sea salt

2 teaspoons minced fresh cilantro leaves

In a blender or food processor, combine the cashew cream, lime juice, spice mix, maple syrup, sea salt, cilantro, and ½ cup water. Blend for 2 to 4 minutes, until smooth and creamy. Store refrigerated in an airtight container for up to 1 week.

"YUM YUM" SAUCE

Makes ¾ cup

While store-bought Yum Yum is made with traditional mayonnaise and has shelf-stabilizing ingredients, my version begins with tangy cashew mayo, a touch of maple syrup, spicy sriracha for kick, and mirin (mildly sweet Japanese rice wine)— some brands of mirin contain high fructose corn syrup, so look for one that has only water, rice, and salt. Drizzle "Yum Yum" Sauce over Tomato "Tuna" Poke Bowls (page 198) or enjoy it as a dip for EZ EWEE Veggies (page 142). For a nut-free sauce, substitute ½ cup plain plant-based yogurt for the cashew mayo.

½ cup Cashew Mayo (page 123) or plain plant-based yogurt

2 garlic cloves, chopped

2 teaspoons sriracha

1 teaspoon mirin (sweet Japanese rice wine)

1 teaspoon maple syrup

¼ teaspoon fine sea salt

In a blender or food processor, combine the cashew mayo, garlic, sriracha, mirin, maple syrup, salt, and ¼ to ½ cup of water, depending on your desired consistency. Blend for 2 to 4 minutes, until smooth and creamy. Store refrigerated in an airtight container for up to 1 week.

EWEE SPICE MIX

Makes about ½ cup

This is my all-purpose spice blend. It includes smoked paprika, which I love for its lightly sweet and smoky flavor. The spice is versatile and bold, so a little goes a long way. Use it to season EZ EWEE Veggies (page 142), Crispy Chickpeas (page 134), Loaded Chipotle Chili (page 185), "Crab" Cakes (page 206), Southwest Dressing (page 126), and BBQ Tofu "Ribs" (page 230).

2 tablespoons smoked paprika

1 tablespoon garlic powder

1 tablespoon onion powder

2 teaspoons mustard powder

2 teaspoons ground cumin

1 teaspoon fine sea salt

1 teaspoon freshly cracked black pepper

In a small jar with a lid, combine the smoked paprika, garlic powder, onion powder, mustard powder, cumin, salt, and pepper. Cover and shake a few times to blend. Store in a cool, dry place for up to 1 year.

ITALIAN SEASONING

Makes about ½ cup

You probably already have most, or all, of these dried herbs in your pantry to make a fragrant, salt-free Italian seasoning for Spaghetti 'n' Beet Balls (page 240), Walnut and Mushroom "Meat" (page 136), and Fantastic Fritters (page 203). Tweak the amounts of one spice over another or omit one, such as the chili flakes, if you don't like too much heat.

2 tablespoons dried oregano

2 tablespoons dried basil

2 tablespoons dried parsley

1 tablespoon dried rosemary

2 teaspoons dried thyme

1 teaspoon garlic powder

½ teaspoon red chile flakes

In a small jar with a lid, combine the oregano, basil, parsley, rosemary, thyme, garlic powder, and chile flakes. Cover and shake a few times to blend. Store in a cool, dry place for up to 1 year.

TACO SEASONING

Makes about ½ cup

The little spice packets that come in store-bought taco kits don't capture the heat and earthiness that are key to a great taco seasoning, and they are also high in sodium. Make this your go-to taco seasoning and adjust the chili powder for more heat and cumin for earthy warmth and a touch of citrus. I use this seasoning in my Walnut and Mushroom "Meat" (page 136), Loaded Chipotle Chili (page 185), and Jackfruit Tacos with Mango-Corn Salsa and Avocado "Cream" (page 253).

2 tablespoons chili powder, or more to taste

1 teaspoon paprika

1 teaspoon ground cumin, or more to taste

1 teaspoon dried oregano

1 teaspoon garlic powder

1 teaspoon fine sea salt

¼ teaspoon freshly cracked black pepper

In a small jar with a lid, combine the chili powder, paprika, cumin, oregano, garlic powder, salt, and pepper. Cover and shake a few times to blend. Store in a cool, dry place for up to 1 year.

TACO
SEASONING

EWEE SPICE
MIX

ITALIAN
SEASONING

EZ HUMMUS

Makes about 1½ cups

Store-bought hummus is pricey as hell for what is essentially seasoned chickpeas that are packaged with tons of sodium and chemical additives. Thick, garlicky chickpea hummus is easy to make for a fraction of the cost. I especially like to dip raw pepper strips in hummus—the vitamin C in the peppers helps your body absorb plant-based iron, called nonheme iron.

One thing to note: Once everything is in the food processor, it may look like the ingredients won't blend into a smooth paste—that's normal! Be patient because as you add the cold water, it churns into a luscious smooth and fluffy dip.

1½ cups cooked chickpeas (garbanzo beans) or 1 15-ounce can chickpeas, drained and rinsed

4 tablespoons tahini

2 large garlic cloves, chopped, or 1 teaspoon garlic powder

½ teaspoon ground cumin, plus more to taste

¼ teaspoon fine sea salt, plus more to taste

3 tablespoons fresh lemon juice (from 1 large lemon)

Crispy Chickpeas (optional; page 134), for garnish

In a food processor, combine the chickpeas, tahini, garlic, cumin, salt, lemon juice, and ¼ cup cold water. Process for a few seconds, until the mixture clumps, also called "seizing." Add 1 tablespoon cold water through the feeder and continue blending for about 1 minute, or until it reaches the consistency of a smooth creamy paste.

Stop and scrape down the sides, add 1 to 2 tablespoons more cold water, and continue blending for about 30 seconds more, or until very smooth. Taste and add more cumin and/or salt if desired. Store refrigerated in an airtight container for up to 1 week.

EZ GUACAMOLE

Makes about 1 cup

The flavor and texture of homemade guacamole beat store-bought versions, which can have a chemical aftertaste from all the preservatives. This homemade guacamole comes together faster than going to the store, and it's bright, clean-tasting, rich, and just a lil' chunky, as I like it. Capsaicin, the chemical that makes jalapeño peppers spicy, is mainly in the seeds and ribs of the pepper, so if you prefer a milder guacamole, just leave them out. Fiber-rich avocados are one of the healthiest sources of monounsaturated fat—a good fat that helps lower cholesterol.

3 avocados, halved and pitted (see Notes)

¼ cup finely chopped red onion

1 tablespoon minced fresh cilantro

½ small jalapeño pepper (seeded if desired for less heat), finely chopped

¼ teaspoon garlic powder

¼ teaspoon fine sea salt, or more to taste

2 tablespoons fresh lime juice (from 2 limes)

Scoop the avocado flesh into a bowl and use the back of a fork to mash the avocado until the texture is slightly chunky.

With a flexible spatula, fold in the onion, cilantro, jalapeño, garlic powder, salt, and lime juice. Serve immediately or store in the fridge (see Notes for the best way to store so it doesn't brown).

NOTES: To prevent freshly cut avocados from browning, leave the pit intact in an avocado half, squeeze fresh lemon juice across the surface of the cut side, then store in an airtight container, cut-side down, in the refrigerator.

To prevent freshly made guacamole from browning, squeeze fresh lemon juice across the surface, store in an airtight container, and refrigerate. Stir before serving.

BEET BBQ SAUCE

Makes about 2 cups

As a lifelong BBQSL (sauce lover), I think this sauce rivals the taste, and surpasses the nutrition, of store-bought brands, which often have caramel coloring, fat, refined sugar, or high fructose corn syrup to enhance their texture and flavor. It's easy to make your own BBQ sauce, but to make it even easier, use canned or precooked beets; both have the same nutritional value as fresh beets. Pair with my BBQ Tofu "Ribs" (page 230), EWEE Beet Burger (page 216), and Mom's Plant Loaf with Skillet Cabbage (page 258).

½ **pound fresh beets (scrubbed, peeled, and quartered), 1 8-ounce package cooked beets (quartered), or 1 14.5-ounce can no-salt-added beets (drained, rinsed, and quartered)**

⅓ **cup organic ketchup**

3 **tablespoons apple cider vinegar**

2 **tablespoons liquid amino acids, reduced-sodium soy sauce, or tamari**

1 **tablespoon mustard powder**

2 **teaspoons smoked paprika**

1 **teaspoon onion powder**

½ **teaspoon garlic powder**

½ **teaspoon fine sea salt**

½ **teaspoon freshly cracked black pepper**

If you are using precooked or canned beets, skip this step. Otherwise, add the fresh beets to a medium saucepan and cover with 3 cups water. Bring to a boil over medium-high heat, then reduce the heat to a simmer and cook for about 25 minutes, or until tender. Drain and rinse under cold water until cool enough to handle. Reserve the saucepan.

In a blender (preferably high-powered), combine the beets, ketchup, vinegar, liquid aminos, mustard powder, smoked paprika, onion powder, garlic powder, salt, and pepper and blend on low speed for 1 to 2 minutes. Then blend on high speed for about 30 seconds more, or until smooth.

Transfer the mixture to the now-empty saucepan. Set over medium-low heat and cook, whisking now and then, for 5 to 7 minutes, until the sauce thickens.

Use immediately or cool completely before storing in an airtight container in the refrigerator for up to 2 weeks.

QUICK PICKLED RED ONIONS

Makes 1 pint

Hello, I am spicy, a little sweet, and I love a beet by my side. No, I am not Dominick Thompson. I am a jar of pickled red onions. I love short walks from your refrigerator to bowls (see EWEE Bowl Guide, page 186), to the Jackfruit Tacos with Mango-Corn Salsa and Avocado "Cream" (page 253), or on sandwiches for a burst of bright flavor. (The small beet in my jar turns me a beautiful color red—and you can eat that, too!)

1½ **cups apple cider vinegar**

2 **garlic cloves, thinly sliced**

1 **teaspoon organic raw sugar**

2 **teaspoons fine sea salt**

1 **large red onion, halved and thinly sliced**

1 **small beet, ends trimmed, peeled and halved**

In a 1-pint glass jar with a tight-fitting lid, stir together the vinegar, garlic, sugar, and salt until the sugar dissolves.

Add the onion to the jar, followed by the beet. Place the lid on the jar, give it a shake, and refrigerate for at least 4 hours, before using. Store sealed and refrigerated for up to 3 weeks.

TOMATO AND BEET MARINARA

Makes 3 cups

My mom added sugar to sweeten her tomato sauce. To be fair, in the '80s, most people didn't yet know all the damage refined white sugar does to our bodies, including increasing the risk of type 2 diabetes, heart disease, and obesity. Now that we're wiser to the detrimental health costs of sugar, I use beets (and a touch of maple syrup) to re-create the sweetness of her sauce. Beets are rich in fiber, so their natural sugars enter your bloodstream more slowly, and therefore don't spike your glucose levels. Make this sauce for Spaghetti 'n' Beet Balls (page 240) or serve it warmed as a dip for Fantastic Fritters (page 203).

¼ cup neutral oil, such as avocado or grapeseed

1 small yellow or white onion, finely chopped (about ½ cup)

3 garlic cloves, minced

1 28-ounce can whole peeled tomatoes

1½ cups Beet Juice (page 167) or store-bought cold-pressed no-sugar-added beet juice such as Pomona

½ teaspoon fine sea salt

½ teaspoon freshly cracked black pepper

¼ teaspoon red chile flakes

2 tablespoons maple syrup

¼ cup packed fresh basil leaves

1 tablespoon chopped fresh parsley

1 tablespoon dried oregano

In a large soup pot, heat the oil over medium-high heat until it shimmers. Add the onion and cook, stirring now and then, for 3 to 5 minutes, until the onions are softened and translucent. Stir in the garlic and cook for about 1 more minute, or until fragrant.

Add the tomatoes, beet juice, salt, black pepper, chile flakes, maple syrup, basil, parsley, and oregano. Increase the heat to high and bring to a boil. Reduce the heat to a simmer and cook for about 15 minutes, or until the sauce thickens.

Remove from the heat and use immediately. Or cool completely before storing in an airtight container in the refrigerator for up to 1 week.

CRISPY CHICKPEAS

Makes 3 cups

A 1-cup serving of chickpeas (garbanzo beans) has 14.5 grams of protein. Consider this: A 3-ounce piece of chicken has 27 grams. When tossed with EWEE Spice Mix (page 127) and roasted, you get a crunchy, protein- and fiber-rich snack or topper for bowls (see EWEE Bowl Guide, page 186) or EZ Hummus (page 130)! Or add them to spaghetti tossed with Tomato and Beet Marinara (page 133).

3 cups cooked chickpeas (garbanzo beans) or 2 15.5-ounce cans, drained and rinsed

2 tablespoons neutral oil, such as avocado or grapeseed

2 teaspoons EWEE Spice Mix (page 127)

Preheat the oven to 400°F. Line a sheet pan with parchment paper or a silicone mat.

Use a paper towel or kitchen towel to blot the chickpeas dry. In a medium bowl, combine the chickpeas, oil, and spice mix. Toss to coat well.

Spread the chickpeas in a single layer on the baking sheet. Bake for 10 minutes.

Gently toss the chickpeas on the sheet pan and continue baking for about 10 more minutes, or until the chickpeas are browned and crunchy.

Cool before storing in an airtight container at room temperature for up to 1 week.

WALNUT AND MUSHROOM "MEAT"

1 cup raw walnuts, soaked and drained (see Note)

10 ounces mushrooms, such as button, cremini, or shiitake, tough stems removed, roughly chopped

2 tablespoons liquid amino acids, reduced-sodium soy sauce, or tamari

½ teaspoon fine sea salt

1 tablespoon Taco Seasoning (page 128) or Italian Seasoning (page 128)

¼ teaspoon freshly cracked black pepper

½ teaspoon garlic powder

½ teaspoon onion powder

2 tablespoons neutral oil, such as avocado or grapeseed

Mushrooms, tempeh, and walnuts each contain all nine essential amino acids found in animal protein—and these amino acids translate into a "meaty" flavor on our palate. Besides being great tasting, readily available, and more economical than faux meat, you'll reap potent health benefits, since walnuts are full of omega-3 fatty acids and mushrooms are a rich source of energy-boosting B vitamins. Use this mixture for a Chicago Taco Bowl (page 196) and in "Beef" 'n' Bean Enchiladas (page 264). Swap the taco seasoning for Italian Seasoning (page 128) to use in Mom's Plant Loaf with Skillet Cabbage (page 258).

In a food processor, pulse the walnuts for a few seconds at a time, or until finely ground, taking care not to overpulse or they will turn into a paste. Transfer to a large bowl and set aside.

To the now-empty food processor, add the mushrooms and pulse 3 or 4 times, stopping as needed to scrape down the sides, until finely chopped. Transfer the mushrooms to the bowl with the walnuts. Stir in the liquid aminos, salt, seasoning mix, pepper, garlic powder, and onion powder and mix well to combine.

In a large skillet, heat the oil over medium-high heat until it shimmers. Add the mushroom-walnut mixture and cook, stirring often, for about 5 minutes, or until the mixture changes color from light to dark brown and the liquid is absorbed.

Use immediately or cool completely and transfer to an airtight container and store in the refrigerator for up to 1 week.

NOTE: Soaking the walnuts first softens their texture. To do so, place the walnuts in a bowl and cover with hot water to cover by 1 inch. Soak for 20 minutes, then drain and proceed with the recipe.

BATCH PREPPING AND COOKING

Adding more whole foods to your diet is good for every type of eater, but they are fundamental to an EWEE journey, no matter which pathway you take. Batch prepping fruits and veggies, and batch cooking beans and whole grains, is a convenient, cost-effective way to make sure you always have them on hand. When you do, making a meal, even if you are just putting veggies on top of a grain with some sauce, is within reach. Try to get in the habit of always having grains and vegetables, fresh or frozen, on hand, and you'll hardly think about heating up processed or other unhealthy and costly food again.

Here's some prepping and cooking I do at the start of my week:

- Wash leafy greens—sturdy greens, such as kale, last the week.

- Wash and dry fruit and cut melons to have on hand for snacking.

- Peel and freeze bananas for smoothies (pages 168–75)—so easy.

- Batch cook sweet potatoes (page 160), grains (page 138), and beans (page 140).

- Make Quick Pickled Red Onions (page 132).

- Make EZ Hummus (page 130).

- Make dressings and sauces, such as Ranch Dressing (page 126), Beet BBQ Sauce (page 132), and Tomato and Beet Marinara (page 133).

- Make EZ EWEE Veggies (page 142) to have as a go-to veggie to add to bowls (see EWEE Bowl Guide, page 186).

BATCH COOKING WHOLE GRAINS 101

1 cup whole grain of your choice (see chart opposite)

Veggie Broth (page 120), store-bought low-sodium vegetable broth, or water (see chart opposite for amounts)

With some planning, a large soup pot, and veggie broth (or water), you can have flavorful whole grains every day, using an absorption method—which means placing the grain in a pot with a specified amount of water until absorbed. You can also batch cook whole grains in an Instant Pot or other electric pressure cooker or rice cooker, if you have one. Follow the cooking time and recommended broth or water volume for your model.

Place the grain in a medium bowl, add warm water to cover by 1 inch, and soak for a minimum of 8 hours or overnight (see Note).

Drain and add the grain to a large pot. Add the amount of broth or water as indicated in the chart. Bring to a boil over high heat. Reduce the heat to a simmer, cover, and cook (resist the urge to lift the lid while cooking—this allows steam to escape) until the liquid is absorbed and the grain is tender, according to the time listed in the chart below.

Once cooked, spread the grains out on a sheet pan to cool completely (this creates more surface area, so they cool down faster). Then transfer to an airtight container and store in the refrigerator for up to 4 days or in the freezer for up to 4 months. Thaw overnight in the refrigerator to use the next day.

NOTE: Soaking grains improves their digestibility and helps release their minerals.

Grain Cooking Chart

GRAIN (1 CUP)	VEGGIE BROTH OR WATER	COOK TIME	YIELD
Amaranth	2 cups	15 to 20 minutes	2½ cups
Barley, pearl	3 cups	45 to 60 minutes	3½ cups
Brown rice	2½ cups	30 minutes	3 cups
Buckwheat	2 cups	20 minutes	4 cups
Bulgur	2 cups	12 minutes	3 cups
Farro, semi-pearled	2½ cups	30 minutes	3 cups
Freekeh	2½ cups	20 minutes	3 cups
Japanese sushi rice	2 cups	20 minutes	4 cups
Quinoa	2 cups	15 minutes	3 cups
Spelt	4 cups	45 minutes	3 cups
Teff	3 cups	20 minutes	2½ cups
Wild rice	3 cups	50 minutes	3½ cups

BATCH COOKING BEANS 101

1 cup dried beans of your choice (see chart opposite)

1 tablespoon fine sea salt

1 celery stalk, halved

1 small onion, halved

2 sprigs woody herbs, such as rosemary, sage, or thyme

Veggie Broth (page 120), store-bought low-sodium vegetable broth, or water

Cracking open a can of beans (or lentils and mung beans, both in the legume family) is an easy shortcut, but cooking dried beans (or what I think of as making beans "from scratch") saves money and gives you control over their texture and flavor with aromatic add-ins. I recommend a 1-hour "quick soak" method for faster cooking and easier digestibility. You can also batch cook beans in an electric pressure cooker, if you have one. Follow the cooking time and recommended broth or water volume for your model.

Batch cook beans, lentils, or mung beans to add to bowls (see EWEE Bowl Guide, page 186) or an EWEE Plate (page 72). Use them for Loaded Chipotle Chili (page 185) and "Beef" 'n' Bean Enchiladas (page 264). Once cooked and cooled, store the beans in their flavorful cooking liquid to keep them moist.

QUICK SOAK: Lentils and mung beans do not need presoaking. For all other beans, pick out any rocks or debris from the dried beans, then rinse and drain well. Place the beans in a large pot and add water to cover by 2 inches. Bring to a boil, then remove the pot from the heat. Add the salt to the water and allow the beans to soak for 1 hour. Drain and rinse.

In a large pot, combine the beans, celery, onion, and herbs. Add broth or water to cover the beans by 1 inch. Bring to a boil over high heat. Reduce the heat to low, cover, and continue cooking, gently stirring now and then and checking the liquid level—if the beans look like they are getting dry, add a bit more water. Cook until the beans are tender, according to the times in the chart. (To test for doneness, fish out a bean and squeeze it between your fingers—if it's soft, it's done.)

Use a spoon to remove the herb stems and discard. Let the beans cool completely in their cooking liquid before transferring them to an airtight glass container. You can keep them in the refrigerator for up to 3 days. If freezing, divide them into 2 servings, store in an airtight container, and freeze for up to 6 months. Reheat them in their liquid or, if using them cold, thaw, drain, and rinse before adding to an EWEE Bowl (page 190) or for using in "Beef" 'n' Bean Enchiladas (page 264).

Bean Cooking Chart

BEAN, OR LENTIL	COOK TIME	YIELD
Black beans	60 to 90 minutes	2¼ cups
Cannellini beans	1 hour	2 cups
Chickpeas (garbanzo beans)	1½ hours	2 cups
Great Northern beans	1½ hours	2½ cups
Kidney beans	1 hour	2¼ cups
Lentils, brown	45 minutes	2¼ cups
Lentils, green	30 minutes	2 cups
Mung beans	1 hour	2 cups
Navy beans	1 hour	2½ cups
Pinto beans	1½ hours	2½ cups

EZ EWEE VEGGIES

2 tablespoons neutral oil,
such as avocado, grapeseed,
or olive oil

2 garlic cloves, thinly sliced

½ pound vegetables of your
choice (see chart opposite)

1 teaspoon EWEE Spice Mix
(page 127)

1 lemon, cut into wedges, or
"Yum Yum" Sauce (page 127)
for dipping

A cast-iron skillet makes quick work of crisp-tender vegetables with lots of flavor, flexibility, and little fuss. Here is an easy guide to making five of my favorite EWEE spiced veggies on the fly or ahead of time so you have them on hand to add to bowls (see EWEE Bowl Guide, page 186).

In a 12-inch cast-iron skillet, heat the oil over medium-high heat until it shimmers. Stir in the garlic and cook for about 30 seconds, or until fragrant.

Add the vegetables, season with the spice mix, and toss. Cook, undisturbed, until the vegetables are crisp-tender and a bit browned, according to the times in the chart.

Transfer to a serving dish and squeeze fresh lemon over the top or serve with "Yum Yum" sauce for dipping.

Skillet Veggies Cooking Chart

VEGETABLE	PREP	COOK TIME
Asparagus	Woody ends trimmed	3 minutes
Brussels sprouts	Tough bottom trimmed, halved	10 minutes; flip after 5 minutes
Carrots	Peeled and halved lengthwise	10 minutes; flip after 5 minutes
Green beans	Trimmed	8 minutes; flip after 5 minutes
Snap peas	Trimmed	4 minutes; flip after 2 minutes

WHEN I WAS NINE, I WAS HOME WITH THE FLU. MY MOM left me with my middle sister, Tonia, who was sixteen years old. Instead of looking after me, she was gossiping with her friends. Since the stove was off-limits to me, I'd asked her numerous times to get off the phone to make me something to eat!

She continued to ignore me, and so I took matters into my own hands and attempted to make my favorite hot wheat breakfast cereal, Malt-O-Meal. I poured it into a pot and tried to flame up the stove when Tonia rushed in with the authority of "big sister." She demanded that I go to my room without anything to eat. The hunger got the best of me, and I lost my temper. I chased Tonia around the kitchen; she ran into our living room, closed the French doors, put her face up to the glass, and stuck her tongue out, teasing me, like a sassy teen. I cocked my fist back to swing a punch at her; instead, I shattered the glass door. I wound up with about one hundred pieces of glass on my wrists and forearm.

Now, the last thing you want to do is call a struggling single Black mother home from her nursing job because her kids are fighting. But she came home, and the first thing she did was take me into the bathroom, set me down, take out her first aid kit, and remove each piece of glass one by one. And *then*, she disciplined my sister and me. But from that day forward, mama said I was allowed to make my own damn grits and go to town!

BREAKFAST

Makes 12 pancakes

SATURDAY MORNING NOSTALGIA PANCAKES

1½ cups oat flour, store-bought or homemade (see Note)

1½ teaspoons baking powder

2 tablespoons flaxmeal

1 tablespoon hemp hearts

1 ripe medium banana

¼ teaspoon fine sea salt

1 teaspoon pure vanilla extract

1 cup plain plant-based milk

1 tablespoon vegan butter, melted

Maple syrup, for serving

Fresh blueberries and/or strawberries (stemmed, hulled, and sliced), for serving

½ cup Sweet Cashew Cream (optional; page 122), for serving

When I was a boy, Saturday mornings were for watching cartoons while devouring my favorite pancake breakfast that my mom or older sisters would cook for me. While I have nostalgia for the adventures of Optimus Prime in *Transformers* ("Bring it on, Decepticons!"), I'd rather forget having to separate the ring of hard, crusty edges from my mom's cast-iron skillet pancakes to get to the tender middle.

I "perfected" my pancake-making by relying on a griddle's flat surface. A griddle allows you to cook pancakes evenly, and fluffily—that's a word. There is no need to add grease to the griddle since the pancake mix has melted vegan butter. I use gluten-free oat flour in my pancake recipe to make it gluten-free and rich with fiber. Mashed banana stars as my "do no harm egg" in this recipe.

Preheat an electric griddle to 375°F or set a cast-iron skillet over medium heat. Preheat the oven to 200°F. Set out a baking sheet.

In a large bowl, whisk together the oat flour, baking powder, flaxmeal, and hemp hearts.

In a medium bowl, use the back of a fork to mash together the banana, salt, and vanilla. Add the milk and melted butter and whisk until the mixture is well combined. Pour the banana mixture into the flour mixture and use a wooden spoon to mix just enough to create a homogenous batter.

Working in batches, pour ¼ cup of the batter onto the griddle, leaving space between the pancakes. Cook the pancakes on one side for about 3 minutes, or until bubbles form on the sides and on the center surface. Use a spatula to flip and cook on the other side for about 1 minute more, or until golden brown.

Transfer the cooked pancakes to the baking sheet and place the baking sheet in the oven to keep the pancakes warm. Continue cooking, holding cooked pancakes in reserve, until you have used up all the batter.

Serve the warm pancakes with maple syrup, strawberries, and blueberries. Drizzle with the sweet cashew cream, if using.

NOTE: To make the oat flour, add 1½ cups old-fashioned rolled oats to a blender and blend until powdered.

"CHEESY" GRITS

These grits are my "grown-up" version—just as cheesy and creamy as the kind from my childhood, but with small and tender baby arugula leaves. When purchasing grits, you'll notice that they can come in white or yellow; the former is made from hominy corn, while the latter is from yellow corn. You can use either one. Steer clear of quick-cooking grits; they are highly processed and the texture is slimy—the extra minutes at the stove are worth it.

1 tablespoon neutral oil, such as avocado or grapeseed

4 scallions (green onions), finely chopped, white and green parts kept separate

2 garlic cloves, minced

2 cups plain plant-based milk

1 teaspoon fine sea salt

1 cup white or yellow corn grits

½ cup vegan cheddar-style shreds

1 cup (packed) baby arugula leaves

In a medium skillet, heat the oil over medium-high heat until it shimmers. Add the scallion whites and the garlic and cook, stirring occasionally, for about 1 minute, or until the scallions are softened and the garlic is fragrant. Set aside.

In a medium saucepan, combine the milk, 2 cups water, and the salt. Bring to a boil over high heat. Add the grits and whisk to combine. Reduce the heat to low and cook, stirring now and then, for about 20 minutes, or until the liquid is absorbed and the grits are thick and creamy.

Using a silicone spatula, stir in the cheddar-style shreds and continue cooking and stirring for about 1 minute more, or until the cheese is melted and the mixture is smooth—add a bit of water or more milk to loosen if the consistency is too thick. Remove from the heat, add the reserved scallion/garlic mixture and the arugula, and stir for about 1 minute to wilt the arugula.

Serve topped with the scallion greens.

BOLD 'N' BEAUTIFUL BEET WAFFLES

1½ cups white whole wheat flour or gluten-free 1:1 baking flour

3 tablespoons flaxmeal

3 tablespoons hemp hearts

2 ripe medium bananas

1 teaspoon pure vanilla extract

1½ cups Beet Juice (page 167) or store-bought cold-pressed no-sugar-added beet juice, such as Pomona

1½ cups plain plant-based milk

⅓ cup thinly sliced fresh strawberries, for serving

¼ cup fresh blueberries, for serving

Maple syrup, for serving

½ cup Sweet Cashew Cream (optional; page 122), for serving

Beets are full of naturally occurring nitrates that your body converts to nitric acid, which regulates blood pressure and improves blood flow. I make Beet Juice (page 167) part of my daily post-workout recovery. And I love to load up on these beet-based waffles before a long bike ride. The hemp hearts are high in omega-3 and omega-6 fatty acids, and the bananas give them a rich texture, making them hearty without feeling heavy.

Preheat a waffle iron.

In a large bowl, whisk to combine the flour, flaxmeal, and hemp hearts.

In a medium bowl, use the back of a fork to mash together the banana and vanilla. Add the beet juice and milk and whisk until the mixture is well combined. Pour the banana mixture into the flour mixture and use a wooden spoon to mix just enough to create a homogenous batter.

Working in batches, pour ¼ to ½ cup of the batter—more or less, depending on the size of your waffle iron—leaving a ½-inch border on all sides. Close the lid and cook for 3 to 5 minutes, until the waffles are crisp and the waffle iron stops steaming.

Transfer to a plate and continue cooking until you have used all the batter.

Serve topped with berries, maple syrup, and cashew cream (if using).

OVERNIGHT OATS

BASE RECIPE

1 cup plain plant-based milk, such as oat, almond, rice, or coconut (see Notes)

1 tablespoon maple syrup

1 to 2 teaspoons of your favorite spice, such as cinnamon, nutmeg, pumpkin pie spice, ground ginger, cardamom, or cocoa powder (see Notes)

1 cup old-fashioned rolled oats

¼ cup fresh or dried fruit, such as berries, banana, mango slices, pineapple, toasted coconut, or finely chopped dates

2 tablespoons nuts, nut butter, Basic Cashew Cream (page 122), or seeds such as hemp or chia

When I was incarcerated, oatmeal was my vegetarian survival food. It was always served in the chow line, and I could buy it at the prison commissary. After working out, I would combine oats, powdered milk, and water in a plastic protein shaker bottle that guys typically use for coffee, let it thicken, then drink it like a protein shake. For years after my release, I couldn't stand oatmeal—it was like kryptonite to me. Eventually, I overcame the repulsion and reintroduced it into my diet because it offers so much nutrition for very little money, and oatmeal's neutral flavor is the perfect canvas for the greatest grab 'n' go breakfast of all time, overnight oats.

I make my overnight oats in one-pint Mason jars, but you can use any repurposed jar and a lid. Also, avoid using instant oats, since they will mush. Here are three of my favorite blends. Each is fresh, healthy, and so good that I forget I am eating more oatmeal.

Pour the milk into a 1-pint glass jar or container with a lid. Add the maple syrup and your choice of spice and stir.

Add the oats and stir to incorporate. Top with your choice of fruit, followed by the nuts, nut butter, or seeds. Cover with the lid and refrigerate for a minimum of 8 hours and up to 5 days. Turn the page for my favorite variations.

NOTES: Coconut milk that comes in a refrigerated carton is intended as a beverage (and is usually marked that way). It differs in fat content and texture from canned coconut milk—which I reserve for baking and Coconut Rice (page 227)—but in a pinch, if all you have is canned coconut milk, use the liquid that separates and settles at the bottom of the can.

Look for the fair-trade mark on the cocoa powder label; it indicates that the product was ethically sourced and made under conditions that guaranteed the livelihood of vulnerable workers.

(recipe continues)

COCOA BERRY OATS: Stir in 1 to 2 teaspoons cocoa powder (see Notes) and top the oats with ¼ cup fresh berries (such as raspberries, blueberries, or blackberries) and ¼ cup slivered almonds or hemp seeds.

"BANANA CREAM PIE" OATS: Stir in 1 to 2 teaspoons cinnamon and top the oats with ½ cup sliced banana (about ½ medium banana) and 2 tablespoons Sweet Cashew Cream (page 122).

HAWAIIAN OATS: Use unsweetened coconut milk for the milk. Stir in 1 to 2 teaspoons ground ginger and top the oats with ¼ cup chopped fresh pineapple or mango and 2 tablespoons hemp seeds, chia seeds, or toasted coconut.

**COCOA
BERRY OATS**

HAWAIIAN
OATS

"BANANA
CREAM PIE"
OATS

THE "DULUTH" OMELET

FOR THE VEGETABLE FILLING:

2 teaspoons neutral oil, such as avocado or grapeseed

6 ounces mushrooms, such as button, cremini, or shiitake, tough stems trimmed, thinly sliced

½ teaspoon fine sea salt

1 cup chopped bell pepper (about 1 medium pepper)

½ cup finely chopped zucchini (½ small zucchini)

2 scallions (green onions), green and white parts, finely chopped

½ cup halved cherry tomatoes

½ cup roughly chopped spinach or kale, stemmed and de-ribbed

¼ teaspoon freshly cracked black pepper

FOR THE OMELET:

½ cup chickpea flour (aka garbanzo bean flour)

1 tablespoon nutritional yeast

¼ teaspoon baking powder

¼ teaspoon fine sea salt

¼ teaspoon freshly cracked black pepper

¼ teaspoon garlic powder

1 teaspoon neutral oil, such as avocado or grapeseed

¼ cup vegan cheddar-style shreds

1 avocado, thinly sliced, for serving

In federal prison in Duluth, Minnesota, I had a full-time job: "pots and pans" kitchen detail. Every two weeks, the prison received a massive delivery of eggs to feed the population of more than one thousand inmates. I took advantage of working in the kitchen to make an omelet loaded with fresh vegetables and some cheese, and it was as close as I got to luxury in my vegetarian meals.

When I went vegan years later, but before the existence of plant-based egg replacers, I re-created that omelet with protein-rich chickpea flour! When the flour is mixed with water, it makes a light batter that, when cooked, results in tender-firm edges and a soft, "eggy" texture in the middle.

I still love a Really Good Tofu Scramble (page 154) for breakfast, but this is my favorite whole-food O.G. option. It's ideal for people who want to take a break from soy or have a soy allergy. And it's convenient if you're looking for an alternative to expensive store-bought egg substitutes.

MAKE THE VEGETABLE FILLING: In a nonstick medium skillet, heat 1 teaspoon of the oil over medium-high heat until it shimmers. Add the mushrooms in a single layer and cook, undisturbed, for about 3 minutes, or until beginning to brown. Add ¼ teaspoon of the salt and continue cooking, stirring now and then, for about 2 minutes more, until they release their liquid and soften. Transfer the mushrooms to a small bowl.

Add the remaining 1 teaspoon oil to the pan along with the bell pepper, zucchini, scallions, and tomato and cook, stirring now and then, for 3 to 5 minutes, until the vegetables are softened. Add the spinach and continue cooking for about 1 minute more, or until the spinach wilts and any remaining water in the pan evaporates. Add the remaining ¼ teaspoon salt and the black pepper and remove from the heat. Transfer the mixture to the bowl with the mushrooms. Reserve the skillet.

MAKE THE OMELET: In a medium bowl, whisk together the chickpea flour, nutritional yeast, baking powder, salt, pepper, and garlic powder. Add ½ cup water and whisk to combine for about 20 seconds, or until air bubbles form.

In the now-empty skillet, heat the oil over medium heat—the pan is still hot, so it won't take long to shimmer. Once shimmering, pour the batter into the pan and immediately swirl the pan to form an even layer. Reduce the heat to low and cook, undisturbed, for about 2 minutes, or until the underside starts to crisp and bubbles start to form in the center. It will remind you of making a pancake.

Add the reserved vegetable filling and cheddar. Use a spatula to fold the omelet. Let stand for 4 minutes to melt the cheese.

Slide the omelet onto a plate and serve with avocado slices.

REALLY GOOD TOFU SCRAMBLE

1 14-ounce package firm tofu, drained and pressed (see Tofu Prep, page 103)

½ teaspoon fine sea salt

½ teaspoon freshly cracked black pepper

1½ teaspoons onion powder

1 teaspoon garlic powder

¼ teaspoon ground turmeric

2 tablespoons neutral oil, such as avocado or grapeseed

1 tablespoon nutritional yeast, or more to taste

Splash of plain plant-based milk or water

1 avocado, sliced, for serving

I start this tofu scramble with a block of tofu sliced in half lengthwise. That increases the surface area of the tofu, resulting in savory, crispy edges and a fluffy center in each bite. Once the tofu has crisped up, I "scramble" or break it up in the pan so each piece absorbs the nutty, earthy flavor of the ground turmeric and "cheesy" nutritional yeast. On weekends, I make a hearty plate with Mushroom "Bacon" and Homie Hash Browns 'cause I love me some potatoes at breakfast. (I also love to scoop this scramble into a sweet potato—page 160.)

Slice the block of tofu in half horizontally. Season on both sides with the salt, pepper, onion powder, garlic powder, and turmeric.

In a nonstick medium skillet, heat the oil over medium-high heat until it shimmers. Add the tofu sheets and cook for 3 to 5 minutes, until the bottoms are golden. Gently flip and continue cooking for 3 to 5 minutes more, until the second side is browned.

Add the nutritional yeast and milk, then gently "scramble" (break up) the tofu into smaller pieces. Increase the heat to high and cook, stirring now and then, for 3 to 5 minutes, until any remaining liquid evaporates.

Serve with avocado slices.

MUSHROOM "BACON"

2 tablespoons neutral oil, such as avocado or grapeseed

2 tablespoons liquid amino acids, reduced-sodium soy sauce, or tamari

2 tablespoons maple syrup

½ teaspoon garlic powder

½ teaspoon onion powder

¼ teaspoon freshly cracked black pepper

½ teaspoon smoked paprika

1 pound portobello mushrooms (5 or 6), stemmed, gills removed (see Note), and cut into slices ½ inch thick

Roasting mushrooms at high heat concentrates their flavor so they morph into smoky "bacon" flavor bombs with a chewy texture. You do not need to buy expensive liquid smoke—a condiment that extracts wood smoke flavor in liquid form isn't great for your body. Instead, smoked paprika lends a nice smoky flavor. Large and "meaty" portobello mushroom caps work well here because they don't pull too much of a Shrinky Dink in the oven (remember those, my '80s babies?). Enjoy as a side to a Really Good Tofu Scramble or anywhere else you'd like a hit of "bacon"—bowls (see EWEE Bowl Guide, page 186) and Mac 'n' "Cheese" (page 242) come to mind. Use the same marinade to create a thicker, crispy protein-rich tofu "bacon" for a Mega Tofu BLT (page 212).

Preheat oven to 400°F. Line a sheet pan with parchment paper or a silicone mat.

In a large bowl, whisk to combine the oil, liquid aminos, maple syrup, garlic powder, onion powder, pepper, and smoked paprika. Add the mushrooms and turn to coat.

Arrange the mushroom slices in a single layer on the pan (pour excess marinade over them). Roast for about 30 minutes, until they are dark in color, crispy, and reduced in size.

Remove from the oven and use immediately or set aside to cool completely before transferring to an airtight container and storing in the refrigerator for up to 5 days.

NOTE: The gills of portobello mushrooms under the caps are dark and soft. Even though they are edible, I choose to gently scrape them away with the back of a spoon, since dirt and debris can hide there. You can leave them intact if you like.

HOMIE HASH BROWNS

1 pound russet potatoes (about 2 large), skin-on and scrubbed

4 tablespoons neutral oil, such as avocado or grapeseed

¼ teaspoon fine sea salt

½ teaspoon onion powder

½ teaspoon garlic powder

Freshly cracked black pepper

Hot sauce, for serving

I fell in love with hash browns hanging out with my homies at IHOP in Chicago and Waffle House when traveling in the South. There, someone else has done the labor of shredding or dicing potatoes! When I have time on weekends, I take pride in making homemade hash browns with crispy outsides and tender insides.

There are three must-dos for success: 1) Use a box grater to grate the potatoes with the skin on (for fiber and iron). The high-powered grating blades on a food processor can make them watery and mushy. 2) Rinse the shredded potatoes in cold water to remove excess starch. 3) Wrap the potatoes in a clean towel and then squeeze out the excess water. This way the oil can stick to the potatoes, which is what makes them crispy. Making a great batch of hash browns will give you EWEE kitchen confidence—it did for me!

Using the largest holes on a box grater, shred the potatoes into a medium bowl. Cover them with cold water and then drain. Repeat one to two more times until the water runs clear (a sign that you have removed all the excess starches).

Transfer the shredded potatoes to a large clean kitchen towel and squeeze to remove excess water.

In a large bowl, toss the potatoes with 2 tablespoons of the oil until well coated—this makes them extra crispy. Add the salt, onion powder, garlic powder, and pepper to taste and toss to coat.

In a large cast-iron skillet, heat the remaining 2 tablespoons oil over medium-high heat until it shimmers. Add the shredded potatoes in an even layer. Reduce the heat to medium and cook, undisturbed, for 5 to 7 minutes, until the bottom is crispy and golden brown.

Use a spatula to break up the potatoes, then flip the pieces and repeat on the other side. Serve immediately with hot sauce.

THINK EWEE: Hash browns are French fries in disguise. You can eat them with an EWEE Burger (page 214) or as a side dish to Mom's Plant Loaf with Skillet Cabbage (page 258).

GOOD MORNING, SWEET POTATO!

7 small to medium (6 to 7 ounces each) Japanese sweet potatoes or orange sweet potatoes (yams), skin-on and scrubbed

2 tablespoons neutral oil, such as avocado or grapeseed

½ teaspoon fine sea salt

I have an undying love for wholesome sweet potatoes. I batch cook them on the weekend so I can enjoy them for breakfast every day. They are a more filling, gluten-free, fiber-rich canvas for sweet or savory toppings than bread. I use Japanese sweet potatoes and orange sweet potatoes interchangeably. Japanese sweet potatoes are purple on the outside and yellow inside. They have a sweeter taste than orange sweet potatoes, which are also called yams. They are also fluffier. Leveled up with sweet cashew cream and berries or nut butter and banana, topped with a lil' crunch from nuts and seeds—I want you to see possibilities in sweet potatoes! Add them to bowls and smoothies or smother them with Loaded Chipotle Chili (page 185) for dinner.

Preheat the oven to 400°F. Line a sheet pan with parchment paper or a silicone mat.

Use a fork to poke holes on all sides of the potatoes. Arrange them on the baking sheet, drizzle the oil over them, tossing to coat evenly, then sprinkle with the salt. Bake for 45 minutes to 1 hour, until they are soft and easily pierced with a knife.

If you're making this to serve right away, slice a still-warm sweet potato down the middle and top with your choice of toppings (see the Variations that follow for ideas). Then turn to your fur-kid or beautiful human in your life and say, "Good morning, Sweet Potato!"

If batch cooking for later, transfer the potatoes to a cooling rack to cool completely before storing refrigerated in an airtight container for up to 1 week.

NOTES: TO REHEAT SWEET POTATOES IN THE MICROWAVE: Wrap a roasted potato in a damp paper towel and place in the microwave to reheat for 2 to 3 minutes.

TO REHEAT IN THE OVEN: Preheat the oven to 350°F. Place a roasted sweet potato on a sheet pan. Bake for 15 minutes to warm through.

TO REHEAT IN AN AIR FRYER: Preheat the air fryer to 350°F. Add 2 to 3 potatoes, depending on the size of the basket, and warm for 15 minutes, shaking halfway through.

Variations:

NUT BUTTER AND BANANA SWEET POTATOES: Fill a warmed potato with 2 tablespoons nut butter, such as cashew, peanut, or almond. Top with banana slices and 1 tablespoon seeds (hemp, pumpkin, or sunflower). Sprinkle with cinnamon to taste.

SWEET CASHEW CREAM, BERRY, AND SEED SWEET POTATOES: Fill a warmed potato with 2 tablespoons Sweet Cashew Cream (page 122), followed by ¼ cup fresh berries, such as blueberries, blackberries, or raspberries. Scatter 1 tablespoon seeds (hemp, pumpkin, or sunflower) over the top.

HOT SWEET POTATO SCRAMBLE: Fill a warmed potato with Really Good Tofu Scramble (page 154). Top with avocado slices and a dash of sriracha or other hot sauce.

FRESH JUICES AND SMOOTHIES ARE A PILLAR OF MY plant-based eating and athletic training since they fill the role of "fast food" in my busy schedule. When I lived in New York, I would return home after my early-morning workout and have only about forty-five minutes to take my fur-daughter, Soca, on a walk, jump in the shower, put on my suit, and head to the L train for my commute from Brooklyn to Manhattan. I'm sure you can relate! No one has enough time in the morning.

Smoothies and juices provide vitamins, enzymes, and micronutrients, and can be prepared quickly and inexpensively. On Sunday and Wednesday prep days, I'd create different juice and smoothie formulas—my "greens" (kale! celery!), my "yellows" (mangoes! bananas!), my "reds" (beets! watermelon!)—and then I would experiment with different combinations of fruits and veggies, my "what the F**K color smoothie concoction is that!?" I'd fill a dozen Mason jars and store them in my refrigerator—stackable airtight containers work, too!

Don't worry if your fruit and veggie combos don't have the aesthetic appeal of a brand-new Crayola crayon; they will still be healthy and taste delicious.

JUICES AND SMOOTHIES

To Juice or to Blend?

Making smoothies and juices in rotation ensures you get a wide range of nutrients. Sometimes it comes down to craving the "clean" feeling of juice or a thicker smoothie's "comforting" feel.

Juicers

A juicer's high-speed sharp blade breaks down the cell walls of a whole fruit or vegetable and extracts just the liquid, leaving behind the fiber and pulp. When you drink juice, you get a boost of energy due to the lack of fiber, which slows down digestion, allowing your body to begin absorbing nutrients within minutes.

WHAT IF I DON'T OWN A JUICER, DOM? You can still make fresh fruit juices using your blender or food processor. Water-rich fruits and vegetables, such as watermelon, beets, cucumbers, peaches, mango, pineapple, citrus, leafy greens, beets, and celery, yield the best results. I have indicated for you in each recipe when you can use a blender or food processor for juicing, so you don't miss out.

Blenders

Blender blades also break down the cell walls of fruits and vegetables, but during this process, more of the fiber and pulp remains intact, which gives smoothies their weight. You will still benefit from all the essential vitamins and nutrients, but it will take your body longer to digest them, and you'll feel full longer because of the fiber. A high-powered blender makes smoothies very creamy, but you can also use a regular blender, taking care to layer the ingredients to maximize its functions.

WHAT IF I DON'T OWN A BLENDER, DOM? Make a smoothie in a food processor by chopping the solid ingredients first, such as greens, nuts, fruits and veggies, and adding the liquid last.

Do You Need Protein Powder in Your Smoothie?

Before the 1960s, whey—a by-product of the cheese-making process—had been dumped in waterways and soil as waste. Because whey is nitrogen-rich, it can cause algae to overbloom, robbing waterways of oxygen and killing fish. Excess whey in the ground can alter pH levels and prevent plants from thriving.

To solve the "whey waste" problem, the dairy industry began isolating liquid whey and drying it in powder form and selling it as protein powders and bars. But to sell it, the dairy industry needed to find an audience that believed they needed extra dairy-derived protein. Whey powders and bars grew in popularity through prolific, bold, and sometimes deceptive marketing aimed at fitness consumers. The industry continued to promote the idea that animal protein is the best food source for building muscle and developing strength.

The Federal Drug Administration does not hold protein powders to the same standards as food since they are classified as dietary supplements. Depending on the brand, they may contain chemical solvents, heavy metals, and pesticides. Consumer-protection organizations, such as Clean Label Project and Informed Choice, verify the safety of whey and vegan protein powders. For a whole-food protein boost, I recommend adding hemp hearts; they have 10 grams of protein per tablespoon, all nine essential amino acids, and a neutral taste, and cost less per serving than a scoopable powder.

How to Freeze Fresh Fruit for Smoothies

Frozen fruit keeps your smoothies cold and makes them creamy. Frozen bananas are my go-to fruit in many of my smoothie blends since they are available year-round, have a mild flavor, and have a lower acid content, which means they play well with higher acid berries and balance out smoothie flavors. But I also love to shop for in-season fruits to freeze and add to my smoothies, saving money on expensive bags of frozen fruit. Follow these steps for easy freezing. Frozen fruit keeps for up to three months.

1. Line a quarter-sheet pan (9½ × 13 inches) with parchment paper.

2. Wash the fruit and pat it dry. If you are freezing stone fruits, such as peaches, nectarines, or cherries, remove any pits. Chop or slice the fruit into even-sized pieces that can easily fit in your blender or food processor. That will save you a step when you're rushing to make the smoothie.

3. Spread the fruit on the prepared sheet pan and place it in the freezer for 1 hour.

4. Transfer the frozen fruit to a plastic freezer bag or airtight container with a lid. Label and freeze until ready to use.

WATERMELON JUICE

Makes about 5 cups

Watermelon juice is the ultimate refresher. I drink it because it is a rich source of citrulline, an amino acid that converts to L-arginine, optimizing blood flow, delivering oxygen and nutrients to muscles, improving recovery. Watermelon is 92 percent water, and a blender juices it fast, with minimal cleanup. I drink watermelon juice every day; and when I am in training mode, I buy them by the truckload—no joke!

9 cups cubed seeded (see Note) watermelon (from about a 6-pound watermelon), chilled

Working in batches, add the watermelon to a blender and blend on high speed for about 30 seconds, or until liquefied. Store refrigerated in a pitcher or sealed glass jars for up to 3 days. Stir or shake or before drinking. If you prefer juice with less pulp, pour it through a fine-mesh sieve before serving.

GREEN JUICE

Makes 2 cups

When juicing kale or spinach, leave it whole, because smaller, chopped pieces may not juice. Instead, scrunch or roll the leaves—you can even process the stems and midribs—into a cylinder shape and feed it to your juicer. You can use any type of kale or cucumber you like.

1 bunch kale, such as curly or lacinato kale, thoroughly washed
1 large cucumber, such as English or 2 to 3 Persian, skin peeled, halved lengthwise and seeded
1 large lemon, peeled, and quartered
4 celery stalks and leaves, well rinsed
2 large green apples, such as Granny Smith, peeled, cored, and quartered

Working in batches, process the kale, cucumber, lemon, celery, and apple in a juicer. Store refrigerated in a sealed glass jar for up to 3 days.

NOTE: To seed a watermelon, lay the melon horizontally and use a sharp knife to slice off the ends. Stand it up on a cutting board and remove the peel and the white rind by slicing downward, following the natural curve of the melon. Lay the naked melon on its side and slice it like a loaf of bread. Working with one slice at a time, gently break it apart by following the natural seed line that runs down the middle. Gently scrape away and discard the inedible and bitter black seeds.

BEET JUICE

Makes 2 cups

I won't lie: Drinking beet juice straight is an acquired taste. If at first the flavor is too strong for you, use it as a liquid base in a smoothie (see EWEE Smoothie Formula, page 174), or blend it with watermelon juice to make a beautiful "red juice." And if you experience beeturia—no, it's not a dance; it's the term for beets turning your urine or poop red—don't worry; it's your body's normal absorption of the beets' pigment.

2 pounds beets, ends trimmed, scrubbed, peeled, and quartered

Working in batches, process the beets in a juicer. Store refrigerated in a sealed glass jar for up to 3 days.

ORANGE-GINGER JUICE

Makes 2 cups

You might know ginger best for its stomach-calming effects. It has other superpowers, too—anti-inflammatory, antioxidant, and antibacterial properties. It's also rich in zinc, a mineral that repairs the cells in our guts, and protects us from cancer-causing pathogens. Ginger brings warm spice to this vitamin C–rich orange and carrot blend. Don't peel the carrots—just scrub them, okay? Their skin contains over half of their phenolic compounds—a type of plant phytochemical that protects our bodies from inflammation.

2 oranges or 1 grapefruit, peeled and quartered

1 large lemon, peeled and quartered

5 medium carrots, unpeeled and scrubbed, leafy tops trimmed off

1 inch fresh ginger, peeled (see Note) and halved

Working in batches, process the oranges, lemon, carrots, and ginger in a juicer. Store refrigerated in a sealed glass jar for up to 3 days.

GREEN MANGO SMOOTHIE

Makes about 1½ cups / Serves 1 or 2

The sweetness of the mango will temper any bitterness in the leafy greens and mask the seaweed flavor of spirulina or chlorella powders. Adding the powders are optional, but they provide good plant sources of omega-3 fatty acids in the form of EPA and DHA, which help prevent heart disease.

1 cup plain plant-based milk or water

1 cup frozen or fresh leafy greens, such as spinach or kale, tough ends discarded, and leaves roughly chopped

¼ cup lightly packed fresh herb of choice, such as basil, mint, parsley, or cilantro leaves

1 tablespoon hemp hearts

1 tablespoon spirulina or chlorella powder (optional)

½ cup banana slices, frozen or fresh

½ cup mango chunks, frozen or fresh

In a blender, combine the milk, leafy greens, herbs, hemp hearts, spirulina powder (if using), banana, and mango and blend on high, until smooth and creamy, scraping down the sides as needed. Store refrigerated in a sealed glass jar for up to 3 days and shake before serving.

NOTE: Use the side of a spoon to peel ginger. The skin is thin and it will scrape right off.

BERRY BEET SMOOTHIE

Makes about 1½ cups / Serves 1 or 2

Berries, leafy greens, beets, this smoothie has it all! Colorful berries are rich in compounds that protect against inflammation and the cell damage that leads to disease.

1 cup Beet Juice (page 167) or store-bought cold-pressed no-sugar-added beet juice, such as Pomona

1 cup frozen or fresh leafy greens, such as spinach or kale, tough ends discarded, and leaves roughly chopped

1 tablespoon hemp hearts

½ cup mixed berries, frozen or fresh

½ cup banana slices, frozen or fresh

1 tablespoon spirulina or chlorella powder (optional)

Ice (optional)

In a blender, combine the beet juice, greens, hemp hearts, berries, banana, spirulina powder (if using), and ice (if using) and blend on high until smooth and creamy, scraping down the sides as needed. Store refrigerated in a sealed glass jar for up to 3 days.

CHOCO POWER
SMOOTHIE

BERRY BEET
SMOOTHIE

BLUEBERRY OATMEAL
SMOOTHIE

GREEN MANGO
SMOOTHIE

STRAWBERRY CASHEW
SMOOTHIE

CHOCO POWER SMOOTHIE

Makes about 1½ cups / Serves 1 or 2

Chocolate makes this sound like a decadent treat, but this creamy, tofu-rich smoothie is loaded with potassium from the banana and dates and almost 4 grams of satisfying fiber from the cocoa powder.

1 cup plain plant-based milk

1 cup frozen or fresh leafy greens, such as spinach or kale, tough ends discarded, and leaves roughly chopped

½ cup soft tofu

1 tablespoon nut butter or tahini

2 soft pitted dates, such as Medjool or Deglet Noor

½ cup banana slices, frozen or fresh

2 tablespoons unsweetened cocoa powder (see Note, page 149)

Ice (optional)

In a blender, combine the milk, greens, tofu, nut butter, dates, banana, cocoa powder, and ice (if using) and blend on high until smooth and creamy, scraping down the sides as needed. Store refrigerated in a sealed glass jar for up to 3 days.

BLUEBERRY OATMEAL SMOOTHIE

Makes about 1½ cups / Serves 1 or 2

Here's a way to get the filling benefits of fiber-rich oatmeal (and blueberries), without thinking you're eating more oatmeal. You can use old fashioned rolled or instant oats for blending.

¼ cup old-fashioned rolled oats or instant oats

1 cup plain plant-based milk or water

½ cup plain plant-based yogurt

1 cup blueberries, frozen or fresh

½ cup banana slices, frozen or fresh

1 tablespoon hemp hearts

½ teaspoon ground cinnamon

Ice (optional)

Add the oatmeal to a blender and blend until it is a fine powder.

Add the milk, yogurt, blueberries, banana, hemp hearts, cinnamon, and ice (if using) and blend on high until smooth and creamy, scraping down the sides as needed. Store refrigerated in a sealed glass jar for up to 3 days.

STRAWBERRY CASHEW SMOOTHIE

Makes about 1½ cups / Serves 1 or 2

This smoothie is one of my O.G. blends—extra creamy from cashews and frozen bananas, and a full cup of sweet strawberries for their vitamin C protection.

⅓ cup raw cashews

1 cup plain plant-based milk or water

1 cup strawberries, frozen or fresh hulled

½ cup banana slices, frozen or fresh

1 tablespoon chia seeds, or hemp hearts

Ice (optional)

Soak the cashews in a bowl of hot water for 20 minutes. Drain well.

In a blender (preferably high-powered), combine the milk, soaked cashews, strawberries, banana, chia seeds, and ice (if using) and blend on high until smooth and creamy, scraping down the sides as needed. Store refrigerated in a sealed glass jar for up to 3 days.

EWEE Smoothie Formula

My nutrient-rich EWEE smoothie formula starts with a scoop of fiber-filled oatmeal, followed by a liquid base, then layers of greens, a protein boost, a healthy fat, and a sweet fruit or vegetable, and then drives you home with spices for extra flavor. Layering the ingredients in the 1-2-3 order listed maximizes your blender's functions—'cause nobody likes leafy greens getting stuck in the blades. Pick and choose ingredients depending on your appetite, what you have on hand, and your flavor preferences.

SMOOTHIE FORMULA LAYERING CHART

ADD OATS (OPTIONAL)

Add ¼ cup old-fashioned rolled oats or instant oats to a blender for added protein and satiating fiber. Blend the oats into a powder first before adding the other ingredients. Or skip the oats and just begin with the liquid base.

CHOOSE A LIQUID BASE

Add 1 cup plain plant-based milk, water, or fresh juice, such as beet or watermelon. Adding liquid first (or after the oatmeal) is key, since it helps create a vortex that pulls fibrous fruits, veggies, hard nuts, and seeds into the blade, ensuring a smooth blend.

GET YOUR GREENS

Add 1 cup chopped dark leafy greens, such as spinach or kale, and/or ¼ cup fresh parsley, mint, or cilantro. The strong flavors of greens and herbs are balanced by the natural sweetness of fruit.

ADD A PROTEIN BOOST (OPTIONAL)

Add ½ cup plant-based yogurt or silken tofu.

ADD A SATISFYING FAT (OPTIONAL)

Add 1 to 2 tablespoons flaxmeal, chia seeds, hemp hearts, hemp powder, soaked and drained cashews (see Note, page 122), nut butter, or tahini, or ¼ avocado. 1 serving of spirulina or chlorella adds satisfying protein and essential omega-3 fatty acids, EPA and DHA, and immune-boosting vitamins.

ADD SWEET FRUITS AND VERSATILE VEGGIES

Add 1 cup cut-up fresh or frozen fruit, such as bananas or berries, or cooked or frozen vegetables, such as cauliflower, Japanese or orange sweet potato, carrots, or summer or winter squash for fiber and vital micronutrients. "Veggies: They're not just for bowls!" (You can quote me on that.)

ICE AND SPICE

If you don't have frozen fruit on hand, add 1 to 2 ice cubes to keep your smoothie cold. Add spices or flavorings to taste, such as ginger, cinnamon, unsweetened cocoa powder, or turmeric here.

AS A KID, I LOVED BROCCOLI CHEDDAR SOUP OR DIPPIN' grilled cheese in canned tomato soup—but mostly, growing up, soup just meant warm broth for sipping when I had a cold. I have since learned to love soup for many more reasons, such as its wholesome goodness and how you can enjoy it year-round—try my recipe for cold Watermelon Gazpacho (page 178) in the summer; so refreshing! I also love how easy and budget friendly vegan soups are to make from scratch. You can double any recipe and make a big batch to eat later or to portion and freeze for later, getting multiple meals from just moments of cooking. Also, unlike prepared soups from a soup shop, you know exactly what ingredients are going into your soup.

You can make most soups with ingredients you already have on hand in your pantry, fridge, or freezer. Use frozen broccoli florets for my "Iron Man" Spinach and Broccoli Soup (page 180), for example, or canned beans for my hearty Loaded Chipotle Chili (page 185), which isn't technically a soup, instead a meal in a bowl, which is precisely how I think of soups today! Soup can be what's for dinner, lunch (take 'em to work in a Thermos), or snack, and that's another "soup-er" reason to make them.

My second favorite all-time go-to meals are bowls. I offer you my favorite bowl recipes on these pages—including my signature EWEE Bowl (page 190). There's a whole world of nutrient-rich goodness, convenience, and customization waiting for you with bowls; Turn to the EWEE Bowl Guide (page 186) now to see what I am talkin' about!

SOUPS AND BOWLS

WATERMELON GAZPACHO

1¾ pounds tomatoes, such as Roma or heirloom, cored, seeded (see Note), and chopped, or 1 28-ounce can whole peeled tomatoes

About 1 medium chopped bell pepper, chopped

½ cup finely chopped red onion (about 1 small)

2 garlic cloves, minced

1 large English cucumber, peeled, seeded, and chopped (about 1½ cups)

3 cups cubed seeded watermelon (about 1 pound)

2 slices any type of vegan bread, or gluten-free vegan sandwich bread, torn into bite-sized pieces

¼ cup chopped fresh herbs, such as basil, parsley, or mint, or a combination of all three, plus more for serving

1½ teaspoons fine sea salt

½ teaspoon freshly cracked black pepper

3 tablespoons red wine vinegar

I always have watermelons on hand in the summer. I blend them with tomatoes, peppers, onions, and cucumber to make my version of cold Spanish gazpacho—I love the fresh, sweet flavor they add. Like tomatoes, watermelon gets its beautiful red color from lycopene, a powerful antioxidant. The best thing about this soup is that it's a no-cook dish; you can even drink it from a mug on a hot day. Bread gives the soup body, so don't skip it—you can use gluten-free bread if you are gluten-sensitive.

In a blender or food processor, working in two batches, add the tomatoes, bell pepper, onion, garlic, cucumber, watermelon, bread, and herbs and blend for about 2 minutes, or until smooth. Combine both batches in a large bowl and add the salt, pepper, and vinegar. Stir to incorporate.

Cover the bowl and refrigerate for at least 3 hours so the flavors meld and the soup chills completely.

Pour into mugs or bowls and top with more herbs, if desired.

NOTE: To core and seed a tomato, slice off both ends, then stand it on a flat end on a cutting board. Slicing downward, cut off the 4 sides of the tomato, leaving the core in the center. Save the tomato core and trimmings for Veggie Broth (page 120).

"IRON MAN" SPINACH AND BROCCOLI SOUP

2 tablespoons neutral
oil, such as avocado or
grapeseed

1 cup thinly sliced leeks
(about 1 large leek), white
part only, well cleaned (see
Note), or 1 medium yellow
onion, finely chopped (about
1 cup)

4 garlic cloves, minced

4 cups Veggie Broth (page
120) or store-bought low-
sodium vegetable broth

1 pound broccoli florets and
stems cut into 1-inch pieces
(from 2 crowns) or 1 1-pound
bag frozen broccoli florets
and stems, thawed

3 cups (loosely packed) fresh
spinach leaves or 1 1-pound
bag frozen spinach leaves,
thawed and squeezed dry

1 teaspoon fine sea salt

½ teaspoon freshly cracked
black pepper

¾ cup Basic Cashew Cream
(page 122)

4 tablespoons hemp hearts
(optional), for serving

1 cup Corn Bread Croutons
(optional; page 234), for
garnish

Spinach is rich in plant-based iron, called nonheme iron. Our bodies absorb animal-sourced heme iron more effectively than nonheme iron, but you can reap all the benefits of plant sources of iron by combining it with a food rich in vitamin C, such as broccoli, because vitamin C aids iron absorption. Broccoli was the only green vegetable I liked and ate as a kid, and my mom always bought frozen bags. Iron-rich spinach, cashews, and hemp hearts meet my favorite childhood veggie and combine their superpowers in this creamy, bright "Iron Man" soup.

In an 8-quart soup pot, heat the oil over medium heat until it shimmers. Add the leeks and cook, stirring occasionally, for about 3 minutes, or until softened. Stir in the garlic and cook for about 1 more minute, until fragrant. Add the broth, broccoli, spinach, salt, and pepper. Stir to incorporate. Cover, increase the heat to high, and bring to a boil. Reduce the heat to a simmer and cook for about 5 minutes, or until the broccoli stems are tender.

Use an immersion blender to blend the soup in the pot until smooth. Stir in the cashew cream and gently cook over low heat for about 2 minutes to warm through.

Ladle the soup into bowls. If desired, garnish with hemp hearts and/or corn bread croutons.

NOTE: To clean leeks: Remove the tough green part and reserve for adding to Veggie Broth (page 120). Then thinly slice the white portion of the leek and place the slices in a bowl. Add cold water to submerge the slices and use your fingers to break apart the tightly bound circles to dislodge any dirt or debris. Drain and repeat until the water in the bowl is clear.

Serves 4

TOMATO SOUP WITH GRILLED "CHEESE"

FOR THE TOMATO SOUP:

2 tablespoons neutral oil, such as avocado or grapeseed

1 small yellow onion, finely chopped (about ½ cup)

2 tablespoons tomato paste

4 cups Veggie Broth (page 120) or store-bought low-sodium vegetable broth

1 28-ounce can whole peeled tomatoes

1½ teaspoons fine sea salt

½ teaspoon freshly cracked black pepper

½ cup Basic Cashew Cream (page 122) or canned full-fat coconut milk

FOR THE GRILLED "CHEESE" SANDWICHES:

6 to 8 tablespoons vegan butter, at room temperature

8 thick slices whole-grain bread or gluten free bread

8 ounces vegan cheese shreds

I don't know any kid (or the kid who lives inside all of us) who doesn't go for the comfort of tomato soup with grilled cheese. They are inseparable. Growing up, dipping my sandwich in the bowl made me feel like I was eating pizza—I loved it. This soup has a zesty tomato flavor and comes together fast. The addition of cashew cream makes it creamy without overdoing it. You can also use full-fat coconut milk, which will give it a rich body and hint of coconut flavor. And if you're looking for a good "cheese-pull" on your grilled "cheese" sandwich, the Chao Creamery plant-based shreds from Field Roast are my go-to brand since they're melty and rich.

MAKE THE TOMATO SOUP: In a large pot, heat the oil over medium heat until it shimmers. Add the onion and cook, stirring occasionally, for 3 to 5 minutes, until softened. Stir in the tomato paste and cook for about 30 seconds, or until the color darkens.

Add the broth, canned tomatoes, salt, and pepper and stir to incorporate. Increase the heat to high and bring to a boil. Reduce the heat to a simmer and cook for 20 minutes to meld the flavors. Stir in the cashew cream and remove from the heat.

Using an immersion blender, blend the soup in the pot until smooth.

MAKE THE GRILLED "CHEESE" SANDWICHES: Slather one side of each slice of bread, crust to crust, with a generous amount of butter.

Heat a large cast-iron skillet or griddle over low heat. Add 4 bread slices, buttered side down. Arrange a mound of the cheese shreds on top of each slice, then cover each with one of the remaining bread slices, buttered side up. Cook for about 4 minutes, or until golden brown on the bottom and the cheese begins to melt. Flip and continue cooking on the other side until golden brown, too, about 2 minutes more.

Transfer the sandwiches to a plate. Warm the soup over low heat and serve with sandwiches for dipping.

MUSHROOM RAMEN NOODLE BOWLS

3 ounces dried mushrooms, such as shiitake or wild mushroom mix

1 inch fresh ginger, grated on a Microplane grater

1 tablespoon kelp powder, or 5 organic nori sheets, powdered (see Note, page 198)

1 cup mirin (sweet Japanese rice wine)

2 3-ounce packages Japanese ramen noodles (seasoning packet discarded!)

1½ cups (packed) baby spinach leaves

8 ounces extra-firm tofu, drained, blotted dry (no need to press it), and cut into small cubes (about 1 cup)

4 tablespoons sesame seeds, for garnish

I survived on a lot of cheap packages of ramen noodles while incarcerated. Ramen noodle seasoning packets contain monosodium glutamate (MSG), a manufactured flavor enhancer often found in canned soups and deli meats. Monosodium glutamate is linked to a host of health troubles, including gastrointestinal issues, obesity, and allergic reactions. However, L-glutamic acid, the natural amino acid that the fake stuff tries to mimic, naturally occurs in many foods, including mushrooms—it's why they taste so damn good. Dried mushrooms have a concentrated umami flavor and all the immune-boosting and micronutrient superpowers of fresh mushrooms. Once rehydrated in water, they become tender again (and they season the liquid they are soaked in), and you can chop them and add them back to the broth for double the deep flavor. Beware: Soft tofu can melt away in hot broth, and firm tofu may get mushy, so make sure to use extra-firm.

In a large soup pot, combine the mushrooms, ginger, kelp powder, mirin, and 12 cups water to make a broth. Bring to a boil over high heat. Reduce the heat to a simmer and cook, uncovered, for 30 minutes—the volume will reduce to about 5 cups.

Set another large pot in the sink. Strain the broth through a fine-mesh sieve into that pot—this helps remove any grit left behind from the mushrooms. Transfer the mushrooms to a cutting board. When cool enough to handle, use a sharp knife to chop them and set aside.

Bring the broth to a boil over high heat. Add the noodles and cook for 1 minute. Reduce the heat to a simmer and continue cooking for 2 minutes more. Stir in the chopped mushrooms, spinach, and tofu and continue cooking for about 30 seconds to wilt the spinach.

To serve, divide evenly among four bowls. Garnish with the sesame seeds.

LOADED CHIPOTLE CHILI

2 tablespoons neutral oil, such as avocado or grapeseed

1 large yellow onion, finely chopped (about 1½ cups)

1 cup chopped bell pepper (about 1 medium pepper)

2 garlic cloves, minced

2 tablespoons Taco Seasoning (page 128)

3 tablespoons tomato paste

2 cups Veggie Broth (page 120) or store-bough low-sodium vegetable broth

1 28-ounce can fire-roasted diced tomatoes, undrained

2 chipotle peppers in adobo sauce, minced (about 2 tablespoons)

1 cup corn kernels, fresh (from about 2 ears) or frozen (no need to thaw)

1 teaspoon fine sea salt

1 teaspoon freshly cracked black pepper

1½ cups cooked pinto beans (page 141) or 1 15.5-ounce can, drained and rinsed

1½ cups cooked kidney beans (page 141) or 1 15.5-ounce can, drained and rinsed

THE "EXTRAS":

½ cup finely diced fresh cilantro

½ cup finely diced red onions

½ cup Sour Cashew Cream (page 123) or vegan sour cream

My mom's traditional meat-based chili always hit the spot, especially when she would spoon it over elbow macaroni for my sister and me. I load my version with beans and a ton of flavorful "extras." But the key to a great-tasting vegan chili begins with the base: Let the tomato paste cook on the bottom of the pot to release its umami flavor; fire-roasted tomatoes and adobo give this chili a spicy backbone that gets cooled by cashew sour cream.

Eating fiber-rich beans protects your health—they are low on the glycemic index and therefore are linked to weight loss and reduced blood sugar and can help lower the risk of heart disease and type 2 diabetes. What's more, growing beans is good for the environment. Beans, lentils, chickpeas, and peas have deep roots that pull carbon out of the atmosphere and store it underground, reducing greenhouse gas emissions.

In a large soup pot, heat the oil over medium heat until it shimmers. Add the onion and bell pepper and cook, stirring occasionally, for about 5 minutes, or until the pepper is softened.

Stir in the garlic and taco seasoning and cook for about 1 more minute, or until fragrant. Stir in the tomato paste and cook for 2 to 3 minutes, until the color changes from bright red to deep red—it's okay if it sticks to the bottom of the pot. Stir in the broth and use a wooden spoon to scrape up any bits stuck to the bottom and incorporate. Cook for 1 more minute.

Stir in the tomatoes and their juices, the chipotle peppers, corn, salt, black pepper, pinto beans, and kidney beans. Cover, increase the heat to high, and bring to a boil. Reduce the heat to a simmer and cook, with the lid ajar, for 15 minutes to thicken the chili.

To serve, top the chili with the cilantro, onions, and cashew sour cream. Or spoon over elbow macaroni, like my mom did, then add the toppings if you wish.

EWEE Bowl Guide

Bowls are the perfect starting point for your plant-based journey. They're fuss-free, adaptable, and great for using on-hand ingredients.

A well-made bowl contains a mix of the macronutrients—protein, carbohydrates, and fat. Begin with a base of dark leafy greens, lettuces, or sprouts—you can also choose fiber-full whole grains.

Next, add a serving of raw and cooked protein-rich plants for a rainbow of color and texture.

Bring it home with nuts and seeds for next-level crunch.

Dress it simply with good quality extra-virgin olive oil or with your favorite EWEE dressing or sauce. Use this guide to create your own bowls. Or try my favorite bowl recipes on the pages that follow.

Leafy Greens

- Beet greens
- Collards
- Dandelion
- Green leaf lettuce
- Kale: lacinato or curly
- Microgreens: the edible young seedlings of vegetables and herbs, including kale, broccoli, arugula, and radish
- Mustard greens
- Radicchio
- Red leaf lettuce
- Romaine lettuce
- Spinach
- Sprouts: the edible germinated seeds of vegetables and herbs, including, broccoli, kale, alfalfa, and sunflower
- Swiss chard
- Turnip greens

Cooked Grain

- Amaranth
- Barley
- Brown rice
- Buckwheat
- Bulgur
- Farro
- Freekeh
- Quinoa
- Spelt
- Teff
- Whole wheat pasta or Mac 'n' "Cheese" (page 242)
- Wild rice

Beans

- Black beans
- Butter beans
- Cannellini beans
- Chickpeas (garbanzo beans)
- Edamame
- Great Northern beans
- Kidney beans
- Lentils: brown or green
- Mung beans
- Navy beans

Protein Add-Ins

- BBQ Tofu "Ribs" (page 230)
- Crispy Chickpeas (page 134)
- "Egg" Salad (page 210)
- Orange "Chicken" (page 251)
- Really Good Tofu Scramble (page 154)

Raw or Cooked Vegetables

- Asparagus
- Avocado
- Broccoli
- Cabbage
- Carrots
- Cauliflower
- Celery
- Corn kernels: fresh or frozen
- Cucumbers
- Radishes
- Red onion, raw, or Quick Pickled Red Onions (page 132)
- Scallions (green onions)
- Snow peas
- Sugar snap peas
- Tomatoes: fresh or sun-dried
- Turnips
- Zucchini or summer squash

Cooked Vegetable Dishes

- Buffalo Cauliflower "Chicken" Wings (page 194)
- EZ EWEE Veggies (page 142)
- Good Morning, Sweet Potato!, plain (page 160)
- Maple-Roasted Brussels Sprouts (page 220)
- Mushrooms, cooked, or Mushroom "Bacon" (page 155)
- Spicy Sweet Green Beans (page 250)

Dressings and Sauces

- Any store-bought plant-based dressing
- Chickpea Caesar Dressing (page 125)
- Extra-virgin olive oil
- Ranch Dressing (page 126)
- Southwest Dressing (page 126)

Nuts and Seeds

- Almonds
- Cashews
- Chia seeds
- Flaxseeds
- Hemp hearts
- Peanuts
- Pecans
- Pine nuts
- Pistachios
- Pumpkin seeds
- Sesame seeds
- Sunflower seeds
- Walnuts

Finishing Touches (Optional)

- Blue corn tortilla chips (such as Garden of Eatin'), crumbled, or tortilla strips
- "Cheese," plant-based
- EZ Guacamole (page 130)
- EZ Hummus (page 130)
- Fruit, fresh and dried, for a touch of sweet, tart, or crunch
- Herbs, fresh, such as basil, cilantro, parsley, and mint
- Mango-Corn Salsa (page 255)
- Nutritional yeast
- Olives
- Smoky "Queso" (page 202)
- Sour Cashew Cream (page 123)

A Guide to Leafy Greens

Leafy greens pack fiber and immune-boosting micronutrients. Choose them as a base for bowls (see EWEE Bowl Guide, page 186). If you are new to "Livin' la Vida Verde" (the Green Life), try adding them to smoothies to get a daily dose. Or use these greens in Kale-L Pesto (page 241) or "Iron Man" Spinach and Broccoli Soup (page 180), or for an "Egg" Salad Collard Wrap (page 210). Or combine their powers and cook them in A Mess of Greens (page 233).

Fresh leafy greens contain dirt and debris, so thoroughly wash them before preparing them. I recommend washing your greens as soon as you get home from the store, so they have plenty of time to dry. Plus, there's nothing like opening your fridge and having washed, fresh greens ready to go.

LEAFY GREEN	FLAVOR AND TEXTURE	SUPERPOWER
Beet greens	Sweet and mild tasting	Excellent source of lutein, an antioxidant that supports eye health
Collards	Cooked and raw collard greens have a mild, earthy taste like spinach	High in fiber (5.3 grams per 1 cup cooked), which keeps you regular, lowers cholesterol, and helps control blood sugar levels
Kale	Strong, earthy flavor that mellows once cooked. Look for lacinato kale, which has more tender leaves.	Rich in vital micronutrients, including vitamins A. K, B, and C. Kale is a prebiotic powerhouse, helping good bacteria flourish in your gut! (see Fiber and Our Gut Microbiome, page 64).
Mustard greens	Flat-leafed Chinese mustard greens are tender and spicy. The curly-leafed Southern mustard green varietal is peppery. When cooked they are full-bodied, like spinach.	High in B vitamins that our bodies need to maintain good energy levels, metabolism, and cell function
Spinach	Large spinach leaves lean toward bitter. Baby spinach leaves are earthy and mildly sweet. Eat it raw or cooked.	Rich in carotenoids (powerful antioxidants) and micronutrients including vitamin C, vitamin K, iron, calcium, and folate (a B vitamin crucial during pregnancy for healthy spine and brain development). It packs 4 grams of fiber per 1 cup cooked.
Swiss chard	Mild tasting with rainbow-colored stems that look like flat celery	Excellent source of vitamin K, which plays a role in helping blood clot.
Turnip greens	Mature greens are very peppery; young greens taste zesty.	One of the highest sources of calcium of all the vegetables: 105 milligrams in 1 cup chopped

EWEE BOWL

½ cup liquid amino acids, reduced-sodium soy sauce, or tamari

¼ cup rice vinegar

2 tablespoons neutral oil, such as avocado or grapeseed

1 8-ounce package tempeh, cut into bite-sized cubes

2 to 3 cups (packed) stemmed, deribbed, and roughly chopped kale, such as curly or lacinato (about 1 large bunch)

¾ cup Ranch Dressing (page 126)

1 Good Morning, Sweet Potato!, halved (page 160)

1 avocado, halved, pitted, flesh removed and cubed

1½ cups Crispy Chickpeas (page 134) or 1 15-ounce can chickpeas, drained and rinsed

1½ cups halved cherry or grape tomatoes, or 2 medium tomatoes, chopped

1 cup pistachios

2 tablespoons hemp hearts, for garnish

I love my EWEE bowl because it's simple to make, filling, and is packed with fantastic texture and fresh, wholesome flavors from Mother Earth—juicy tomatoes, buttery avocado, nutty hemp seeds, and an elephant-sized amount of fiber and protein from tempeh, pistachios, Japanese sweet potato, and crispy chickpeas. Yeah, this is my signature bowl and the one I would make for you if we were hanging out. I'd even wrap leftovers for you to take home the next day, or hey, you could come back over.

MARINATE THE TEMPEH: In a large bowl, whisk together the liquid aminos, vinegar, and 1 tablespoon of the oil. Add the tempeh and marinate at room temperature for 20 minutes.

In a large nonstick skillet, heat the remaining 1 tablespoon oil over medium-high heat until it shimmers. Arrange the tempeh in a single layer, along with any remaining marinade, and cook, undisturbed, for 2 to 3 minutes, until golden brown and crispy. Flip and continue cooking, about 2 minutes more, until all sides are crispy. Remove from the heat and set aside.

ASSEMBLE THE BOWLS: In a large bowl, combine the kale and ½ cup of the ranch dressing. Toss until the greens are well coated. Divide the dressed kale between two bowls. Add the prepared tempeh, sweet potato, avocado, crispy chickpeas, tomatoes, and pistachios. Garnish with the hemp hearts and drizzle each bowl with some of the remaining ¼ cup dressing before serving.

CRISPY, CRUNCHY, CREAMY CHICKPEA CAESAR BOWLS

4 cups (packed) chopped romaine hearts (about 2 large hearts)

4 cups (packed) stemmed, deribbed, and roughly chopped kale, such as curly, or lacinato (about 1 large bunch)

¾ cup Chickpea Caesar Dressing (page 125)

1 cup Crispy Chickpeas (page 134) or 1 15-ounce can chickpeas, drained and rinsed

1½ cups halved cherry or grape tomatoes

¼ cup nutritional yeast

I love different varieties of kale, including my favorite, lacinato (aka dinosaur kale)—it's darker and more tender than curly kale. While you can juice and cook kale without removing the midribs—the thick and fibrous vein that runs up the middle of the leaves—they are tough to chew in a salad, so it's best to cut them out of the leaf. I combine kale with crisp romaine lettuce for the base of this bowl, then make chickpeas do double-duty in both the creamy Caesar dressing and the garnish of crispy chickpeas for spicy crunch.

In a large bowl, combine the lettuce, kale, and dressing. Toss until the greens are well coated.

Divide the dressed greens among four bowls. Add the crispy chickpeas and tomatoes. Sprinkle the nutritional yeast over the top.

THINK EWEE: Hey! Are you craving a chicken Caesar salad on your Fake It Till You Make It! Pathway (page 86)? Add a faux meat to this bowl, such as Chick'n Tenders from Gardein.

BUFFALO CAULIFLOWER "CHICKEN" WINGS BOWLS

2 flax eggs or 2 egg replacers, such as Bob's Red Mill (see page 101)

FOR THE CAULIFLOWER WINGS:

1 cup almond flour

1 cup chickpea flour (aka garbanzo bean flour)

2 tablespoons stone-ground medium-grind cornmeal

1 teaspoon garlic powder

2 teaspoons onion powder

1 tablespoon paprika

1 teaspoon fine sea salt

½ teaspoon freshly cracked black pepper

1 tablespoon maple syrup

4 cups cauliflower florets (from 1 large head), cut into "wing"-sized pieces, about 2 inches across

3 tablespoons vegan butter

1½ cups hot sauce

FOR ASSEMBLY:

8 cups (packed) stemmed, deribbed, roughly chopped kale, such as curly or lacinato (about 3 large bunches)

¾ cup Ranch Dressing (page 126)

¼ cup hemp hearts, for garnish

¼ cup sesame seeds, for garnish

This is one of my favorite bowls to make for nonvegans, because it packs all the crispy, saucy deliciousness from traditional chicken wings, but without the grease, fat, and too-full feeling. I make these all the time during football season and serve them with a hard cider—they're the perfect "good-time" food. And they feel good, too, since you can enjoy the sensory experience of wings without the harm to animals or to your own body.

Use leftover cauliflower wings to make a "Soul" Bowl (page 236).

Before beginning the recipe, prepare the flax egg or egg replacer (see How to Prepare a "Flax Egg" or Egg Replacer, page 101).

MAKE THE CAULIFLOWER WINGS: Preheat the oven to 400°F. Line a sheet pan with parchment paper or a silicone mat.

In a large bowl, use a whisk to combine the almond flour, chickpea flour, cornmeal, garlic powder, onion powder, paprika, salt, and pepper. Add the maple syrup, flax egg (or egg replacer), and 2 cups water and gently whisk until a smooth, thick batter forms. If it's too thick, add more water, a tablespoon at a time to thin it out, if necessary.

Using tongs, or your clean hands, dip a cauliflower floret into the batter until well coated and place on the baking sheet. Repeat with the remaining florets, arranging them on the baking sheet in an even layer.

Transfer to the oven and bake for 10 to 15 minutes, until lightly browned. Remove the pan from the oven and using tongs, gently rotate the florets. Continue baking for 10 to 15 more minutes, until tender but not mushy.

Meanwhile, in a large saucepan, melt the butter over medium heat. Reduce the heat to low, add the hot sauce, and stir until well incorporated.

Remove the sheet pan from the oven and slowly pour the hot sauce mixture over the cauliflower. Gently toss to coat. Continue baking for about 10 minutes more for the flavors to meld. Remove from the oven and let cool slightly.

Assemble the bowls: In a large bowl, combine the kale and dressing and toss until the greens are well coated. Divide the dressed kale among four bowls. Add the cauliflower wings. Scatter the hemp hearts and sesame seeds over the top.

THINK EWEE: Serve cauliflower wings on a platter instead, alongside fresh carrot and celery sticks, with ranch dressing alongside for dipping.

CHICAGO TACO BOWLS WITH WALNUT AND MUSHROOM "MEAT"

Serves 4

8 cups (packed) chopped leafy greens, your choice (see A Guide to Leafy Greens, page 188)

¾ cup Southwest Dressing (page 126)

Walnut and Mushroom "Meat" (page 136)

1½ cups cooked black or pinto beans or 1 15.5-ounce can, drained and rinsed

1 cup cooked brown rice (see Grain Cooking Chart, page 139)

12 cherry or grape tomatoes, halved

1 cup EZ Guacamole (page 130) or 2 avocados, sliced

8 ounces crumbled vegan queso fresco cheese, such as Forager Project

16 jarred pickled jalapeño peppers, drained

1 cup crumbled blue corn tortilla chips, such as Garden of Eatin'

Chicago's Mexican demographic was, at one time, among the highest in the US, and aside from having Mexican roots in my bloodline—my grandmother Sophie's father was Mexican—I have many childhood friends and colleagues of Mexican descent. I love their food and their culture! This bowl is an ode to Sophie's roots and the spicy, tangy, sour, "cheesy," salty flavors and textures of Mexican cuisine. Finely ground walnuts and mushrooms seasoned with taco seasoning are satisfying and healthy—a swap so perfect for beef that if you're starting on your plant-based journey, I promise you won't miss it.

In a large bowl, combine the greens and ½ cup of the Southwest dressing. Toss until the greens are well coated.

Divide the dressed greens among four bowls. Add the "meat," beans, brown rice, tomatoes, guacamole, cheese, and jalapeños. Scatter the tortilla chips over the top and drizzle each bowl with some of the remaining ¼ cup dressing before serving.

THINK EWEE: Hey! Are you following the Fake It Till You Make It Pathway (page 86)? Enjoy the goodness of the leafy greens and whole grains in this bowl, but swap the homemade "meat" for store-bought ground "meat" crumbles, such as Beyond Meat.

TOMATO "TUNA" POKE BOWLS WITH "YUM YUM" SAUCE

FOR THE TOMATO "TUNA":

8 large Roma tomatoes

½ cup liquid amino acids, reduced-sodium soy sauce, or tamari

2 tablespoons toasted sesame oil

2 teaspoons sriracha

2 tablespoons mirin (sweet Japanese rice wine)

2 large scallions (green onions), white and green parts, sliced

1 tablespoon kelp powder or 5 organic nori sheets, powdered (see Note)

FOR ASSEMBLY:

4 cups cooked Japanese sushi rice (see Grain Cooking Chart, page 139)

4 cups shelled edamame, cooked according to the package directions if frozen

1 cup cubed fresh mango

1 cup cubed fresh pineapple

1 cup diced avocado (from about 1 large)

1 cup finely chopped cucumber (from 1 medium cucumber)

"Yum Yum" Sauce (page 127)

¼ cup sesame seeds

Poke means "to slice" in Hawaiian and refers to cubing freshly caught raw bigeye or ahi tuna. Commercial fishers overfish the world over, disrupting and destroying the delicate ocean ecosystem. This bowl carries poke's fresh flavors but does not harm the fish, or the environment. You'll blanch and peel the skin off hearty Roma tomatoes—a technique that takes less than five minutes. After a quick marinade, the tomatoes take on a silky texture and umami flavor. Look for frozen shelled edamame at the grocery store and follow the directions on the bag to cook them. Or grab precooked shelled edamame from the refrigerated section.

MAKE THE TOMATO "TUNA": Bring a medium pot of water to boil. Set up an ice bath by filling a large bowl with cold water and ice cubes.

Using a sharp knife, score an X on the bottom of each tomato. Gently place the tomatoes in the boiling water for 1 minute. Using a slotted spoon, remove them and plunge them in the ice bath. Allow to sit for 1 minute, then peel the skins—they will slide right off.

Cut the tomatoes into cubes and place them in a medium bowl. Add the liquid aminos, sesame oil, sriracha, mirin, scallions, and kelp powder. Stir to combine. Cover the bowl and refrigerate for 30 minutes.

ASSEMBLE THE BOWLS: Divide the rice among four bowls. Add the tomatoes, edamame, mango, pineapple, avocado, and cucumber. Drizzle each bowl with "Yum Yum" sauce and scatter the sesame seeds over the top.

NOTE: To make the nori powder, cut the sheets into 1-inch pieces and grind in a food processor to a fine powder. Store in an airtight container in a cool, dry place for up to 2 months.

THINK EWEE: Hey! Are following the Fake It Till You Make It Pathway (page 86)? Enjoy the goodness of this bowl, but make it yours by adding plant-based tuna, such as Good Catch brand.

A VEGAN DIET CHANGES HOW YOU SEE VEGETABLES. NO longer will you relegate them to side-dish status. They will be in every corner of your plate. Here you'll find small-plate dishes that provide for a light meal, or options to mix and match for something more substantial: Summertime Sweet Corn 'n' Jalapeño Fritters (page 205) make a great lunch on their own, or set them on the table with some Maple-Roasted Brussels Sprouts (page 220) or EZ EWEE Veggies (page 142). Many of the dishes in this chapter take less time to create than main dishes and include lunch and brunch favorites, such as my do no harm "Crab" Cakes with Rémoulade Sauce (page 206), Mega Tofu BLT (page 212), and "Egg" Salad Collard Wraps (page 210).

Change is good. And on your EWEE journey, change is delicious.

SMALL PLATES, SANDWICHES, AND BURGERS

SMOKY "QUESO"

1 cup Basic Cashew Cream (page 122)

½ cup nutritional yeast

2 tablespoons liquid amino acids, reduced-sodium soy sauce, or tamari

1 teaspoon garlic powder

1 teaspoon onion powder

½ teaspoon ground turmeric

½ teaspoon fine sea salt

¼ teaspoon freshly cracked black pepper

1 to 2 chipotle peppers in adobo sauce, depending on the level of heat you want

Blue corn tortilla chips or fresh cut vegetables, such as broccoli florets, carrot sticks, cauliflower, or snap peas, or a combination

Traditional queso is a Tex-Mex cheese dip made with melted, often processed, cheese, milk, and heavy cream. In addition to causing harm to animals, it usually has artificial food coloring and high amounts of sodium. My version has no saturated fat, is wonderfully creamy, and gets a spicy and smoky kick from chipotle peppers. The natural deep orange color of ground turmeric—a healing spice native to South Asia that has anti-inflammatory properties—gives this "queso" its cheddar color. You can adjust the spice by using more or less chipotle pepper. Dip fresh vegetables in it and call it lunch.

In a blender, combine the cashew cream, nutritional yeast, liquid aminos, garlic powder, onion powder, turmeric, salt, black pepper, chipotle peppers, and ½ cup water. Blend until smooth.

Transfer the mixture to a medium saucepan. Whisk constantly over medium heat for about 3 minutes to warm through. Transfer to a bowl and serve with tortilla chips or fresh vegetables alongside for dipping.

THINK EWEE: To make a vegan queso fundido—which is queso traditionally topped with spicy chorizo—top this with ¾ cup Walnut and Mushroom "Meat" (page 136) seasoned with Taco Seasoning (page 128).

FANTASTIC FRITTERS

Fritters are small, pan-fried veggie cakes that are easy to make. Once you mix the batter, add your favorite herbs and spices or whatever fresh or frozen veggies you have on hand, including leftovers. Stir them up, then drop them into a hot pan! Sizzle, sizzle. Within minutes you have a crunchy on the outside and tender on the inside savory cake. Chickpea flour combined with ground cornmeal makes a delicious gluten-free batter.

FOR THE BATTER:

1 flax egg or 1 egg replacer, such as Bob's Red Mill (see page 101)

½ cup chickpea flour (aka garbanzo bean flour)

¼ cup stone-ground medium-grind cornmeal

1 teaspoon garlic powder

1 teaspoon fine sea salt

¼ teaspoon freshly cracked black pepper

1 cup plain plant-based milk

1 teaspoon apple cider vinegar

FOR THE FRITTERS:

1 cup cut-up vegetables of your choice

1 tablespoon dried seasonings, your choice, such as Italian Seasoning (page 128)

2 tablespoons minced fresh herbs, such as dill, parsley, or chives

Shredded vegan cheese (optional)

Neutral oil, such as avocado or grapeseed, for frying

½ cup dressing or sauce (see Variations on page 205 for suggestions), for dipping

Preheat the oven to 200°F.

MAKE THE FRITTER BATTER: Before beginning the recipe, prepare the flax egg or egg replacer (see How to Prepare a "Flax Egg" or Egg Replacer, page 101).

In a large bowl, whisk to combine the chickpea flour, cornmeal, garlic powder, salt, and pepper. Add the flax egg, milk, and vinegar. Whisk until a thick batter forms.

MAKE THE FRITTERS: Add your choice of vegetables, seasonings, and/or fresh herbs (see Variations on page 205 for some suggestions). Stir well to combine.

Line a large plate with a paper towel and set aside. Pour just enough oil into a large cast-iron skillet to coat the bottom and heat over medium-high heat until it shimmers. Working in batches, drop fritters (about 3 heaping tablespoons each) into the skillet 1 inch apart. Cook, undisturbed, for 2 to 3 minutes, until the undersides are browned. Flip, then gently press down with the back of a spatula to flatten and cook for about 2 more minutes, until the other side is golden brown.

Transfer the fritters to the paper towel–lined plate. Add more oil to the skillet as needed to coat the bottom and repeat with the remaining batter.

Arrange the fritters on a baking sheet and warm in the oven for 5 minutes before serving with your choice of dressing or sauce for dipping.

NOTE: Zucchini has a high water content, so make sure to remove excess moisture before adding it to the fritter batter, otherwise they won't get crispy. Grate the zucchini over the center of a clean kitchen towel, then wrap it up tightly. Wring out the liquid over the sink.

THINK EWEE: Fritters are fantastic anytime. Enjoy them with a Really Good Tofu Scramble (page 154) for breakfast, or for a light lunch or dinner with a side of leafy greens.

(recipe continues)

Variations:

SWEET CORN 'N' JALAPEÑO FRITTERS:
Make the batter and add 1½ cups corn kernels (fresh—from 2 ears—frozen, or canned, drained and rinsed), 2 finely chopped jalapeños, and 2 teaspoons finely chopped fresh chives. Pan-fry as directed and serve with ½ cup Ranch Dressing (page 126).

ZUCCHINI 'N' HERB FRITTERS: Make the batter. Coarsely grate ½ pound zucchini (about 2 medium) and squeeze it dry (see Note on page 203). Add the zucchini to the batter along with 2 tablespoons chopped fresh herbs (such as basil, parsley, or mint) or 1 teaspoon Italian Seasoning (page 128) Pan-fry as directed and serve with ½ cup Rémoulade Sauce (page 208).

BROCCOLI 'N' "CHEESE" FRITTERS: Make the batter and add 2 cups broccoli florets, cut into 1-inch pieces and cooked, or 2 cups thawed frozen broccoli, thawed, and ½ cup vegan cheddar-style shreds. Pan-fry as directed and serve with ½ cup warmed Tomato and Beet Marinara (page 133) or jarred marinara.

"CRAB" CAKES WITH RÉMOULADE SAUCE

Rémoulade Sauce (page 208)

FOR THE "CRAB" MIXTURE:

1 tablespoon neutral oil, such as avocado or grapeseed, plus more as needed

1 celery stalk, plus leaves, finely chopped (about ½ cup)

½ medium bell pepper, finely chopped (about ½ cup)

½ small yellow onion, finely chopped (about ¼ cup)

1 teaspoon EWEE Spice Mix (page 127) or Old Bay seasoning

1½ cups cooked chickpeas or 1 15-ounce can, drained and rinsed

1 15-ounce can hearts of palm, drained

1 tablespoon kelp powder or 5 organic nori sheets, powdered (see Note, page 198)

1 tablespoon Dijon mustard

2 tablespoons Cashew Mayo (page 123) or 2 tablespoons vegan mayonnaise

1 teaspoon celery seed

½ teaspoon celery salt

½ teaspoon fine sea salt

½ teaspoon freshly cracked pepper

Grated zest and juice of 1 lemon

2 cups whole wheat panko bread crumbs or gluten-free panko

From 1970 to 1985, my grandmother Sophie owned Sophie's Fishery—a fried fish and chicken shack across the alley from her house in Chicago's Holy City neighborhood. As a little boy, I lived for her fish sticks and ketchup, along with fried Buffalo perch, catfish, jack salmon, and white fish. Sundays were always "fry day" in my family, and now I keep the tradition alive by creating a plant-based "fish" fry once a week with my "crab" cakes. The addition of kelp powder to the hearts of palm and chickpea blend gives these a seafood taste. Fry them or bake them, but what you won't do is cause harm to marine life.

Make the rémoulade sauce first, since it needs about 1 hour to chill in the refrigerator before serving.

MAKE THE "CRAB" MIXTURE: In a medium skillet, heat the oil over medium heat until it shimmers. Add the celery, bell pepper, onion, and spice mix and cook, stirring occasionally, for about 5 minutes, or until the vegetables are softened. Transfer to a small bowl. Refrigerate until chilled, about 15 minutes.

Meanwhile, in a large bowl, combine the chickpeas, hearts of palm, and kelp powder and use a fork to break them up until just combined.

In a small bowl, stir together the mustard, mayo, celery seed, celery salt, salt, black pepper, lemon zest, and lemon juice. Stir into the chickpea mixture. Fold in the chilled sautéed vegetables and the panko and stir once more to combine.

COOK THE "CRAB" CAKES: You have two choices for cooking the cakes: in the oven or in a skillet. If using the oven method, preheat the oven to 400°F and line a sheet pan with parchment paper or a silicone mat.

With wet hands, divide the mixture into 8 equal portions (about ½ cup each) and form each into a patty about 1 inch thick.

(recipe and ingredients continue)

2 tablespoons neutral oil (if pan-frying), such as avocado or grapeseed, plus more as needed

Choose your method for cooking the "crab" cakes:

OVEN METHOD: Arrange the patties on the lined sheet pan. Bake for about 15 minutes, or until the underside is golden and crispy. Remove the sheet pan from the oven, flip the "crab" cakes, and return to the oven. Continue baking for another 6 to 8 minutes, until the tops are golden.

SKILLET METHOD: In a large cast-iron skillet, heat the oil over medium-high heat until it shimmers. Working in batches, add the patties in a single layer and cook, undisturbed, for 5 minutes, until the bottom is crispy. Flip and cook for 5 minutes, or until the second side is crispy. Continue with the remaining cakes, adding more oil to the skillet, if necessary.

Serve immediately with the rémoulade sauce.

RÉMOULADE SAUCE

Makes about ½ cup

Traditional French rémoulade sauce is used to dress Louisiana Cajun and Creole dishes, such as fried fish, crab cakes, and oyster po'boy sandwiches. It tastes like a cross between mayonnaise and tartar sauce, and the best ones, in my opinion, have heat, sweet, and a smack of tang from capers.

4 tablespoons Dijon mustard, or 2 tablespoons mustard powder

2 tablespoons organic ketchup

2 tablespoons Cashew Mayo (page 123) or 2 tablespoons vegan mayo

1 teaspoon hot sauce, plus more to taste

1 teaspoon liquid amino acids, reduced-sodium soy sauce, or tamari

2 tablespoons fresh lemon juice (from 1 small lemon)

2 tablespoons chopped fresh parsley

1 garlic clove, minced

2 tablespoons capers

½ teaspoon fine sea salt

½ teaspoon smoked paprika

¼ teaspoon freshly cracked black pepper

In a small bowl, whisk to combine the mustard, ketchup, mayo, hot sauce, liquid aminos, and lemon juice. Add the parsley, garlic, capers, salt, paprika, and pepper and stir to combine. Taste and season with more hot sauce if you like. Refrigerate for at least 1 hour before serving.

"EGG" SALAD COLLARD WRAPS

FOR THE "EGG" SALAD:

1 16-ounce package firm tofu, drained and pressed (see Tofu Prep, page 103)

¼ cup Cashew Mayo (page 123) or ¼ cup vegan mayonnaise

1½ tablespoons Dijon mustard or 1 teaspoon mustard powder

2 tablespoons nutritional yeast

1 garlic clove, minced

¾ teaspoon black salt (kala namak) or fine sea salt

¼ teaspoon freshly cracked black pepper

½ teaspoon ground turmeric

1 cup chopped bell pepper (about 1 medium pepper)

1 celery stalk, finely chopped

FOR THE WRAPS:

4 large collard leaves, washed, patted dry, and stemmed (see Note)

Collard greens are associated with Southern cooking and "soul" food (see A Mess of Greens, page 233). They're usually cooked down with ham hocks or bacon. But you can enjoy them raw! All it takes is a quick trim of their tough stems and midribs, and the large, sturdy leaves (which, when laid out on my cutting board, remind me of elephant ears!) become a nutrient-dense wrap for a tofu "egg" salad. Firm tofu gives the right boiled egg texture, but black salt (kala namak) is the secret ingredient for the eggy taste. It will still taste delicious if you skip it, though.

MAKE THE "EGG" SALAD: Place the tofu in a medium bowl and use a fork to break it up into small pieces. Stir in the mayo, mustard, nutritional yeast, garlic, black salt, pepper, and turmeric until well combined. Add the bell pepper and celery and stir to combine.

ASSEMBLE THE WRAPS: Lay the collard greens flat on a clean work surface. Working with one collard green at a time, place a ¼-cup scoop of the salad at the base and roll up, like a burrito, tucking in the sides as you roll. Cut in half and serve.

NOTE: To stem a collard green and remove the midribs, place the collard leaf on a cutting board, rib-side up. Use a sharp knife to cut on either side of the midrib to remove it and the stem completely.

MEGA TOFU BLT

4 ounces extra-firm tofu, drained and blotted dry

3 tablespoons neutral oil, such as avocado or grapeseed

¼ cup liquid amino acids, reduced-sodium soy sauce, or tamari

2 tablespoons maple syrup

¼ teaspoon garlic powder

¼ teaspoon onion powder

¼ teaspoon freshly cracked black pepper

¼ teaspoon smoked paprika

1 large tomato (about 7 ounces), such as beefsteak or heirloom

¼ teaspoon fine sea salt

¼ teaspoon freshly cracked black pepper

2 tablespoons Cashew Mayo (page 123) or vegan mayonnaise

3 slices whole-grain or gluten-free bread, lightly toasted

4 lettuce leaves, such as romaine, rinsed and patted dry

1 small avocado, mashed

I eat this protein-packed tofu "bacon," lettuce, and tomato sandwich weekly, paired with baked potato chips, a pickle, and sparkling water. It's big and juicy, which I love, and I think it stands up to any sandwich sourced from animals. And I've had every animal-based fast-food, sit-down, in the car, out the car, Chicago-style iteration of traditional sandwich you can possibly think of. You do not need to press the extra-firm tofu. By blotting it dry, it will crisp in the skillet like traditional bacon but retain a moist and chewy middle.

MAKE THE TOFU "BACON": Slice the tofu into four 1-ounce slices.

In a small bowl, whisk to combine 2 tablespoons of the oil, the liquid aminos, maple syrup, garlic powder, onion powder, pepper, and smoked paprika. Add the tofu slices and turn to coat. Let sit at room temperature for 10 minutes.

In a nonstick medium skillet, heat the remaining 1 tablespoon oil over medium-high heat until it shimmers. Arrange the tofu slices in a single layer and cook for about 5 minutes, or until browned on the underside. Flip and continue cooking for about 3 minutes more, until golden brown on the other side. Remove from the heat and set aside.

ASSEMBLE THE SANDWICH: Using a serrated knife, slice the tomato crosswise into 4 thick slices and place them on a paper towel to absorb some of their moisture. Season both sides of the tomato slices with the salt and pepper and set aside.

Spread 1 tablespoon of the mayo on 1 slice of the bread, followed by 2 lettuce leaves, followed by 2 slices of tomato, and 2 slices tofu "bacon." Top the bacon with half of the avocado mash and cover with the second slice of toasted bread. Spread the remaining 1 tablespoon of mayo on top of the middle slice of bread, followed by the remaining 2 lettuce leaves, remaining 2 slices of tomato, remaining 2 slices of tofu "bacon," and remaining avocado mash. Cover with the third slice of toasted bread. Use a serrated knife to cut in half before chowing down.

EWEE BURGERS TWO WAYS

Hey, heads up: You'll spend some time creating these bad boys!

Plant-based products like Beyond Meat and Impossible Burger offer convenience when you crave a burger. But there is so much more satisfaction in creating a hearty, tender, tasty whole-food burger: mixing, seasoning, forming the patty, and grilling it up—sounds like a cookout to me! Plus, a whole-food burger is healthier than the two alternatives: animals (nahh) or highly processed plant-based foods (on occasion). Here are two of my all-time favorite foods, beets and chickpeas, spun into another favorite food—burgers. The beet burger is earthy and sweet and gets a smack of my beet BBQ sauce. The chickpea burger is a little bit smoky, savory, and topped with creamy tahini sauce.

I hope you will feel a sense of pride in making these and that you will delight in knowing you can eat them often, without causing harm to animals or your health. Nothing feels better than that, except enjoying them with crispy maple-roasted brussels sprouts.

(recipe continues)

EWEE BEET BURGERS

Makes 4 burgers

FOR THE BURGERS:

1 flax egg or 1 egg replacer, such as Bob's Red Mill (see page 101)

2 tablespoons neutral oil, such as avocado or grapeseed

4 small beets, scrubbed and grated (see Note)

1 cup cooked white beans, such as cannellini, Great Northern, or navy (see Bean Cooking Chart, page 141), or 1 cup canned beans, drained and rinsed (from a 15-ounce can; reserve the remaining beans for another use)

¼ cup cooked lentils (see Bean Cooking Chart, page 141) or no-salt-added canned lentils, drained and rinsed (from a 14-ounce can; reserve the remaining lentils for another use)

¼ cup old-fashioned rolled oats

2 tablespoons flaxmeal

2 garlic cloves, minced

1 tablespoon dried thyme

½ teaspoon cayenne pepper

½ teaspoon fine sea salt

½ teaspoon freshly cracked black pepper

FOR SERVING:

4 vegan whole wheat burger buns, lightly toasted

¼ cup Beet BBQ Sauce (page 132) or ¼ cup store-bought no-sugar-added vegan BBQ sauce, such as Sweet Baby Ray's

4 romaine lettuce leaves

Fresh tomato slices

Maple-Roasted Brussels Sprouts (page 220)

Before beginning the recipe, prepare the flax egg or egg replacer (see How to Prepare a "Flax Egg" or Egg Replacer, page 101).

MAKE THE BURGERS: In a cast-iron skillet, heat the oil over medium heat until it shimmers. Add the beets and cook, stirring occasionally, for about 10 minutes, or until softened. (If cooking the burgers in a skillet—see Burger Cooking Methods—keep the skillet available.)

In a food processor (fitted with the S blade), combine the flax egg, cooked beets, beans, lentils, oats, flaxmeal, garlic, thyme, cayenne, salt, pepper, and ¼ cup water and pulse 2 to 3 times, until the mixture just comes together. Transfer the mixture to a medium bowl, cover, and refrigerate for 15 minutes to firm up.

Wet your clean hands—so the mixture doesn't stick—and form 4 burgers ½ inch thick and place them on a plate.

Choose your method for cooking the burgers (see Burger Cooking Methods (page 218).

TO SERVE: Divide the burgers among the toasted buns and top each with 1 tablespoon of the BBQ sauce, lettuce, and tomato. Serve with the brussels sprouts.

NOTE: You do not need to peel the beets before grating if they are well scrubbed! To grate, use the shredding disc in your food processor or a box grater.

EWEE CHICKPEA TAHINI BURGERS

Makes 4 burgers

FOR THE BURGERS:

1 flax egg or 1 egg replacer, such as Bob's Red Mill (see page 101)

2 tablespoons neutral oil, such as avocado or grapeseed

1 medium red onion, finely chopped (about 1 cup)

3 medium carrots, grated (about 1 cup)

1½ cups cooked chickpeas (see Bean Cooking Chart, page 141) or 1 15-ounce can chickpeas, drained and rinsed

⅓ cup cooked brown rice, quinoa, or farro (see Grain Cooking Chart, page 139)

¼ cup old-fashioned rolled oats

2 tablespoons flaxmeal

6 oil-packed sun-dried tomatoes, blotted dry and roughly chopped

2 teaspoons nutritional yeast

2 garlic cloves, minced

1 tablespoon smoked paprika

½ teaspoon fine sea salt

¼ teaspoon freshly cracked black pepper

FOR SERVING:

4 vegan whole wheat burger buns, lightly toasted

¼ cup Tahini Sauce (page 218), plus more to taste

Romaine lettuce leaves

Fresh tomato slices

Maple-Roasted Brussels Sprouts (page 220)

Before beginning the recipe, prepare the flax egg or egg replacer (see How to Prepare a "Flax Egg" or Egg Replacer, page 101).

MAKE THE BURGERS: In a cast-iron skillet, heat the oil over medium heat until it shimmers. Add the onion and carrots and cook, stirring occasionally, for 3 to 5 minutes, until the carrots are softened. (If cooking the burgers in a skillet—see Burger Cooking Methods—keep the skillet available.)

In a food processor, combine the flax egg, cooked carrot mixture, chickpeas, rice, oats, flaxmeal, sun-dried tomatoes, nutritional yeast, garlic, smoked paprika, salt, pepper, and ¼ cup water and pulse 2 to 3 times, until the mixture just comes together. Transfer the mixture to a medium bowl, cover, and refrigerate for 15 minutes to firm up.

Wet your clean hands—so the mixture doesn't stick—and form 4 burgers ½ inch thick and place them on a plate.

Choose your method for cooking the burgers (see Burger Cooking Methods (page 218).

TO SERVE: Divide the burgers among the toasted buns and top each with 1 tablespoon or more of the tahini sauce, some lettuce, and tomato. Serve with the brussels sprouts.

Burger Cooking Methods

Pan-Fried

Wipe out the now-empty skillet. Heat 2 tablespoons neutral oil (such as avocado or grapeseed) over medium heat until it shimmers. Add the burgers and cook, undisturbed, for 3 to 5 minutes, until the bottoms are browned and crispy. Flip and continue cooking for, 3 to 5 minutes more, until the undersides are golden brown and crispy.

Oven-Baked

Preheat the oven to 350°F. Line a sheet pan with parchment paper or a silicone liner. Arrange the burgers on the pan and bake for 7 minutes. Remove the sheet pan from the oven and flip the burgers and continue baking 6 to 7 more minutes.

Grilled

Preheat an outdoor grill to 400°F. Place the burgers directly on clean, oiled grill grates in a single layer. Grill for 2 to 3 minutes per side, until char marks appear.

TAHINI SAUCE

Makes about 1 cup

½ cup tahini

¼ cup fresh lemon juice (from 1 to 2 lemons)

2 teaspoons liquid amino acids, reduced-sodium soy sauce, or tamari

1 small garlic clove, minced

1 tablespoon finely chopped fresh herbs, such as dill, parsley, or chives

¼ teaspoon fine sea salt

In a small bowl, whisk to combine the tahini, lemon juice, liquid aminos, garlic, herbs, salt, and 1 to 2 tablespoons cold water. The mixture will clump or "seize," but continue adding 1 to 2 more tablespoons of water, whisking constantly until smooth.

LENTIL SLOPPY JOES

2 tablespoons neutral oil, such as avocado or grapeseed

6 ounces mushrooms, such as button, cremini, or a combination, stemmed and thinly sliced

1 cup chopped bell pepper (about 1 medium pepper)

½ teaspoon fine sea salt

¼ teaspoon freshly cracked black pepper

1½ cups cooked green lentils (see Grain Cooking Chart, page 139) or 1 14-ounce can lentils, drained and rinsed

1 tablespoon chili powder

1¼ teaspoons ground cumin

1 tablespoon Dijon mustard or 1 teaspoon mustard powder

¾ cup Tomato and Beet Marinara (page 133) or store-bought marinara

4 vegan soft sesame seed buns or 4 vegan soft sandwich rolls, such as Nature's Own, lightly toasted

⅓ cup Quick Pickled Red Onions (page 132), drained, for serving

Dill pickle chips, for serving

My Auntie Valerie introduced all the kids in my family to the classic Hunt's Manwich sauce. It was a staple in the '80s, and she used it to make tangy, sweet sandwiches on sesame buns. I loved the richness of the sauce and the comfort of the soft bun—and since the ground meat was not attached to a bone, I wasn't bothered the way I was when I saw the bird's wing on my plate. I devoured them whenever Valerie prepared a Manwich sloppy joe.

This fiber-rich lentil, mushroom, and bell pepper version carries the nostalgia of my childhood. Pickle chips and thinly sliced pickled red onions give a little grown-up crunch. If using a store-bought marinara sauce, look for one with a short ingredient list—organic tomatoes or tomato paste, herbs, and very little to no added oil.

In a large skillet, heat the oil over medium heat until it shimmers. Add the mushrooms, bell pepper, salt, and black pepper and cook, stirring now and then, for about 10 minutes, or until the peppers are softened and the liquid in the pan evaporates.

Stir in the lentils, chili powder, cumin, mustard, and marinara. Increase the heat to medium-high and cook until the mixture begins to bubble. Reduce the heat to medium and cook, stirring now and then, for 5 more minutes to thicken the mixture. Remove from the heat and allow to cool for 10 minutes.

Divide the mixture among the lightly toasted buns and serve topped with pickled onions and pickle chips.

MAPLE-ROASTED BRUSSELS SPROUTS

2 pounds brussels sprouts, yellow outer leaves removed, tough ends trimmed, halved

2 tablespoons neutral oil, such as avocado or grapeseed

¼ teaspoon fine sea salt

¼ teaspoon freshly cracked black pepper

¼ cup maple syrup

Some people order a round of tequila for the table when they go out to eat with friends; I order a round of brussels sprouts! Brussels sprouts belong to the cruciferous family of veggies, a diverse-looking bunch that includes broccoli, cabbage, cauliflower, collard greens, kale, and turnips. Cruciferous veggies contain a compound associated with decreased inflammation, lowering cancer risk. And since the cruciferous family is so varied, you can make sure you get some every day—in bowls (see EWEE Bowl Guide, page 186), smoothies (see EWEE Smoothie Formula, page 174), and brussels sprouts to enjoy with an EWEE burger. Preheating your oven (at least twenty minutes) is essential for roasting vegetables, because they need high heat to crisp up.

Preheat the oven to 425°F. Line a sheet pan with parchment paper or a silicone mat.

In a medium bowl, toss the brussels sprouts with the oil, salt, and pepper. Arrange the sprouts cut-sides down in a single layer on the prepared baking sheet. Roast for about 15 minutes, or until the sprouts are browned.

Remove the sheet pan from the oven, drizzle the maple syrup over the top, and gently turn to coat. Return the brussels sprouts to the oven and continue roasting for another 5 minutes, or until the leaves are crispy and the inside is fork-tender.

BBQ PULLED MUSHROOM SANDWICHES

3 tablespoons neutral oil, such as avocado or grapeseed

1 10-ounce cluster oyster mushrooms, cleaned and pulled (see Note)

½ teaspoon fine sea salt

½ cup Beet BBQ Sauce (page 132) or store-bought no-sugar-added vegan BBQ sauce

2 vegan soft sandwich rolls, such as Nature's Own, lightly toasted

½ cup Creamy Coleslaw (page 232), for serving

Once you try pulled oyster mushrooms, I don't think you'll go back to pulled pork sandwiches! Oyster mushrooms are generally available at grocery stores; they are cultivated indoors year-round. In the spring they pop up at farmers' markets.

First, you shred or "pull" the mushrooms, then cook them, and within minutes, their delicate texture turns velvety and their edges get satisfyingly crispy. Add beet BBQ sauce to give them a thick 'n' perfectly sweet coating. If using store-bought sauce, look for a brand with a short ingredient list and organic sugar—some brands use honey and refined sugar, which are not vegan. Top off the pulled mushrooms with creamy coleslaw for magic on a lightly toasted bun. Can you tell I am excited for you?

In a large cast-iron skillet, heat the oil over medium-high heat until it shimmers. Arrange the mushrooms in a single layer. Cook, undisturbed, for about 5 minutes, or until beginning to brown. Add the salt, stir, and continue cooking for about 3 minutes, or until their liquid is absorbed. Continue cooking, stirring now and then, for about 5 minutes more, or until some of the edges crisp.

Stir in the BBQ sauce and continue cooking, stirring, for about another 2 minutes, until the sauce bubbles and reduces to a thick coating.

Divide the mushrooms between the rolls and top with coleslaw.

NOTE: Oyster mushrooms grow in a cluster on wood logs, so they don't have much dirt, making them easy to clean. With a clean towel, gently wipe the mushroom caps and central stem free of any dirt. Leave the cluster intact and use your hands to pull downward, shredding the mushrooms through to the stem—they will come apart easily. If the stem is tough, lay it on a work surface and run the back of a fork downward against it to shred it—don't worry, you can't mess this up.

THE ORIGIN STORY OF SOUL FOOD, THOSE DOWN-HOME deep Southern dishes passed to us from our ancestors—including chitlins, pork ribs, fried fish, fatback, ham hocks, hog jowl, offal, and oxtail—is rooted in white supremacy. Those meals were created in Southern kitchens by enslaved Black cooks, who did what they had to do to feed their families from the discarded, less nutritious parts of animals that wealthy plantation owners refused to eat.

During the great migration of Blacks fleeing the Jim Crow South to northern and Midwestern cities like New York and Chicago, from 1916 through the 1970s, these foods represented a feeling of "stick togetherness" that Black people from all over the country needed in a time of segregation and civil unrest. I grew up with soul food at family cookouts—maybe you did, too?

Cooking and sharing the traditional Southern dishes Black people brought from the South created income opportunities. Black-owned chicken shacks, fish shacks, and restaurants serving Southern fare sprung up in urban cities, and soul food became part of the Black culture and identity.

But the identity of soul food and the animal-based culinary practices forged from them was born of trauma. And even though the dishes are bound up in love and community tradition, when we cook and eat them, we repeat the trauma of their origins. We hurt our hearts, health, and bodies.

Here is what "soul food" means to me today: It's food that comes from the heart—prepared with

"SOUL FOOD" REDEFINED

the best intentions for all humans and non-human species. My redefined "soul food" is full of "live" plant energy. It fuels you and keeps you moving forward—physically, mentally, emotionally, and spiritually.

It's okay to pay tribute to the nostalgia and comfort that traditional soul foods may have filled at one time in our lives—and my EWEE "soul food" dishes have a look, flavor, and feel that honors their Southern origins and my family. But they are also an expression of how we can evolve on our journey. The question persists: What can we learn from our past to inform strong choices about who we are today as a species/culture/Black person/human?

I believe that seeing soul food dishes through a vegan lens and cooking and sharing them is essential to dismantling the destructive mindset of domination that continues to hurt humans and nonhuman species. This is more important than ever for Black communities, where poor-quality food, food scarcity, and poverty are issues that contribute to chronic disease and illness.

With these "soul food" dishes, I wish for you to travel forward on your journey, in and out of the kitchen, following a path paved with love for all.

COCONUT RICE AND PLANTAINS

FOR THE COCONUT RICE:

1 13.5-ounce can full-fat coconut milk

1 tablespoon maple syrup

½ teaspoon fine sea salt

2 cups long-grain jasmine rice, rinsed

FOR THE PLANTAINS:

4 large dark yellow (some black spots are okay) plantains (about 6 ounces each)

2 tablespoons neutral oil, such as avocado or grapeseed, plus more as needed

Fine sea salt

Creamy coconut rice is made sweeter by adding plantains, and that sweetness counters the heat of the jerk tempeh. Plantains look like large thick bananas and are just as inexpensive. Their flavor is a cross between a starchy potato and a sweet banana. To assess how ripe they are, look at the color of the skin: Green plantains are unripe, sour, starchy, and traditionally pounded and twice-fried for a Caribbean dish called tostones. The color of plantains ranges from unripe green to very ripe black, with yellow in the middle. I look for yellow plantains that have some black spots. To my taste, they have the right level of starch and sweetness, and they cook fast!

MAKE THE COCONUT RICE: In a medium saucepan, stir together the coconut milk, 1 cup water, maple syrup and the salt. Bring to a boil over medium-high heat. Stir in the rice and return to a boil. Reduce the heat to low, cover, and cook for about 15 minutes, or until the liquid has been absorbed. Remove from the heat and let stand, covered, while you make the plantains.

MAKE THE PLANTAINS: Use a paring knife to slice through the plantain's thick skin, then peel it like a banana. Slice each plantain in half lengthwise and set aside.

Line a plate with paper towels. In a large cast-iron skillet, heat the oil over medium-high heat until it shimmers. Working in batches, add the plantains cut-side down in a single layer and cook, undisturbed, for about 3 minutes per side, until golden brown and slightly crispy. Transfer to the paper towel–lined plate. Repeat with the remaining plantains, adding more oil to the pan, as needed, to lightly coat the bottom.

Fluff the coconut rice with a fork and transfer to a serving platter. Drape the plantains across the top, sprinkle with salt to taste, and serve.

Jerk Tempeh
Cooking Methods

Pan-Fried

In a large cast-iron skillet, heat the oil over medium-high heat until it shimmers. Working in batches, add the tempeh in a single layer and cook, undisturbed, for about 8 minutes per side, until both sides are crispy. Transfer the tempeh to a cutting board and continue with the remaining tempeh, adding 1 tablespoon more oil to the skillet, if necessary.

Oven-Baked

Turn on the oven's exhaust fan. Preheat the oven to 350°F. Place the tempeh in a covered baking dish in the oven and bake for about 40 minutes, or until the tempeh is crispy. Let stand 5 minutes before transferring the tempeh to a cutting board.

Grilled

Preheat an outdoor grill to 400°F. Place the tempeh directly on clean grill grates in a single layer. Grill for 5 to 8 minutes per side, until char marks appear. Transfer the tempeh to a cutting board and let stand 5 minutes.

NOTE: When preparing any hot peppers, such as Scotch bonnet or jalapeños, be sure to wear gloves for protection. The fiery heat in the peppers comes from capsaicin, a naturally occurring chemical primarily concentrated in the seeds and ribs of chiles. Though capsaicin can be used medicinally as a great anti-inflammatory to alleviate arthritis and joint pain, the raw compound in chiles can burn your skin and be easily transmitted from your bare hands to your eyes.

Serves 6

YALONDA'S JERK TEMPEH WITH COCONUT RICE AND PLANTAINS

FOR THE MARINADE:

FOR THE MARINADE:

8 whole garlic cloves, peeled

2 Scotch bonnet peppers or jalapeño peppers, stemmed (see Note on page 228)

¼ cup extra-virgin olive oil

2 tablespoons maple syrup

2 tablespoons fresh lime juice (from 2 limes)

1 tablespoon liquid amino acids, reduced-sodium soy sauce, or tamari

1 tablespoon tamarind paste

¾ tablespoon molasses

2 teaspoons ground allspice

1 teaspoon smoked paprika

1 teaspoon onion powder

1 teaspoon dried thyme or 2 tablespoons fresh thyme leaves

½ teaspoon ground cloves

½ teaspoon ground cinnamon

½ teaspoon fine sea salt

½ teaspoon freshly cracked pepper

FOR THE TEMPEH, COOKING, AND SERVING:

3 8-ounce packages tempeh, each piece halved to make 6 equal squares

2 tablespoons neutral oil, such as avocado or grapeseed, plus more as needed

Coconut Rice and Plantains (page 227)

When my sister Yalonda bought her first home in the Broadview section of Chicago, she launched a tradition of inviting family to gather in her backyard. The only rule was that you could never show up empty-handed. (Once my nephew showed up with just a date; it didn't count. She chewed him out.) Yalonda set her grill on a small concrete strip and we all sat in the grass. Growing up, I always steered clear of meat with a bone attached, but I couldn't resist the flavor of her grilled jerk-marinated bone-in chicken breasts. Jerk marinade has its roots in Jamaican culture, and Yalonda makes a mean one! Her recipe has the warmth of allspice and cloves, the sweetness of molasses, and a punch of heat from Scotch bonnet peppers. I get all the flavors I love by making this jerk tempeh. Boiling the tempeh is essential to help it soak up the marinade, so don't skip it.

MAKE THE MARINADE: In a blender or food processor, combine all the ingredients and blend for about 2 minutes, or until smooth.

PREPARE THE JERK TEMPEH: Bring a medium pot of water to boil. Add the tempeh and boil for 10 minutes. Drain and transfer the tempeh to a 9 × 13-inch baking dish.

Pour the jerk marinade over the tempeh. With gloved hands (see Note on page 228), massage the marinade into each square. Cover with foil and marinate at room temperature for at least 30 minutes and up to 1 hour.

COOK THE TEMPEH: Choose your cooking method (see Jerk Tempeh Cooking Methods, page 228). Cook the tempeh and let stand as directed.

TO SERVE: Slice the cooked tempeh crosswise into ¼-inch-thick slices. Arrange them on a serving plate. Serve with the coconut rice and plantains alongside.

BBQ TOFU "RIBS" WITH SOPHIE'S "FAMOUS" POTATO SALAD

2 16-ounce packages extra-firm tofu, drained and blotted dry

1 tablespoon EWEE Spice Mix (page 127)

1 cup Beet BBQ Sauce (page 132) or store-bought no-sugar-added vegan BBQ sauce

2 tablespoons neutral oil, such as avocado or grapeseed

Sophie's "Famous" Potato Salad (page 231), for serving

If you had a snapshot of nineteen-year-old Dominick in my sister's backyard, you'd see a husky, out-of-shape guy with a plate of chicken and a pile of my grandmother's famous potato salad. My younger self is far away now. But what hasn't changed is my love for my family. I express that, and my reverence for tradition, by aligning it with the values that define me as a protector of health and all living beings.

I've been making tofu "ribs" for a long time now—they're so easy. I season the tofu with my spice mix for a layer of flavor and then marinate them in beet BBQ sauce—warming the BBQ sauce first helps the tofu soak up the flavor. They turn out sticky, smoky, and satisfyingly dense.

Slice each tofu block lengthwise into six 1-inch-thick planks for a total of 12 tofu ribs Arrange the ribs in a single layer in a 9 × 13-inch baking dish. (You should have 2 rows of 6 ribs each.) Season all over with the spice mix and set aside.

In a medium saucepan, warm the BBQ sauce over medium-high heat, stirring now and then, for about 1 minute, or until bubbling.

Pour the sauce over the ribs and turn to coat. Cover the dish tightly with foil and refrigerate for at least 2 hours or up to overnight.

When ready to cook, move a rack to the center of the oven and turn on the broiler. Line a sheet pan with aluminum foil and drizzle with oil. (You can also make these on the grill; see Note.)

Arrange the "ribs" on the prepared sheet pan about 1 inch apart (leave any excess BBQ sauce in the baking dish). Broil for 3 to 5 minutes, until the tops of the tofu are browned and sticky, keeping a close eye on them, so they don't burn. Remove the pan from the oven, flip the tofu, return to the oven and continue broiling for about 3 minutes more, until crispy and dark in spots.

Arrange the "ribs" on a serving platter. Serve with the potato salad alongside.

NOTE: To grill the "ribs," preheat an outdoor grill to 400°F. Place the tofu directly on clean grill grates in a single layer. Grill for about 2 minutes, or until char marks appear on the bottom and the tofu easily releases. Flip and continue grilling on the other side for about 2 minutes.

THINK EWEE: Serve BBQ "ribs" with Creamy Coleslaw (page 232) or use leftover "ribs" to create a BBQ "rib" bowl—for ingredient ideas, turn to page 186.

Serves 6

SOPHIE'S "FAMOUS" POTATO SALAD

1½ pounds tiny red or yellow potatoes, or larger red or yellow potatoes, cut into 1-inch pieces

Fine sea salt

2 tablespoons yellow mustard

¼ cup Cashew Mayo (page 123) or ¼ cup vegan mayonnaise

2 tablespoons maple syrup

¼ cup vegan sweet relish

1 small red onion, finely chopped (about ½ cup)

1 cup chopped bell pepper (about 1 medium pepper)

¼ teaspoon freshly cracked black pepper, or more to taste

When it came to sharing my grandmother's perfectly creamy, chunky, crunchy, tangy, sweet potato salad—all the reasons it was "famous"—I had to text my mom for her recipe. She wrote: *red potatoes, chopped onion, bell pepper, plain mustard, a lil' sugar, very lil' salt, black pepper, Heinz sweet relish, and mayo.* I immediately knew my swaps: cashew mayo, maple syrup, and vegan relish (most crispy cucumber and cabbage blends have honey or high fructose corn syrup).

Is there a traditional meat, fish, or dairy dish for *you* that you associate with family love and "stick togetherness?" Do you think you won't be able to enjoy them again by choosing a plant-based or vegan path? Check in on your "why," focus on the journey, learn from your mistakes, be curious, and see possibilities instead of limitations—even in potato salad.

Prepare an ice water bath by filling a large bowl with cold water and ice cubes (see Note). Set aside.

In a large pot, combine the potatoes with enough cold water to cover by 1 inch. Bring to a boil over high heat, add 1 tablespoon salt, then reduce the heat to a simmer and cook for about 10 minutes, or until the potatoes are fork-tender.

Drain the potatoes in a colander, then immediately transfer to the prepared ice water bath and let sit until cool enough to handle, 2 to 4 minutes. Drain and set aside.

In a large bowl, whisk to combine the mustard, mayonnaise, maple syrup, and relish. Add the cooled potatoes to the bowl and stir gently to coat. Add the onion, bell pepper, salt to taste, and black pepper.

Cover the bowl and refrigerate 1 to 2 hours before serving.

NOTE: Dunking the cooked potatoes in an ice water bath helps speed up the cooling process before you dress them.

CREAMY COLESLAW

1 medium head red cabbage (about 2 pounds), wilted outer leaves discarded, quartered, and cored (see Note)

1 medium carrot, peeled and grated

2½ teaspoons fine sea salt

¼ cup Cashew Mayo (page 123) or ¼ cup vegan mayonnaise

2 teaspoons apple cider vinegar

1 teaspoon celery seed

¼ teaspoon freshly cracked black pepper

¼ cup Quick Pickled Red Onions (page 132), or more to taste, drained

Choosing between a plate full of Sophie's "Famous" Potato Salad (page 231) or coleslaw at a family gathering was like choosing between Prince and Michael Jackson. Even though they both delivered the good vibes that make you want to dance, just one captured the deep flavor and texture I craved. But I've come to appreciate the possibilities that Michael Jackson—uh, I mean coleslaw—offers. For starters, red cabbage, which looks more purple, is an immune-booster rich in antioxidant vitamin C. The carrots, too, add beautiful color and contain the antioxidant beta-carotene, which protects your eyes. I prefer to make this dish a few hours ahead of time, allowing the veggies to soften in the apple cider vinegar dressing and vegan mayo, which makes coleslaw creamy. I also added pickled red onions for the tang I love. Salting the cabbage and carrots is the first step to release their water and prevent the coleslaw from becoming watery.

Place a cabbage wedge cut-side down on a cutting board and use a sharp knife to cut lengthwise into fine ribbons. Repeat with the remaining wedges. (Alternatively, fit a food processor with the shredding disc, and working in batches, shred each wedge.)

Place the shredded cabbage and grated carrots in a large colander, sprinkle with 2 teaspoons of the salt, and use your hands to gently massage it into the cabbage mixture. Set aside to drain for 1 hour.

In a large bowl, whisk to combine the mayo, vinegar, celery seed, remaining ½ teaspoon salt, and the pepper. Add the cabbage, carrots, and pickled onions and toss thoroughly to coat. Refrigerate for 1 hour before serving.

NOTE: To quarter and core a cabbage, use a sharp knife to cut the head in half through the core, then cut the halves through the core again to make 4 quarters. Locate the core at the bottom of each quarter and use the knife to make two cuts at an angle on either side to cut out the wedge of tough core. Discard.

A MESS OF GREENS

3 tablespoons neutral oil, such as avocado or grapeseed

1 small red onion, finely chopped (about ½ cup)

2 garlic cloves, minced

1½ pounds leafy greens, such as collard greens (or a combination of collards, turnip, mustard greens, and kale), tough leaves, stems, and midribs removed, coarsely chopped (about 4½ cups packed)

¼ teaspoon fine sea salt

¼ teaspoon red chile flakes (optional)

1½ cups Veggie Broth (page 120), store-bought low-sodium vegetable broth, or water

Mothers, grandmothers, and *their* mothers have been cooking collards and other greens in Black communities for generations. A *mess* of greens refers to their size—a pile big enough to feed a whole family. Historically, collard greens, and other cruciferous greens, such as turnip, kale, and mustard greens, were easy to grow on plots of Southern plantation land permitted for private gardening among enslaved people. Traditional Southern-style collard greens always included the addition of ham hocks, bacon drippings, or lard to the greens, which, besides adding saturated animal fat, makes them salty.

My version includes a mess of my favorite greens, allowing the importance of collard greens in Black culture to shine without weighing down their wholesome goodness—because they are perfect as they are. Make this with just collards or mix in other greens for a range of flavors (see A Guide to Leafy Greens, page 188). Simmering the greens with liquid in a covered pot to trap the heat is a technique called braising—it makes the greens tender and won't dry them out.

In a large sauté pan with a tight-fitting lid, heat the oil over medium-high heat until it shimmers. Add the onion and cook, stirring now and then, for about 5 minutes, or until the onion is softened and translucent.

Stir in the garlic and cook about 1 more minute, or until fragrant. Add the greens, salt, chile flakes (if using), and broth. Increase the heat to high and bring to a boil. Reduce the heat to a simmer, cover, and cook, stirring now and then, for about 20 minutes, or until the greens are wilted and tender.

Arrange the greens on a serving platter and serve hot.

SWEET CORN BREAD

Neutral oil, such as avocado
or grapeseed, for greasing

1½ cups plain oat milk

1 tablespoon apple cider
vinegar

1 cup stone-ground medium-
grind cornmeal, such as Bob's
Red Mill

¾ cup white whole wheat
flour or ¾ cup 1:1 gluten-free
baking flour

½ cup organic coconut sugar

1½ teaspoons baking powder

½ teaspoon baking soda

¼ teaspoon fine sea salt

½ cup unsweetened
applesauce

6 tablespoons unsalted
vegan butter, melted and
cooled

The origin of Southern-style corn bread belongs to Indigenous Native American tribes. With corn as their most widely grown crop, Native Americans combined ground cornmeal with water and cooked it over an open fire, making a cake called *apone*, or "bread" in Algonquin, which became known in English as pone.

European settlers and enslaved African cooks made food that was heavily influenced by Native people, who would also make this style of cake, sometimes called hot water cakes, johnny cakes, or hoe cakes. Those enslaved Black cooks who had access to butter, eggs, and milk in plantation kitchens, evolved "corn pone" into a fluffier corn bread that later became a dish associated with traditional Southern soul food. There is an ongoing debate among Southerners about the "right" way to make corn bread, with or without the addition of sugar.

I believe the "right" way is the way *you* like to eat it, and I want sweet corn bread, which is what you get here! Making vegan buttermilk by combining vinegar and oat milk makes the corn bread fluffy and crumbly. Unsweetened applesauce as an egg replacer keeps it moist. Make corn bread croutons with day-old corn bread and add them to "Iron Man" Spinach and Broccoli Soup (page 180) and bowls (see EWEE Bowl Guide, page 186).

Preheat the oven to 400°F. Lightly grease an 8 × 8 baking pan with oil.

In a small bowl, stir to combine the milk and vinegar. Let sit for 10 minutes.

In a large bowl, whisk to combine the cornmeal, flour, coconut sugar, baking powder, baking soda, and salt. Stir in the applesauce and melted butter, then slowly add the milk mixture. Whisk until well combined. Pour the batter into the prepared pan.

Bake for 30 to 35 minutes, until the edges are browned and a toothpick inserted into the center comes out clean. Transfer to a cooling rack. Let cool for 30 minutes in the pan before serving.

FOR CORN BREAD CROUTONS: Preheat the oven to 350°F. Line a sheet pan with parchment paper or a silicone mat. Cut day-old corn bread into bite-sized pieces. Arrange the pieces on the sheet pan and gently toss with 1 tablespoon or more neutral oil. Bake until golden brown, 15 to 20 minutes, tossing halfway through.

"SOUL" BOWL

1½ cups A Mess of Greens (page 233), warmed, or 1½ cups fresh leafy greens, such as kale or mustard greens, dressed with your choice of dressing

1 serving Mac 'n' "Cheese" (page 242), warmed

1 serving BBQ Tofu "Ribs" (page 230), warmed

1 serving Buffalo Cauliflower "Chicken" Wings (optional; page 194)

½ cup cooked red kidney beans or canned beans, drained and rinsed

½ cup corn kernels, fresh or canned, drained and rinsed

An EWEE "Soul" Bowl is what you get when you throw a feast of plant-based "soul food" dishes and you have a little bit of something here and something there leftover. Warm them up and bring them together again. It's just for you.

Place the greens in a bowl. Arrange the mac 'n' "cheese" on top, followed by the tofu "ribs," "chicken" wings (if using), beans, and corn. That's it.

IN MY VEGAN COMMUNITY I SEE A LOT OF MOMS AND dads preparing tasty, whole-food vegan meals for their kids, and those little ones gobble them up with a smile. Maybe *you're* the head of the house and in charge of cooking meals. And I bet it's dinner that you have the most control over, right? If so, why not open palates to new flavors with EWEE meals as you move forward on your journey? The recipes in this chapter include some of the dinners my mom used to make me as a kid but that I now enjoy in a plant-based version. Shout out to my mom for always doing her best to protect me. And shout out to all y'all out there doing your best on your EWEE journey, and whose "why" includes protecting those they love.

(Auntie Valerie, if you're reading this, your Stuffed Peppers, page 256, got the EWEE makeover, but the vibes are all you: comforting and colorful.)

Feed your fam my EWEE versions of old-school traditional favorites in this chapter, such as "Beef" 'n' Bean Enchiladas (page 264) and Mom's Plant Loaf with Skillet Cabbage (page 258). You may find a new favorite to fall in love with, such as my Jackfruit Tacos with Mango-Corn Salsa and Avocado "Cream" (page 253). Taco Tuesday at your house will never be better—for you, your loved ones, animals, other people, and the environment.

Look out. I'm comin' over for dinner.

And I'm makin' Soft-Serve Banana Nice Cream (page 274) for dessert.

MAINS

SPAGHETTI 'N' BEET BALLS

I used to live a hard and fast life, pounding late-night Italian meatball subs and deli meat–filled sandwiches. It never even crossed my mind to cook a meal. This simple dish is my vegan take on a classic pairing and reminds me that I have accepted my past and now make choices that reflect who I am today. My beet marinara has the sweetness I like, and the beets, beans, and walnuts bind for a savory, comforting ball with lots of texture.

FOR THE BEET BALLS:

½ pound fresh beets, scrubbed, peeled, and quartered, or 1 8-ounce package cooked beets, quartered, or 1 14.5-ounce can no-salt-added beets, drained, rinsed, and quartered

½ cup walnuts, soaked and drained (see Note)

1 small yellow onion, finely chopped (about ½ cup)

1½ cups cooked red kidney beans or 1 15-ounce can, drained and rinsed

2 teaspoons Italian Seasoning (page 128)

1 teaspoon fine sea salt

⅔ cup whole wheat panko bread crumbs or gluten-free panko

FOR THE SPAGHETTI:

Fine sea salt

1 pound whole-grain spaghetti or gluten-free brown rice spaghetti

1½ cups Tomato and Beet Marinara (page 133) or store-bought marinara

¼ cup grated vegan Parmesan (from a block)

Preheat the oven to 375°F. Line a sheet pan with parchment paper or a silicone mat.

MAKE THE BEET BALLS: If using already cooked or canned beets, omit this step In a medium saucepan, combine the fresh beets with water to cover. Bring to a boil over medium-high heat. Reduce the heat to a simmer and cook for about 25 minutes, or until tender. Drain and rinse under cold water until cool enough to handle.

Add the beets (fresh cooked, precooked, or canned) to a food processor and process until finely chopped. Transfer to a medium bowl.

In the now-empty food processor (no need to wipe it out), combine the walnuts and onion and process until the walnuts are the texture of fine crumbs. Add the beans to the mixture and pulse 3 to 4 times, until just incorporated. Transfer the mixture to the bowl with the beets.

To the beet mixture in the bowl, add the Italian seasoning, salt, and panko and mix well to combine. With wet hands, form balls the size of golf balls (about 2 tablespoons each) and place them on the prepared sheet pan. You should have about 16 beet balls.

Transfer to the oven and bake for about 15 minutes, or until the beet balls are lightly browned on the bottom. Remove the sheet pan from the oven, gently flip the beet balls, and continue baking for about 10 more minutes, until the other side is lightly browned and the beet balls are firm. Remove from the oven and transfer to a plate.

MEANWHILE, MAKE THE SPAGHETTI: In a large pot, bring 4 quarts of generously salted water to a boil over high heat. Add the spaghetti and cook to al dente according to the package directions. Drain and return to the pot. Add the marinara and stir over low heat for about 5 minutes to warm through.

Serve the spaghetti topped with vegan parmesan and the beet balls alongside.

NOTE: Soaking the walnuts first softens their texture. Place the walnuts in a bowl and add enough hot water to cover by 1 inch. Soak for 20 minutes, then drain and proceed with the recipe.

KALE-L PESTO PASTA

FOR THE KALE-L PESTO:

¼ cup pine nuts, sunflower seeds, hemp hearts, unsalted almonds, or walnuts (see Note)

2½ cups (packed) roughly chopped kale (from about 1 bunch), spinach, beet greens, Swiss chard, or fresh basil leaves

½ cup nutritional yeast

2 garlic cloves, peeled but whole

½ teaspoon fine sea salt

1 cup extra-virgin olive oil

FOR THE PASTA:

Fine sea salt

1 pound whole-grain short pasta, such as bow ties, fusilli, or shells, or gluten-free brown rice pasta, such as Jovial

¼ cup grated vegan parmesan, for serving

Freshly cracked black pepper, for serving

My "Kale-L" pesto gets its name from the combination of kale and my favorite superhero, Superman, whose birth name was Kal-El. When I first started endurance racing, I would make this super-nutritious pasta a couple of days before the race, loading my body with carbohydrates to store and use for energy. I like to use raw kale for vibrant color and earthy flavor, but you can use another leafy green if you like, including fresh basil leaves for a more traditional pesto. Save the leafy tops of the beets, called beet greens, to make an earthy-sweet pesto, or try Swiss chard. I pair my pesto with a short pasta shape, such as bow ties, fusilli, or shells, because the thick pesto clings to their nooks. Explore possibilities by making pesto with any nut you have on hand, or make it nut-free by using sunflower seeds or hemp hearts. If you use walnuts or almonds, soaking them for 20 minutes first helps soften their texture.

MAKE THE KALE-L PESTO: In a food processor, combine the pine nuts, kale, nutritional yeast, garlic, salt, and olive oil and process for about 45 seconds, or until thick and smooth. Use a flexible spatula to scrape down the sides and pulse 2 to 3 more times to incorporate. Set aside.

COOK THE PASTA: Bring a large pot of generously salted water to a boil over high heat. Add the pasta and cook to al dente according to the package directions. Drain and return to the pot.

Stir the pesto into the pasta and warm over low heat for 2 minutes. Divide among bowls and garnish with grated vegan Parmesan and black pepper. Serve hot.

THINK EWEE: Add pesto to a Good Morning, Sweet Potato! (page 160) or bowl (see EWEE Bowl Guide, page 186). Use it as a sandwich spread or to make a pesto dip: Stir 2 tablespoons or more pesto into 1 cup thick plain plant-based yogurt.

NOTE: Soaking nuts first softens their texture for blending. Place the walnuts or almonds in a bowl and add enough hot water to cover by 1 inch. Soak for 20 minutes, then drain and proceed with the recipe.

MAC 'N' "CHEESE"

¾ cup raw cashews

Fine sea salt

1 pound whole-grain elbow macaroni or gluten-free brown rice macaroni

½ pound yellow potatoes, such as Yukon Gold, peeled and quartered (about 1¾ cups)

1 small yellow onion, quartered

1 large carrot, peeled and halved lengthwise

½ cup nutritional yeast, plus more to taste

1 tablespoon fresh lemon juice (from ½ lemon)

1 teaspoon smoked paprika

Freshly cracked black pepper

I enjoy mac 'n' "cheese" as a side dish, adding scoops to my "Soul" Bowl (page 236), and I also take it to the next level as a satisfying dinner. My version has a from-scratch "cheese" sauce base, made with creamy Yukon Gold potatoes and bright orange carrots, which, surprisingly, is just as colorful and sharp tasting as traditional dairy cheddar. Cashews offer the vegetable base a nondairy richness and comfort. This mac is a long way from the "cheesy spaghetti" my sisters and I made by melting Velveeta cheese into angel hair pasta!

Soak the cashews in a bowl of hot water while you cook the pasta (but for at least 20 minutes).

Bring a large pot of generously salted water to a boil over high heat. Add the macaroni and cook to al dente according to the package directions. Drain in a colander and return to the cooking pot.

Meanwhile, in a medium saucepan, combine the potatoes, onion, carrot, and 5 cups water. Bring to a boil, then reduce the heat to a simmer and cook for about 10 minutes, or until the potatoes are fork-tender.

Use a slotted spoon to transfer the vegetable mixture to a blender. (Reserve the hot water, you will use it to blend the sauce.) Drain the cashews and add to the blender along with the nutritional yeast, lemon juice, smoked paprika, and ½ cup of the reserved hot water. Blend for about 5 minutes, or until smooth and creamy. (Add more of the reserved hot water if needed to thin the sauce to your desired consistency.) Taste for seasoning, adding salt and pepper to taste, or more nutritional yeast for a "cheesier" taste, if desired.

Pour the "cheese sauce" over the drained macaroni and warm over low heat. Serve hot.

THINK EWEE: Serve this mac 'n' "cheese" as a side dish with Mom's Plant Loaf with Skillet Cabbage (page 258). Folding in ½ cup Mushroom "Bacon" (page 155) just before serving wouldn't be a bad idea.

MUSHROOM "CREAM" PENNE

Fine sea salt

1 pound whole-grain penne pasta or gluten-free brown rice penne

10 ounces mixed mushrooms, such as button, cremini, or shiitake, or a combination, tough stems trimmed, thinly sliced

2 tablespoons neutral oil, such as avocado or grapeseed

1 medium yellow onion, finely chopped (about 1 cup)

4 garlic cloves, minced

½ cup dry white wine, such as Sauvignon Blanc

⅓ cup Veggie Broth (page 120) or store-bought low-sodium vegetable broth

¾ cup Basic Cashew Cream (page 122)

1 tablespoon vegan butter

¼ teaspoon dried thyme

Freshly cracked black pepper

I used to hate mushrooms when I was a kid. Mushrooms—and onions, too—when grilled and shriveled felt like worms on my tongue . . . as if I knew what worms tasted like, right? For years, anything associated with soil was a turn-off. Can you believe it? But once I expanded my palate, I joined the Mushroom Mafia (it's just people who love mushrooms)! Mushrooms are loaded with fiber and micronutrients and, like tofu, they quickly absorb a marinade and provide a richly flavored dish.

Bring a large pot of generously salted water to a boil over high heat. Add the penne and cook to al dente according to the package directions. Drain in a colander and return to the pot.

Meanwhile, set a large cast-iron skillet over medium heat. Add the mushrooms in a single layer and cook, undisturbed, for about 5 minutes, or until beginning to brown. Add ½ teaspoon salt, stir, and continue cooking about 3 minutes, until the mushrooms are tender and their liquid is absorbed. Continue cooking, stirring occasionally, for another 2 minutes, or until tender. Transfer to a plate.

Add the oil to the same skillet and heat over medium heat until it shimmers. Add the onion and cook, stirring now and then, for about 5 minutes, or until softened. Stir in the garlic and cook for 1 minute, or until fragrant.

Add the white wine, increase the heat to high, bring to a boil, and cook for 3 to 5 minutes to reduce the wine by half. Stir in the broth and cashew cream, reduce the heat to a simmer, and cook for about 5 minutes, or until the sauce thickens.

Stir in the butter until melted, about 2 minutes. Stir in the thyme and reserved cooked mushrooms. Taste for seasoning, adding pepper to taste and more salt if needed.

Pour the mushroom cream sauce over the pasta and warm over low heat. Serve hot.

A Guide to Mushrooms

There are more than ten thousand known species of mushrooms, and the edible ones contain all nine essential amino acids and have potent anti-inflammatory and cancer-fighting properties.

MUSHROOM	FLAVOR AND TEXTURE	SUPERPOWER	RECOMMENDED PREPARATION
Button or white	Mild and neutral tasting with a hearty texture	High in potassium, which helps maintain our body fluid levels (223 mg per sliced cup)	Mushroom "Cream" Penne (page 243), Mushroom Brown Gravy (page 263)
Cremini	Also known as baby bellas, they are less mature portobello mushrooms. More savory tasting, darker in color, and meatier than button mushrooms.	High in ergothioneine, a potent amino acid linked to preventing age-related illnesses. Rich in folate, which is essential for healthy cell growth, especially during pregnancy.	Add to bowls (see EWEE Bowl Guide, page 186), Mushroom "Cream" Penne (page 243), or Mushroom Brown Gravy (page 263)
Oyster	Mild tasting, lightly savory, with a hint of saline—like oysters! Delicate texture.	High in niacin, a micronutrient that keeps your nervous system, digestive system, and skin healthy	BBQ Pulled Mushroom Sandwiches (page 222)
Portobello	Fully grown cremini mushrooms with wide, firm, dense caps and deep savory flavor	Rich in the B vitamins niacin and riboflavin, which are essential in energy metabolism	Mushroom "Bacon" (page 155)
Shiitake, fresh and dried	Strong, earthy flavor with a spongy texture when fresh	Rich in copper, which helps your body make red blood cells and keeps nerve cells and your immune system healthy	Mushroom Brown Gravy (page 263), Mushroom "Cream" Penne (page 243), Mushroom Ramen Noodle Bowls (page 184)

Serves 4

SPAGHETTI SQUASH WITH CAULIFLOWER ALFREDO

FOR THE SPAGHETTI SQUASH:

2 medium spaghetti squash, halved lengthwise and seeded

½ teaspoon fine sea salt

¼ teaspoon freshly cracked black pepper, plus more to taste

When I was a kid, a fancy dinner out was ordering thick and creamy fettuccine Alfredo with chicken or shrimp at Red Lobster. If we craved it at home, we'd buy jarred Alfredo sauce that looked more like a white gravy since it's full of oil and heavy cream. I loved it anyway. But at its best, fettuccine or linguine with Alfredo sauce should be silky and cheesy—not heavy and gloppy. My version of fettuccine Alfredo is smooth and light and served over spaghetti squash, which, when roasted, has a deeply sweet flavor and texture that holds up like spaghetti. Cashews are the base for this silky sauce that gets an extra creamy boost from adding cauliflower and chickpeas. Nutritional yeast, which has the umami flavor of Parmesan, gives my sauce a rich, cheesy flavor. This plant-based version is so good, it's almost sinful.

Preheat the oven to 425°F. Line a sheet pan with parchment paper or a silicone mat.

ROAST THE SPAGHETTI SQUASH: Season the insides of the squash with the salt and pepper and place them cut-side down on the pan. Roast for 35 to 40 minutes, until the squash strands are tender. Check for doneness by removing from the oven and using tongs to turn over one half. Drag a fork across the top of the squash. If you can pull away spaghetti-like strands, it is ready. (If you prefer the strands to be softer, return to the oven and continue cooking in 5-minute increments, until it reaches your preferred level of tenderness.)

FOR THE CAULIFLOWER ALFREDO:

½ cup raw cashews

1 tablespoon neutral oil, such as avocado or grapeseed

1 small yellow onion, finely chopped (about ½ cup)

2 garlic cloves, minced

1½ cups small cauliflower florets (about 8 ounces)

¼ cup cooked chickpeas/ garbanzo beans (see Bean Cooking Chart, page 141) or ¼ cup canned chickpeas, drained and rinsed

2 tablespoons nutritional yeast

½ teaspoon smoked paprika

2 teaspoons fresh lemon juice (from ¼ lemon)

½ teaspoon fine sea salt, plus more to taste

MEANWHILE, MAKE THE CAULIFLOWER ALFREDO: Soak the cashews in a bowl of hot water for 20 minutes.

In a medium skillet, heat the oil over medium-high heat until it shimmers. Add the onion and cook, stirring now and then, for 3 to 5 minutes, until softened. Stir in the garlic and cook for about 1 minute, or until fragrant. Remove from the heat.

In a medium saucepan, combine the cauliflower and 3 cups water. Bring to a boil over high heat. Reduce the heat to a simmer and cook for 5 to 7 minutes, or until the cauliflower is fork-tender.

Use a slotted spoon to transfer the cauliflower to a blender (reserve the hot water, you will use it to blend the sauce). Drain the cashews and add to the blender along with the onion/garlic mixture, chickpeas, nutritional yeast, smoked paprika, lemon juice, salt, pepper, and ¼ cup of the reserved hot water. Blend for about 5 minutes, or until smooth and creamy. Add more of the reserved water, if needed, to thin the sauce to your desired consistency. Taste for seasoning and add salt and pepper as needed.

Discard any remaining water in the saucepan and wipe it dry. Pour the Alfredo sauce to the now-empty saucepan and warm over low heat.

Using tongs, transfer the squash to a plate, spoon the sauce over the top, and serve immediately.

THINK EWEE: Make this sauce to serve over your favorite whole-grain fettuccine or gluten-free noodle.

ALMOND-CRUSTED TOFU "SALMON"

1 16-ounce package firm tofu, drained and pressed (see Tofu Prep, page 103)

1 cup Beet Juice (page 167) or store-bought cold-pressed no-sugar-added beet juice, such as Pomona

¼ cup rice vinegar

2 tablespoons liquid amino acids, reduced-sodium soy sauce, or tamari

1 tablespoon kelp powder or 5 organic nori sheets, powdered (see Note, page 198)

2 garlic cloves, minced

½ cup almonds, soaked and drained (see Note)

⅓ cup whole wheat panko bread crumbs or gluten-free panko

Spicy Sweet Green Beans (page 250), for serving

I was inspired to make tofu "salmon" after ordering it for vegan take-out. I added my spin to it by creating a marinade with beet juice, which turns the tofu pink. And I made it garlicky. You can get fancy and add fake salmon "skin" by attaching nori sheets to the bottom of the tofu—no judgment, but that's not my thing. Instead, I keep it simple and roll the tofu in a coating of crushed almonds and panko for a baked fish vibe! The moist and tender tofu gets a briny "from the sea" flavor from the addition of kelp powder in the marinade. I love it served with spicy sweet green beans.

Cut the tofu lengthwise into 4 thick slabs. Each slab will be about 5 × 2 inches and about 1 inch thick. Make 6 diagonal cuts (being careful not to cut all the way through) on top of each piece—for both a "flaky" appearance and to allow the marinade to permeate.

In a large bowl, stir together the beet juice, vinegar, liquid aminos, kelp powder, and garlic. Add the tofu and turn to coat. Cover the bowl and refrigerate for at least 1 hour and up to overnight.

In a food processor, combine the almonds and panko and pulse 4 to 5 times, until the almonds are finely ground and the mixture looks like sand. Transfer the mixture to a shallow bowl.

Preheat the oven to 400°F. Line a sheet pan with parchment paper or a silicone mat.

Working with one piece of marinated tofu at a time, dip the tofu into the almond mixture and turn to coat on all sides, pressing to create a crust. Arrange the pieces on the sheet pan.

Bake for about 15 minutes, or until the underside is golden brown. Remove the pan from the oven, gently flip, and continue baking for another 15 minutes, until golden and crispy.

Serve immediately with green beans alongside.

NOTE: Soaking almonds first helps soften their texture. Place the almonds in a bowl and add enough hot water to cover by 1 inch. Soak for 20 minutes, then drain and proceed with the recipe.

SPICY SWEET GREEN BEANS

1 pound green beans or sugar snap peas, ends trimmed, or 1 pound broccoli florets, florets cut into 1-inch pieces (from 2 crowns)

½ teaspoon fine sea salt

¼ teaspoon freshly cracked black pepper

2 tablespoons toasted sesame oil

2 garlic cloves, minced

2 tablespoons liquid amino acids, reduced-sodium soy sauce, or tamari

2 tablespoons rice vinegar

2 tablespoons maple syrup

1 teaspoon sriracha

¼ cup sesame seeds, for garnish

Fresh green beans—also known as string beans and snap beans—are available year-round but best in the summer. Look for bright, firm, smooth green beans that snap when you bend them. This Asian-inspired sauce gets heat from sriracha and sweet from maple syrup for a veggie sidekick to go with almost every tofu dish I can think of, especially Almond-Crusted Tofu "Salmon" (page 248), BBQ Tofu "Ribs" (page 230), and Orange "Chicken" (page 251). The sauce is great over roasted broccoli florets, too, so I've included that option here! To keep the vegetables from getting mushy as they roast, spread them out on the pan. If piled on top of each other, they will steam instead of roast.

Preheat the oven to 425°F. Line a sheet pan with parchment paper or a silicone mat.

Arrange the vegetables on the prepared baking sheet in an even layer. Sprinkle with the salt and pepper and toss well. Roast for about 10 minutes, or until the vegetables begin to soften.

Meanwhile, in a small bowl, stir together the sesame oil, garlic, liquid aminos, vinegar, maple syrup, and sriracha.

Remove the sheet pan from the oven, pour the sauce over the vegetables, toss to coat, and return to the oven. Continue roasting until the vegetables are crisp-tender and slightly charred in spots, another 8 to 10 minutes for the beans and 10 to 12 minutes for the broccoli.

Sprinkle the sesame seeds over the top before serving.

ORANGE "CHICKEN"

FOR THE "CHICKEN":

1 16-ounce package extra-firm tofu, frozen overnight (see Note), then thawed the next day in the refrigerator, drained, and blotted dry

¼ cup cornstarch

¼ cup neutral oil, such as avocado or grapeseed

FOR THE ORANGE SAUCE:

1 tablespoon grated orange zest

1 cup orange juice (from about 4 large oranges) or store-bought cold-pressed organic orange juice

2 tablespoons liquid amino acids, reduced-sodium soy sauce, or tamari

2 tablespoons rice vinegar

2 tablespoons maple syrup

1 teaspoon sriracha

2 small garlic cloves, minced

¼ teaspoon ground ginger

1 tablespoon cornstarch

FOR SERVING:

2 cups cooked brown rice or other whole grain, such as quinoa or farro (see Grain Cooking Chart, page 139)

¼ cup sesame seeds

My favorite dish to order when my mom could afford to take us out for Chinese food was bite-sized crispy orange-glazed chicken over white rice. VeGreen Restaurant in Atlanta gives me my vegan orange "chicken" fix. But I have also learned to make a healthy orange tofu "chicken" in my EWEE kitchen. It is super crispy and costs a fraction of the restaurant dish.

The secret to making this? Freeze the tofu! Once thawed, the ice crystals that formed inside the block of tofu melt and make it chewy and spongy. When baked, the tofu crisps in the oven like you wouldn't believe. The orange sauce hits the sour, sweet, and tangy flavors I love. Serve over brown rice—or now's a good time to try a new whole grain (see Batch Cooking Whole Grains 101, page 138).

Preheat the oven to 425°F. Line a sheet pan with parchment paper or a silicone mat.

MAKE THE "CHICKEN": Using your hands, tear the thawed tofu into large, equal-sized pieces and place them in a bowl. Scatter the cornstarch over them and gently toss to coat.

Arrange the pieces in a single layer on the sheet pan and drizzle with the oil. Bake for about 20 minutes, or until browned and crispy.

MEANWHILE, MAKE THE ORANGE SAUCE: In a medium saucepan, whisk to combine the orange zest, orange juice, liquid aminos, vinegar, maple syrup, sriracha, garlic, and ginger. Bring the sauce to a boil over medium-high heat. Reduce the heat to low and cook for 1 minute. Whisk in the cornstarch and continue cooking, whisking constantly, for about 30 seconds, or until the sauce bubbles and thickens.

Remove the sheet pan from the oven and transfer the "chicken" pieces to the saucepan and gently toss to coat.

TO SERVE: Spoon the "chicken" over brown rice and top with sesame seeds.

NOTE: To freeze tofu, place an unopened package in the freezer overnight. Thaw in the refrigerator the next day. You will notice that the color turns yellow while frozen—that's normal—it will fade once it thaws. Drain excess water and blot dry with a clean towel—no need to press it.

"CLEAN" DIRTY RICE

2 tablespoons neutral oil, such as avocado or grapeseed

1 small yellow onion, finely chopped (about ½ cup)

2 celery stalks with leaves, finely chopped

1 cup chopped bell pepper (about 1 medium pepper)

½ teaspoon fine sea salt

¼ teaspoon freshly cracked black pepper

10 ounces mushrooms, such as button, cremini, or a combination, tough stems removed, thinly sliced

½ teaspoon smoked paprika

2 tablespoons liquid amino acids, reduced-sodium soy sauce, or tamari

2 cups brown rice

4 cups Veggie Broth (page 120) or store-bought low-sodium vegetable broth

1½ cups cooked kidney beans (see Bean Cooking Chart, page 141) or 1 15.5-ounce can kidney beans, drained and rinsed

4 scallions (green onions), white and green parts, finely chopped, for serving

When I was incarcerated in Duluth, Minnesota, an inmate from one of my "cars" (a brotherhood of inmates who are typically from the same town) and I would partner at least twice a week to make our version of "dirty rice." The dish has its origins in Cajun cooking and gets its name from the muddled color the rice takes on from spices and ground meat. The daunting process went like this: We would place some rice, and whatever seasonings we could find, in one of the plastic bags given to us each week for trash cans in our cells. Then we would add 180°F water from the coffeemaker in our unit, tie the bag, and then toss it back and forth for ten to fifteen minutes so the rice could "cook." I have pots now. And my one-pot dirty rice—full of "meaty" mushrooms, kidney beans, brown rice and the "holy trinity" of bell peppers, onions, and celery—leaves me feeling clean.

In a large soup pot, heat the oil over medium heat until it shimmers. Add the onion, celery, bell peppers, salt, and black pepper and cook for about 5 minutes, or until the vegetables are softened. Add the mushrooms, smoked paprika, and liquid aminos and continue cooking for about 5 minutes, or until the mushrooms change color from light to dark brown and the liquid is absorbed.

Stir in the rice and toast, stirring, for about 1 minute, or until fragrant. Add the broth and bring the mixture to boil. Reduce the heat to a simmer, cover, and cook for 20 to 22 minutes, until the rice has absorbed the broth and is tender.

Stir in the kidney beans, then remove the pot from the heat and let sit, covered, for 5 minutes. Serve topped with the scallions.

Serves 4

JACKFRUIT TACOS WITH MANGO-CORN SALSA AND AVOCADO "CREAM"

FOR THE AVOCADO "CREAM":

1 medium avocado, halved and pitted

2 garlic cloves, chopped

2 tablespoons chopped fresh cilantro leaves and tender stems

2 tablespoons fresh lime juice (from 2 limes)

½ teaspoon ground cumin

¼ cup Cashew Mayo (page 123) or ¼ cup vegan mayonnaise

FOR THE JACKFRUIT:

1 20-ounce can "young" or unripe green jackfruit in brine, drained and rinsed

2 tablespoons neutral oil, such as avocado or grapeseed

1 small yellow onion, finely chopped (about ½ cup)

1 garlic clove, minced

1½ teaspoons Taco Seasoning (page 128)

¼ teaspoon freshly cracked black pepper

¼ cup Veggie Broth (page 120) or store-bought low-sodium vegetable broth

FOR SERVING:

8 6-inch corn tortillas, warmed

Mango-Corn Salsa (page 255)

I love tacos with jackfruit because its texture is "meaty," easy to shred, and much lighter and better for you than pork or chicken. Here, the fresh mango and corn salsa get a hit of fresh cilantro and lime, and the avocado "cream" brings it all home. The salsa and avocado "cream" can be made up to 1 day in advance.

MAKE THE AVOCADO "CREAM": Scoop the avocado flesh into a blender or food processor. Add the garlic, cilantro, lime juice, cumin, and mayo and process until smooth and creamy. Transfer to a small bowl. Cover and refrigerate until serving.

MEANWHILE, MAKE THE JACKFRUIT: Jackfruit pieces contain a tender core attached to a tougher stem. Shred the core by breaking it apart in your hands, discarding the seeds. Use a knife to roughly chop the tougher stem. Set aside.

In a medium skillet, heat the oil over medium heat. Add the onion and cook, stirring now and then, until the onion is softened, about 5 minutes. Stir in the garlic and cook until fragrant, about 1 more minute. Add the jackfruit, taco seasoning, pepper, and broth and increase the heat to medium-high. Cook, stirring frequently, for about 8 minutes, or until the liquid is absorbed and some of the edges of the jackfruit begin to crisp. Remove from the heat and set aside.

TO SERVE: Divide the jackfruit evenly among the tortillas and top with salsa and avocado "cream."

(recipe continues)

MANGO-CORN SALSA

Makes about 4 cups

Eat this on its own as a snack, if you like, with some blue corn tortilla chips.

1 large mango, cut into ½-inch cubes (1½ cups)

½ cup corn kernels, fresh (from about 1 ear) or thawed frozen corn

1 cup cooked black beans (see Bean Cooking Chart, page 141) or 1 cup canned black beans, drained and rinsed

½ small red onion, finely chopped (about ¼ cup)

¼ cup fresh cilantro leaves and tender stems, finely chopped

2 jalapeño peppers (seeded, if desired), chopped, or ½ cup chopped bell pepper (about ½ medium pepper)

2 tablespoons fresh lime juice (from 2 limes)

1 teaspoon fine sea salt

¼ teaspoon freshly cracked black pepper

2 tablespoons maple syrup

In a medium bowl, stir to combine the mango, corn, beans, onion, cilantro, jalapeños, lime juice, salt, black pepper, and maple syrup. Cover the bowl and refrigerate until serving.

AUNTIE VALERIE'S STUFFED PEPPERS

2 tablespoons neutral oil, such as avocado or grapeseed, plus more for greasing

½ small yellow onion, finely chopped (about ¼ cup)

2 medium celery stalks with leaves, finely chopped

2 medium tomatoes, such as plum or Roma, finely chopped

4 garlic cloves, thinly sliced

½ cup cooked green lentils (see Bean Cooking Chart, page 141) or ½ cup canned lentils, drained and rinsed

½ cup cooked quinoa (see Grain Cooking Chart, page 139) or ½ cup frozen quinoa (see Note)

¼ cup finely chopped fresh parsley

¼ cup finely chopped fresh basil

½ teaspoon fine sea salt

¼ teaspoon freshly cracked black pepper

4 bell peppers, halved lengthwise through the stem and seeded (see Notes)

¼ cup Sour Cashew Cream (page 123), for serving

My Auntie Valerie, my mom's youngest sister, made her stuffed green peppers at least once a month when we all lived in our family building on North Lockwood Ave and West Crystal Street. (For years, I didn't know any other color pepper existed; now I love to use red, yellow, and orange peppers interchangeably; they are all high in vitamin C and iron.) While Aunt Valerie stuffed her green peppers with ground beef and rice, I fill mine with a hearty quinoa/lentil mixture enhanced with aromatic veggies and fresh herbs.

Preheat the oven to 400° F. Lightly grease a 9 × 13-inch baking dish with oil.

In a medium skillet, heat the oil over medium heat until it shimmers. Add the onion, celery, and tomatoes and cook, stirring occasionally, for about 5 minutes, or until the vegetables are softened. Stir in the garlic and cook until fragrant, about 1 more minute.

Scrape the mixture into a large bowl and add the lentils, quinoa, parsley, basil, salt, and black pepper. Stir to mix well.

Arrange the 8 bell pepper halves cut side up in the prepared baking dish. Dividing evenly, fill them with the lentil mixture. Bake for 15 to 20 minutes, until the pepper skin softens and ripples.

Serve the stuffed peppers drizzled with sour cashew cream.

NOTES: If using frozen quinoa, thaw it on the counter for 30 minutes before starting this recipe.

Use a spoon to scrape out the seeds and ribs from the cut peppers.

MOM'S PLANT LOAF WITH SKILLET CABBAGE

2 tablespoons neutral oil, such as avocado or grapeseed, plus more for greasing

½ small yellow onion, finely chopped (about ½ cup)

2 garlic cloves, minced

1 medium carrot, finely chopped (about ½ cup)

1 celery stalk with leaves, finely chopped (about ½ cup)

2 tablespoons chopped fresh parsley

1 tablespoon dried thyme

1½ teaspoons fine sea salt

1 teaspoon freshly cracked black pepper

Walnut and Mushroom "Meat" (page 136)

2 cups cooked brown rice, quinoa, farro, or barley (see Grain Cooking Chart, page 139)

½ cup tomato paste

1 cup whole wheat panko bread crumbs or gluten-free panko

1 cup Beet BBQ Sauce (page 132) or store-bought no-sugar-added vegan BBQ sauce

Skillet Cabbage (recipe follows), for serving

When I was growing up, my mom would make her meatloaf and serve it covered in a tangy and sweet BBQ sauce with mac 'n' cheese and skillet cabbage on the side—it was great! My plant loaf is hearty like hers, from a base of walnut and mushroom "meat" seasoned with Italian seasoning, and blended with veggies, chewy whole grains, and herbs.

Preheat the oven to 350°F. Lightly grease a 9 × 5-inch nonstick loaf pan with neutral oil and line with parchment paper with overhang along the two long sides.

In a large cast-iron skillet, heat the oil over medium heat until it shimmers. Add the onion, garlic, carrot, and celery and cook, stirring now and then, for about 5 minutes, or until the vegetables are softened. Stir in the parsley, thyme, salt, and pepper and continue cooking about 30 more seconds. Remove from the heat.

Scrape the cooked vegetables into a large bowl. Add the walnut and mushroom "meat," brown rice, tomato paste, and panko. Stir until you have a homogenous mixture. Spoon the mixture into the loaf pan, using the back of the spoon to make it compact.

Cover the pan with foil and bake for about 30 minutes, or until the plant loaf is firm.

Remove the pan from the oven, discard the foil, and pour the BBQ sauce over the top. Return to the oven uncovered and bake for about 10 minutes more, until the sauce is bubbling and looks like a glaze. Transfer the loaf pan to a cooling rack and cool for 15 minutes.

To serve, lift the loaf out of the pan with the overhanging parchment paper. Slice and serve with cabbage alongside.

THINK EWEE: For a comforting plant-based meal, serve the plant loaf alongside Creamy Mashed Potatoes with Mushroom Brown Gravy (page 262).

SKILLET CABBAGE

Serves 4

1 medium head green cabbage (about 2 pounds), wilted outer leaves discarded, quartered, and cored (see Note)

2 tablespoons neutral oil, such as avocado or grapeseed

1 tablespoon fine sea salt

3 tablespoons apple cider vinegar

Place a cabbage wedge cut side down on a cutting board and use a sharp knife to cut lengthwise into fine ribbons. Repeat with the remaining wedges. (Alternatively, fit a food processor with the shredding disc and work in batches to shred the wedges.)

In a large cast-iron skillet, heat the oil over medium-high heat until it shimmers. Add the cabbage and cook, stirring often, for about 6 minutes, or until it begins to wilt. Sprinkle the salt across the top and reduce the heat to medium-low. Continue cooking and stirring for about 5 minutes, or until softened.

Add the vinegar and continue cooking and stirring for another 5 minutes, until some of the edges are browned. Remove from the heat.

NOTE: To quarter and core a cabbage, use a sharp knife to cut the head vertically through the middle or core, then cut the halves through the core again to make 4 quarters. Locate the core at the bottom of each quarter and use the knife to make two cuts at an angle on either side to cut out the wedge of tough core. Discard.

CREAMY MASHED POTATOES WITH MUSHROOM BROWN GRAVY

3 pounds Yukon Gold potatoes, peeled and cut into ¾-inch-thick rounds

3 teaspoons fine sea salt, plus more to taste

3 tablespoons vegan butter

1½ cups oat milk

1 teaspoon freshly cracked black pepper, plus more to taste

Mushroom Brown Gravy (recipe follows)

There is no reason to give up creamy mashed potatoes and gravy on your journey—but I guarantee there is a better way to enjoy them. In my EWEE kitchen, vegan drives the car, but delicious calls the front seat. For the mashed potatoes: Swap the dairy for plant-based milk and vegan butter—you won't taste the difference. And here's a trick to get your mashed potatoes pillowy soft: First, set a fine-mesh sieve over a large bowl, then working in batches, pass hand-mashed potatoes through the sieve using the back of a wooden spoon, scraping the bottom of the sieve as you work. It takes a little elbow grease, but your "why" is worth it.

In a large pot, combine the potatoes with enough cold water to cover by 1 inch and season with 2 teaspoons of the salt. Bring to a boil over high heat. Reduce the heat to a simmer and cook for about 10 minutes, or until fork-tender. Drain.

In the now-empty pot, melt the butter over low heat. Whisk in the milk, increase the heat to medium-low, and bring the mixture to a simmer. Turn off the heat.

Return the potatoes to the pot and use whatever tool you have on hand—a potato masher, large fork, or balloon whisk—to mash them until they are lump free and creamy. (Alternatively, pass the potatoes through a ricer, back into the pot, and stir well, until smooth and creamy. Or use a fine-mesh sieve, as directed in the headnote.) Season with the remaining 1 teaspoon salt and the pepper. Adjust the seasoning to taste.

Serve the potatoes family-style covered with warmed brown gravy.

MUSHROOM BROWN GRAVY

Makes about 3 cups

We gotta talk about the gravy. My plant-based version of traditional brown gravy is silky-smooth with a glossy shine and a "lick the spoon" umami flavor from nutritional yeast, liquid amino acids, and mushrooms.

1 tablespoon vegan butter

3 tablespoons cornstarch

3 cups Veggie Broth (page 120) or store-bought low-sodium vegetable broth

½ teaspoon onion powder

½ teaspoon garlic powder

¼ cup nutritional yeast

3 tablespoons liquid amino acids, reduced-sodium soy sauce, or tamari

1 teaspoon Dijon mustard or ¼ teaspoon mustard powder

Fine sea salt and freshly cracked black pepper

1 tablespoon neutral oil, such as avocado or grapeseed

6 ounces mushrooms, such as button, cremini, shiitake, or a combination, tough stems removed, thinly sliced

In a medium saucepan, melt the butter over medium-low heat. Once the butter is melted, add the cornstarch, whisking vigorously until a thick paste forms, a few seconds.

Add 1 cup of the broth and continue whisking for about 30 seconds, or until all the lumps are dissolved. Add the remaining 2 cups broth, the onion powder, garlic powder, nutritional yeast, liquid aminos, and mustard, whisking vigorously to incorporate.

Increase the heat to high and bring to a boil, then reduce the heat to a simmer and cook, whisking now and then, for about 5 minutes, or until the gravy is thick enough to coat the back of a spoon and is smooth and glossy. Taste for seasoning, adding salt and pepper, as needed. Remove from the heat and set aside.

In a large nonstick skillet, heat the oil over medium-high heat until it shimmers. Arrange the mushrooms in a single layer and cook, undisturbed, for about 3 minutes, or until beginning to brown. Add ¼ teaspoon salt and continue cooking, stirring now and then, for about 2 minutes more, or until they release their liquid and soften.

Stir the mushrooms into the prepared brown gravy and set aside.

THINK EWEE: Enjoy mushroom brown gravy over anything else you like, such as Homie Hash Browns (page 158).

"BEEF" 'N' BEAN ENCHILADAS

FOR THE ENCHILADA SAUCE:

3 tablespoons white whole wheat flour or 1:1 gluten-free baking flour

½ teaspoon chili powder

½ teaspoon ground cumin

1 tablespoon unsweetened cocoa powder (see Note, page 149)

½ teaspoon fine sea salt

¼ teaspoon freshly cracked black pepper

3 tablespoons neutral oil, such as avocado or grapeseed

1 6-ounce can tomato paste

2½ cups Veggie Broth (page 120) or store-bought low-sodium vegetable broth

When I was a kid, for my birthday I always asked my mom to make me her special enchiladas. The recipe came from my mom's grandmother and her connection to her Mexican roots, but my mom has a special touch with enchiladas—her sauce is the real deal. The secret to its deep flavor is the spices and cocoa powder, and to really cook down the tomato paste to bring out its umami flavor. The enchilada filling is loaded with fresh veggies, beans, and plant-based walnut and mushroom "meat," making them worthy of a celebration. Warming the tortillas in oil for a few seconds prevents them from absorbing too much sauce and falling apart!

Preheat the oven to 350°F. Set out a 9 × 13-inch baking dish. Set out a large cutting board.

MAKE THE ENCHILADA SAUCE: In a small bowl, whisk to combine the flour, chili powder, cumin, cocoa, salt, and pepper. In a medium saucepan, heat the oil over low heat until it shimmers. Add the flour mixture and cook, whisking constantly, until a smooth paste forms and the mixture is fragrant, about 1 minute.

Add the tomato paste and cook, whisking constantly, for about 30 seconds, or until the color of the tomato paste turns deep red. Slowly pour in the broth, whisking constantly to prevent lumps from forming. Increase the heat to high and bring to a boil. Reduce the heat to low and cook for about 5 minutes, or until the mixture is thick enough to coat the back of a wooden spoon. Ladle some of the enchilada sauce on the bottom of the baking dish—just enough for a thin coating. Set aside.

FOR THE ENCHILADAS:

2 tablespoons plus ¼ cup neutral oil, such as avocado or grapeseed

1 small red onion, finely chopped (about ½ cup)

1½ cups chopped bell peppers (about 1½ medium peppers)

2 garlic cloves, minced

8 10-inch corn tortillas

1½ cups Walnut and Mushroom "Meat," (page 136)

1½ cups cooked black beans (see Bean Cooking Chart, page 141) or 1 15.5-ounce can, drained and rinsed

1½ cups vegan Mexican-style cheese shreds

FOR SERVING:

Fresh cilantro leaves

Quick Pickled Red Onions (page 132)

EZ Guacamole (page 130) or sliced avocado

½ cup Sour Cashew Cream (page 123) or vegan sour cream

MAKE THE ENCHILADAS: In a cast-iron skillet, heat 2 tablespoons of the oil over medium heat until it shimmers. Add the onion and bell peppers and cook, stirring now and then, for about 5 minutes, or until the peppers are softened. Stir in the garlic and cook for 1 more minute, or until fragrant. Transfer the onion/pepper mixture to a small bowl.

In the now-empty skillet, warm the remaining ¼ cup oil over very low heat. Working with one tortilla at a time, use tongs to dip them in the warm oil for 5 to 8 seconds, until the tortilla is warmed through. Immediately dip the tortilla into the saucepan of enchilada sauce and turn to coat, then transfer to the prepared cutting board. Repeat with the remaining tortillas, laying them flat on the cutting board—it's okay to stack them if they don't all fit.

Working with one tortilla at a time, and using the cutting board as your work surface, place 3 tablespoons of "meat" mixture down the center, followed by 3 tablespoons of the onion/pepper mixture, 3 tablespoons of the beans, and 3 tablespoons of the cheese. Roll the tortilla by pinching in the sides and folding it over to close. Place the rolled tortilla seam-side down in the prepared baking dish. Repeat the process with the remaining tortillas.

Cover the tortillas with the remaining enchilada sauce and scatter the remaining ½ cup of cheese across the top. Bake for about 20 minutes, or until the cheese is melted and lightly browned.

TO SERVE: Top the enchiladas with cilantro and pickled red onions. Serve the guacamole and sour cashew cream alongside.

When I was seven—long before I was allowed to flame up the stove to make my own grits—I was allowed to bake. I'd get two boxes of Jiffy brownie mix (they cost around 45 cents a box!), a couple of eggs, and a bit of water and turn out rich, chocolatey brownies. I would eat the whole batch in one sitting. Vegan treats are all about nostalgia for me—and I am sure they are for you, too. Who doesn't crave a bite of homemade birthday cake? Or an old-fashioned Lemon Loaf (page 272) or Peach Cobbler (page 280) your grandma might have thrown down, like mine did.

I'm not gonna lie; I love baked goods—you tell me you found a place that sells a great vegan blueberry muffin, and I am on it! But the truth is too much sugar, in any form, harms our health, so I limit my baked goods, saving them for a special occasion. When I do bake, I stick to molasses, maple syrup, and coconut sugar for my recipes since, unlike refined white sugar, which has no nutritional value, these sugars enter our bloodstream more slowly and contain trace vitamins, minerals, and antioxidants. But I also thought it would be a good idea to include whole-food sweet treats that rely on Mother Nature's sweetest treat—fruits. Try Banana Nice Cream (page 274) or Date and Fig Energy Balls (page 277) for a snack.

And the next time you roll up to a picnic, nobody will turn down the Roasted Stone Fruit with Sweet Cashew Cream (page 269) you're gonna bring—the soft, juicy fruit and creamy hit of cashew cream is a winner. That's right; this chapter is a bit of the old "feels," and a segue to starting new sweet treat traditions.

SWEET TREATS

BROWNIES IN A "JIFFY"

3 flax eggs or 3 egg
replacers, such as Bob's Red
Mill (see page 101)

Coconut oil for the baking
pan

1 cup white whole wheat flour
or 1:1 gluten-free baking flour

⅔ cup unsweetened natural
cocoa powder

1 teaspoon baking powder

¼ teaspoon fine sea salt

½ cup plain oat milk

1½ cups coconut sugar

½ cup coconut cooking oil or
regular coconut oil, melted
(see Note)

1 teaspoon pure vanilla
extract

I created this fudgy vegan brownie version as a tribute to that little boy inside of me who did what he could with what he was working with before the Universe set him on a path of "do no harm." One bite takes me back (in a jiffy?) to our house in the Austin neighborhood. I no longer eat the whole pan in one sitting, as I did in junior high. Instead, I save them for a rare vegan treat. Here's proof that with the right ingredients and mindset, transformation is just as possible in life, as it is in brownies.

Before beginning the recipe, prepare the flax eggs or egg replacers (see How to Prepare a "Flax Egg" or Egg Replacer, page 101).

Preheat the oven to 350°F. Lightly grease an 8 × 8-inch baking pan with coconut oil and line it with parchment paper.

In a medium bowl, whisk to combine the flour, cocoa powder, baking powder, and salt.

In a separate medium bowl, whisk to combine the oat milk and flax eggs. Add the coconut sugar, coconut oil, and vanilla and whisk to thoroughly combine.

Add the oat milk mixture to the flour mixture and whisk to form a thick batter and until no lumps remain. Scrape the batter into the prepared pan with a silicone spatula and spread the batter in an even layer.

Bake for about 20 minutes, or until the top is set and a toothpick inserted in the center comes out with moist crumbs. Transfer the pan to a cooling rack and let cool completely in the pan before cutting into brownies.

NOTE: Coconut oil for cooking is sold in liquid form and is usually labeled "cooking oil." If you have regular coconut oil, which is solid at room temperature, you can melt it in the microwave in 15-second increments, stirring after each, until liquefied. Allow to come to room temperature before using.

Serves 4

ROASTED STONE FRUIT WITH SWEET CASHEW CREAM

8 medium stone fruits (about 3 pounds), such as peaches, nectarines, plums, or apricots, halved and pitted (see Note)

3 tablespoons maple syrup

3 tablespoons vegan butter, cut into tiny pieces

1 teaspoon ground cinnamon

1 cup Sweet Cashew Cream (page 122), for serving

I add a touch of maple syrup and vegan butter to stone fruits—any fruit with thin skins and large pits—and roast them. The high heat concentrates their natural sugars, turning them into a caramelly, sweet, and wholesome treat to enjoy on their own, or as a topping for plant-based yogurt. Serve roasted fruit with Sweet Cashew Cream for a fancy dessert to impress friends who think all you ever eat is Banana Nice Cream (page 274)—oh wait, those are my friends. Use ripe fruit since they will release their juices easily.

Preheat the oven to 350°F.

Arrange the fruit halves cut-side up and close to one another in a 9 × 13-inch baking dish. Pour ¼ cup water into the dish. Drizzle the fruit with the maple syrup, dot the tops with the butter, and sprinkle with the cinnamon.

Roast for about 30 minutes, or until the fruit is soft and their juices look like syrup.

Serve with cashew cream on the side.

NOTE: To pit stone fruit, cut in half and twist the halves in opposite directions. If you need to scoop out the pit, use a spoon rather than a knife so you don't risk cutting yourself.

LEMON LOAF WITH LEMON ICING

1 flax egg or 1 egg replacer, such as Bob's Red Mill (see page 101)

FOR THE LEMON LOAF:

Neutral oil, such as avocado or grapeseed, for the pan

2 cups white whole wheat flour or 1:1 gluten-free baking flour

1 tablespoon baking powder

1 teaspoon fine sea salt

1 cup plain almond milk, at room temperature

1 tablespoon apple cider vinegar

2 tablespoons grated lemon zest

½ cup fresh lemon juice (from about 3 large lemons)

1 cup organic cane sugar

1 cup extra-virgin olive oil

FOR THE LEMON ICING:

1 large lemon

1 cup organic powdered sugar or ¾ cup organic cane sugar, powdered (see Note)

This lemon loaf has all the "feels" of a lemon loaf from your favorite coffee shop. Save your money and make your own with pantry staples. Its texture is rich and "buttery" from extra-virgin olive oil, and it has a double hit of the fresh zing of lemon that I love in the cake *and* the icing.

Before beginning the recipe, prepare the flax egg or egg replacer (see How to Prepare a "Flax Egg" or Egg Replacer, page 101).

MAKE THE LEMON LOAF: Preheat the oven to 350°F. Lightly grease a 9 × 5-inch loaf pan with oil and line it with parchment paper with paper overhanging the 2 long sides.

In a medium bowl, whisk to combine the flour, baking powder, and salt. Set aside.

In a separate medium bowl, whisk to combine the almond milk and vinegar. Set aside until the almond milk curdles, about 10 minutes. Add the prepared flax egg, lemon zest, and lemon juice and gently whisk until well combined. Add the sugar and olive oil and whisk to combine.

Add the milk mixture to the flour mixture and gently whisk until no dry spots remain. Scrape the batter into the prepared pan with a silicone spatula.

Bake for 1 hour, or until a toothpick inserted in the center comes out clean. Remove the loaf from the oven and transfer to a cooling rack to cool in the pan for 30 minutes.

MAKE THE LEMON ICING: Grate the zest from the lemon until you have 1 tablespoon and set aside. Juice the lemon and measure out 3 tablespoons. In a small bowl, combine the powdered sugar and lemon juice and gently stir until smooth and creamy.

Pour the icing over the cooled lemon loaf and spread to cover completely. Scatter the reserved lemon zest across the top.

NOTE: Blend the cane sugar in a blender until it has the fineness of powdered sugar.

SOFT-SERVE BANANA NICE CREAM WITH CHOCOLATE SAUCE

3 to 4 tablespoons plain plant-based milk

Frozen slices of 3 medium bananas (about 2 cups)

¼ teaspoon fine sea salt

OPTIONAL TOPPINGS:

Chocolate Sauce (page 276)

Roasted Stone Fruit (page 269)

Fresh berries

Cinnamon

Vegan semisweet chocolate chips

Nuts, such as slivered almonds or peanuts

Unsweetened toasted coconut flakes

Chia seeds

Hemp hearts

The creamy texture of this "nice cream" comes from just two blended ingredients: frozen bananas and a splash of plant-based milk. It's nicer than traditional ice cream since it doesn't harm animals or people and contains no saturated fat to hurt your health. It's cheap to make, too! Add cocoa to the base for a rich chocolate flavor, or frozen mango for a tropical twist. Add toppings!

In a blender, combine the milk, frozen bananas, and salt and blend on high, scraping down the sides as needed, until smooth and creamy, about 5 minutes—if you think you need to add more milk, add up to 1 more tablespoon, but don't overdo it, or you will make a smoothie.

Divide the nice cream between two bowls. Top with your desired toppings and serve immediately.

CHOCOLATE SAUCE

Makes about ½ cup

Whisk up an easy to make rich 'n' chocolatey sauce to drizzle over any flavor of nice cream. You like hot fudge? Warm it in the microwave for 30 seconds, then pour. Craving chocolate milk? Stir 1 heaping tablespoon (or more, depending on your choco-meter) into a glass of plain plant-based milk, and that's what you'll get.

¼ cup maple syrup

½ cup unsweetened cocoa powder

3 tablespoons plain plant-based milk

½ teaspoon pure vanilla extract

Pinch of fine sea salt

In a medium bowl, gently whisk together the maple syrup, cocoa powder, milk, vanilla and salt until smooth and glossy. The cocoa powder takes a little extra time to dissolve, but it will give in, so just keep whisking. Use immediately or transfer to an airtight container and store refrigerated for up to 1 week.

Variations:

CHOCOLATE NICE CREAM: Add 3 tablespoons unsweetened cocoa powder.

MANGO NICE CREAM: Add 1 cup chopped frozen mango (from about ½ medium mango).

DATE AND FIG ENERGY BALLS

1½ cups soft pitted dates, such as Medjool or Deglet Noor (about 15)

1 cup raw almonds or cashews

¼ cup maple syrup

1 teaspoon pure vanilla extract

¼ teaspoon fine sea salt

1 teaspoon ground cinnamon

½ cup raisins or dried cherries

½ cup old-fashioned rolled oats

¼ cup pumpkin seeds, sunflower seeds, or chia seeds

¼ cup unsweetened shredded coconut

I used to eat bananas and dates rolled up into a snack for energy during tri-athlons—biking, swimming, and running long distances. These sticky balls are inspired by that snack and are a tasty way to see you through a long day. Use naturally sweet and sticky dates as a base and any dried fruit, nut, or seed you have in your pantry. Rolled oats and a touch of maple syrup also help bind them. Before you scoop the mixture, wet your hands, which makes it easier to roll the sticky mixture. You can make this nut-free, too, if you like.

In a food processor, combine the dates, almonds, maple syrup, vanilla, salt, and cinna-mon and process until the almonds are finely ground and the mixture sticks together, about 1 minute. Add the raisins, oats, pumpkin seeds, and coconut and pulse 4 to 5 times, until well combined.

With wet hands, form walnut-sized balls (about 1 heaping tablespoon each) and place them on a large plate or sheet pan. You should have about 24 balls.

Transfer to an airtight container and store in the refrigerator for up to 1 week.

PUMPKIN CHOCOLATE CHIP COOKIES

1 flax egg or 1 egg replacer, such as Bob's Red Mill (see page 101)

1½ cups white whole wheat flour, or 1½ cups 1:1 gluten-free baking flour

½ teaspoon baking soda

½ teaspoon fine sea salt

1 tablespoon pumpkin pie spice

8 tablespoons (1 stick/ 4 ounces) vegan butter, at room temperature

1 teaspoon pure vanilla extract

1 tablespoon organic molasses

½ cup organic cane sugar

½ cup canned pure pumpkin puree

¾ cup vegan semisweet chocolate chips

These cookies don't spread when cooked. Their texture is soft and pillowy in the middle, while the edges and bottoms get golden brown. They are more like mini cakes. Canned pumpkin puree is just cooked and mashed pumpkin without added seasoning or sugar, and it will be labeled as 100 percent pure pumpkin, pumpkin puree, solid pack pumpkin, or simply "pumpkin." The pumpkin pie spice mix—a combination of cinnamon, cloves, nutmeg, and ginger—makes your EWEE kitchen smell great while they bake.

Before beginning the recipe, prepare the flax egg or egg replacer (see How to Prepare a "Flax Egg" or Egg Replacer, page 101).

Preheat the oven to 350°F. Line a baking sheet with parchment paper or a silicone mat.

In a medium bowl, whisk to combine the flour, baking soda, salt, and pumpkin pie spice. Set aside.

In a separate medium bowl, use a wooden spoon to vigorously combine the butter, vanilla, molasses, and sugar until creamy, smooth, and fluffy. Add the flax egg and pumpkin puree and stir well to combine. Add the flour mixture and stir until fully combined, then fold in the chocolate chips.

Scoop the dough into 1 heaping tablespoon portions and place 1 inch apart on the prepared pan. Bake for 13 to 15 minutes, until the edges and bottoms are golden brown.

PEACH COBBLER

2 pounds ripe peaches (see Note), such as freestone or semi-freestone peaches (about 6 medium)

2 tablespoons fresh lemon juice (from 1 small lemon)

¼ cup organic cane sugar

3 tablespoons cornstarch

¼ teaspoon fine sea salt

FOR THE BISCUIT TOPPING:

2 cups white whole wheat flour or 1:1 gluten-free baking flour

⅓ cup stone-ground medium-grind cornmeal

½ cup plus 1 tablespoon organic cane sugar

½ teaspoons baking powder

1 teaspoon ground cinnamon

¼ teaspoon fine sea salt

5 tablespoons unsalted vegan butter, cold and cut into cubes

1 teaspoon pure vanilla extract

½ cup plain plant-based milk

My Grandma Sophie would bring her incredible peach cobbler—a deep-dish, casual fruit pie—to cookouts, uncovering it to reveal a rich biscuit topping over soft, juicy peaches. Peaches are the official fruit of my adopted home of Georgia, and during early summer super-sweet freestone peaches (peaches whose flesh easily breaks away from the pit) come into season. When I make this, I don't peel the peaches because their skin softens and melts into the fruit while cooking.

Precooking the peaches is the way to a great peach cobbler; the piping hot peaches help cook the underside of the biscuit topping.

Preheat the oven to 425°F.

PREPARE THE PEACHES: Halve and pit the peaches and cut each half into ½-inch wedges. In a large bowl, combine the peaches, lemon juice, sugar, cornstarch, and salt, stirring well to coat. Transfer the peach mixture to a 2-quart 2-inch-deep glass baking dish and cover with foil.

Bake for about 25 minutes, or until the peaches soften.

MEANWHILE, MAKE THE BISCUIT TOPPING: In a large bowl, whisk to combine the flour, cornmeal, ½ cup of the sugar, the baking powder, cinnamon, and salt. Add the butter and use your fingertips to work the butter into the flour mixture until it looks like coarse bread crumbs. Add the vanilla and milk and stir until just combined.

Reduce the oven temperature to 350°F. Remove the baking dish from the oven. Uncover and drop heaping tablespoons of the biscuit dough over the peaches, leaving a 1-inch space between them. They will spread. Scatter the remaining 1 tablespoon sugar across the top.

Return the dish to the oven and bake, uncovered, for about 20 minutes, or until the biscuits are golden brown.

Transfer to a cooling rack to allow the juices to settle, about 15 minutes. Serve warm.

NOTES: To choose ripe peaches, look for ones that are dark yellow in color and have some "give" when you gently squeeze them. If it's dead of winter, or you can't find ripe fresh peaches, use two 16-ounce bags frozen sliced peaches. You don't need to thaw the peaches beforehand, but the cobbler filling's texture may be looser.

THINK EWEE: Use this cobbler recipe as a template for other stone fruits, such as nectarines or apricots—they all provide essential vitamins, minerals, and fiber.

Makes 1 dozen muffins

BLENDER BERRY MUFFINS

Coconut oil for the muffin tin

1 cup white whole wheat flour
or 1:1 gluten-free baking flour

2 teaspoons baking powder

½ cup organic cane sugar

¾ cup oat flour (see Note)

1 cup plain oat milk

2 ripe medium bananas

½ cup coconut cooking oil or
regular coconut oil, melted
(see Note, page 268)

1 teaspoon pure vanilla
extract

1 cup blueberries,
cranberries, raspberries,
blackberries, or sliced
hulled strawberries, or a
combination

2 tablespoons hemp seeds,
pumpkin seeds, sunflower
seeds, or chia seeds

I love eating fresh, seasonal berries all by themselves, but sometimes, I crave a berry muffin—especially blueberry. I use a blender for a no-fuss muffin template that allows you to toss in blueberries, blackberries, raspberries, strawberries, and even tart fresh cranberries—or any combination. All those recipes that tell you to first "flour" the berries so they don't sink in the batter? . . . it's a lie; they still sink to the bottom. Instead, add plain batter to the muffin cup first, fold the berries into the remaining batter, and you'll have berry in every bite. Domz got your back.

Preheat the oven to 350°F. Lightly grease 12 cups of a muffin tin with coconut oil.

In a large bowl, whisk to combine the flour, baking powder, and sugar. Set aside.

In a blender, combine the oat flour, milk, bananas, coconut oil, and vanilla and blend on high speed until smooth.

Add the banana mixture to the flour mixture and stir until well combined.

Fill each muffin cup about one-third of the way with plain batter. Fold the berries into the remaining batter and continue filling each muffin cup with batter until halfway full, taking care not to overfill. Sprinkle the hemp seeds over the tops of the muffins.

Bake for about 30 minutes, or until golden or until a toothpick inserted in the center of a muffin comes out clean.

Set the muffin tin on a cooling rack and allow to cool for 10 minutes before removing the muffins from the tin to cool completely. Store in an airtight container in the refrigerator for 3 days or in the freezer for up to 3 months.

NOTE: You can make ¾ cup oat flour in a blender by blending 1 cup old-fashioned rolled oats or instant oats on high speed until powdered.

ACKNOWLEDGMENTS

As my wonderful editor, Doris Cooper, says, it truly takes a village to make a book—and she is absolutely right! Doris, I simply can't thank you enough for taking a chance on me. I appreciate you more than you know. And to my copilot, Theresa Gambacorta, who co-created this incredible book with me, words simply are not enough to express my gratitude for you and your hard work. To my amazing agent, Janis Donnaud, you are a legend and, to this day, the person who has represented my best interests to the fullest. I truly adore you for your hard work and passion to bring the best people together to get things done! Thank you to Caitlin Bensel for the photography, and to Christine Keely and M. McLean. Finally, thank you, too, to the incredible team at Simon Element, without whom this book would not be out in the world: Richard Rhorer, Jessica Preeg, Ingrid Carabulea, Elizabeth Breeden, Katie McClimon, Jackie Seow, Jen Wang, Kristina Juodenas, Jessie McNiel, Allison Har-zvi, Jaime Putorti, and Frances Yackel.

RESOURCES

Here is a list of recommended books, documentaries, and websites that cover a range of topics I'm passionate about and that I hope will further support your "why": nutrition, animal and human rights, environmental sustainability and food justice, and athletic performance.

Books

- *Fast Food Nation: The Dark Side of the All-American Meal* by Eric Schlosser
- *Food Politics: How the Food Industry Influences Nutrition and Health* by Marion Nestle, PhD
- *How Not to Die: Discover the Foods Scientifically Proven to Prevent and Reverse Disease* by Michael Gregor, MD, and Gene Stone
- *Mindset: The New Psychology of Success* by Carol S. Dweck, PhD
- *The Chain: Farm, Factory, and the Fate of Our Food* by Ted Genoways
- *The China Study: The Most Comprehensive Study of Nutrition Ever Conducted and the Startling Implications for Diet, Weight Loss, and Long-Term Health* by T. Colin Campbell and Thomas M. Campbell
- *The Jungle* by Upton Sinclair
- *Veganism in an Oppressive World: A Vegans-of-Color Community Project* by Julia Feliz Brueck
- *Why Vegan: Eating Ethically* by Peter Singer

Documentaries

- *Earthlings*, 2018, director Shaun Monson. This film contains behind-the-scenes footage of animal agriculture and may be difficult to watch due to the violence and abuse enacted on animals and the inhumane conditions of the people who work in the animal agriculture industry in the name of "food," power, and money.
- *The Game Changers*, 2019, director Louie Psyhoyos. This film presents science-backed research and stories of elite athletes who credit their increased recovery time and powerful overall performance to plants.
- *What the Health*, 2021, Kip Andersen and Keegan Kuhn. This moving, groundbreaking documentary contains a wealth of information exposing the corruption in government and big businesses related to health care.

Meal Planner, Food, and Nutrition Apps

Need more meal planning ideas? I got you. Need a vegan meal on the road, stat? That too. Are you asking where the farmers' market is? I know how to find it. Wanna put on your glasses and brush up on the latest nutrition research? I know you do. Here are my favorite resources for all of that:

- **THE EAT WHAT ELEPHANTS EAT FOOD NUTRITION AND WELLNESS PROGRAM:** I created this program to support my mission to feed the world affordable plant-based food. As a member, you'll receive delicious, simple recipes customized to you, a meal planner, and support from food coaches. https://kitchen .eatwhatelephantseat.com/.
- **HAPPYCOW:** This vegan community and food app helps you find vegan restaurants near you, or while traveling.
- **NUTRITIONFACTS.ORG:** A science-based nonprofit organization founded by Michael Greger, MD FACLM that provides free updates on the latest in nutrition research. On this site, check out Dr. Greger's checklist of the healthiest plant foods to include every day, called Dr. Greger's Daily Dozen. https://nutritionfacts.org/.
- **LOCALHARVEST.ORG/CSA:** A great resource for community-supported agriculture and farm-fresh foods near you.

Joining a Herd

As you move forward on your EWEE journey, you may want to connect with like-minded vegans, or, as I like to say, Join a Herd! It feels good to be part of a compassionate collective.

- **MEETUP:** Search for local vegan community events and activities, and make some vegan friends!
- **GRAZER:** Find meat-free dates and friends.
- **LAST CHANCE FOR ANIMALS:** Volunteer with animal activist groups. lcanimal.org.
- **GLOBAL FEDERATION OF ANIMAL SANCTUARIES:** Find accredited sanctuaries and rescue centers around the world and donate or get involved. sanctuaryfederation.org.
- **THE FOOD EMPOWERMENT PROJECT:** Volunteer to raise awareness about how food choices can change the world. foodispower.org.

NOTES

CHAPTER 2: OUR EAT WHAT ELEPHANTS EAT (EWEE) JOURNEY BEGINS

1. "The New Food Fights: US Public Divides Over Food Science," Pew Research Center, Washington, DC, December 1, 2016, https://www.pewresearch.org/science/2016/12/01/the-new-food-fights/.

2. Jessica Kate Knight and Zoe Fritz, "Doctors Have an Ethical Obligation to Ask Patients about Food Insecurity: What Is Stopping Us?" *Journal of Medical Ethics* 48, no. 10 (July 2021): 707–11, doi: 10.1136/medethics-2021-107409.

3. Neel Ocean, Peter Howley, and Jonathan Ensor, "Lettuce Be Happy: A Longitudinal UK Study on the Relationship between Fruit and Vegetable Consumption and Well-Being," *Social Science & Medicine* 222 (February 2019): 335–45, doi: 10.1016/j.socscimed.2018.12.017.

4. Ibid.

5. Djawad Radjabzadeh et al., "Gut Microbiome-Wide Association Study of Depressive Symptoms," *Nature Communications* 13, no. 1 (December 2022): 7128, doi: 10.1038/s41467-022-34502-3.

6. Massimo Filippi, Gianna C. Riccitelli, Laura Vacchi, and Maria A. Rocca, "Cognitive Processes Underlying Vegetarianism as Assessed by Brain Imaging," in François Mariotti, ed., *Vegetarian and Plant-Based Diets in Health and Disease Prevention* (Academic Press, 2017), 71–91.

CHAPTER 3: CONNECTING THE DOTS

1. *Climate Change 2022: Impacts, Adaptation and Vulnerability*, Sixth Assessment Report, Intergovernmental Panel on Climate Change, February 28, 2022.

CHAPTER 6: PROTECT YOUR HEALTH: EWEE NUTRITION

1. National Academies of Sciences, Engineering, and Medicine, Health and Medicine Division, Food and Nutrition Board, Committee on the Dietary Reference Intakes for Energy, *Dietary Reference Intakes for Energy* (Washington, DC: National Academies Press, 2023), https://doi.org/10.17226/26818.

INDEX

ABOUT THE AUTHOR

DOMINICK THOMPSON is a leading voice in the ethical vegan and No-Meat Athlete movements. An Ironman® triathlete and social entrepreneur, Dom reentered the workforce after his imprisonment and began competing in endurance races, including marathons, triathlons, and ultra-races. He eventually became an executive at a leading health care company, where he saved enough money to launch Eat What Elephants Eat, an online nutrition and wellness program that gives subscribers a personalized plant-based plan with daily meal recommendations.

SIMON
ELEMENT

An Imprint of Simon & Schuster, LLC
1230 Avenue of the Americas
New York, NY 10020

For information about special discounts for bulk purchases,
please contact Simon & Schuster Special Sales at 1-866-506-1949
or business@simonandschuster.com.

The Simon & Schuster Speakers Bureau can bring authors to your live
event. For more information or to book an event, contact the Simon &
Schuster Speakers Bureau at 1-866-248-3049 or visit our website at
www.simonspeakers.com.

Interior design by Jen Wang

Manufactured in China

10   9   8   7   6   5   4   3   2   1

Library of Congress Cataloging-in-Publication Data has been applied
for.

ISBN 978-1-6680-0529-3
ISBN 978-1-6680-0530-9 (ebook)